BISON
BOOKS

FARM

A Year in the Life
of an American Farmer

RICHARD RHODES

ILLUSTRATIONS BY BILL GREER

UNIVERSITY OF NEBRASKA PRESS
LINCOLN AND LONDON

"Billy Bayou," by Roger Miller. Copyright © 1958 Tree Publishing Co., Inc.
Copyright renewed. All rights reserved. International copyright secured. Used by
permission of the publisher.

⊖ The paper in this book meets the minimum requirements of American National
Standard for Information Sciences—Permanence of Paper for Printed Library
Materials, ANSI Z39.48-1984.

First Bison Books printing: 1997
Most recent printing indicated by the last digit below:
10   9   8   7   6   5   4   3   2   1

Library of Congress Cataloging-in-Publication Data
Rhodes, Richard.
Farm: a year in the life of an American farmer / Richard Rhodes; illustrations by Bill
Greer.
p.   cm.
Originally published: New York: Simon and Schuster, c1989.
ISBN 0-8032-8965-0 (pbk.: alk. paper)
1. Farm life—Missouri.   2. Family farms—Missouri.
3. Agriculture—Missouri.   I. Title.
S521.5.M8R48   1998
630.9778—dc21   97-17687
                                                                                        CIP
Reprinted from the original 1989 edition by Simon & Schuster, Inc., New York.
As with the original, chapter one begins on arabic page 17; no material has been
omitted from this Bison Books edition.

AUTHOR'S NOTE

The story that follows is based on detailed notes I kept in forty-two spiral notebooks during most of a year spent visiting and working on a family farm in central Missouri. Events and dialogue are authentic. Nothing is made up except names, including some place names, to protect the privacy of people generous enough to allow this intimate intrusion into their lives. I think the world of them, as they know, and thank them here again for their cooperation and their friendship.

For George and Frances Berkemeier

CONTENTS

The philosopher's stone of an American farmer is to do everything within his own family, to trouble his neighbors by borrowing as little as possible, and to abstain from buying European
commodities. He that follows that golden rule and has a good
wife is almost sure of succeeding.

J. Hector St. John de Crevecoeur
Thoughts of an American Farmer
on Various Rural Subjects, c. 1782

I
HARVEST

ONE

Running a combine before dawn in the dead of winter in a strange field was damned spooky. Inside the big cab it was warm enough. The tilted picture window that started overhead and disappeared below the floor divided him off from the blowing snow that swirled in the headlights. But he didn't know the references, didn't know the trees silhouetted in the distance against the night sky that might serve as markers, didn't know where the rows came out that wandered with the terraces, and watching the saw-toothed cutter bar tripping up soybeans was hypnotic. A man could lose his bearings in the dark in a strange field.

A wet November had caught a neighbor's four hundred acres of soybeans unharvested. The neighbor had to wait until the ground froze in January to finish up. Tom Bauer had finished his own harvest by then and had some slack time, so he and two other neighbors pitched in to help, four combines in all.

Beans were a bigger challenge to pick anyway than corn. Cornstalks carried their heavy ears waist high, but the brown, rattling bean pods marched down their stiff stalks nearly to the ground. To leave a clean field you had to work the cutter bar close to the roots. You watched it like a hawk when you didn't know the field.

They'd commence at four in the morning and run straight through until ten, when it thawed enough to make the ground

17

slick. The combines would start skidding off the sides of the ter-races in the greasy mud and bang down at the bottom. The men left their machines parked in the field then, drove their pickups home, did their own days' work and went out again of an evening until ten or eleven at night. Then they'd catch four or five hours of sleep before going at it once more.

Tom's wife, Sally, sometimes drove out during that marathon and rode with her husband, talking to him to help him keep his eyes open. Back at the house she'd shout at him over the two-way radio before she went to bed to see if he was still awake. The neighbor who owned the beans worked twenty-four hours non-stop, took a nap over lunch and worked seventeen hours more. Then he fell asleep at the wheel and ran his combine into a slope and tore up one side. Tom told him it wasn't worth killing himself to get his beans in.

They picked beans in the darkness for four days before the work was done. No one said anything about getting paid.

That was the end of last season. Tom remembered it now be-cause of the mud. It was the beginning of September, nearly time for another harvest. He'd been tired enough when he put away his big red Case International 1460 combine last January that he'd left it muddy instead of steam-cleaning and waxing it the way he usually did. He'd have run it last June to thresh wheat, but the same fall weather that kept the neighbor from getting to his beans kept the Bauers from planting any wheat at all. So when Tom wheeled the big 1460 from the cool darkness of its storage shed out into the summer heat, the mud was still there, caked and dried all over the sides where the tires had flung it up. It shamed him a little. He wondered if he was slowing down. It didn't seem to him he worked as hard as he used to. He used to work eighteen or twenty hours a day. They weren't knocking at the poorhouse door yet, though, and he'd get around to the mud. The combine needed servicing before he started in on the corn. He'd clean it then.

Tom Bauer was a Missouri farmer, six feet three, two hundred forty pounds, most of the weight muscle even at forty-six. With his massive head and long jaw, his powerful presence and easy walk, he could have doubled for Sheriff Matt Dillon on the old *Gun-*

smoke television series. He was Western in the same way, big and physically confident, courteous, with a voice he could make deep and drawling, quick to grin. He looked less like a television star and more like just plain Tom when he took off his seed cap, which he only did indoors. Then his high white forehead shone above the dark weathering of his neck and face. He was losing his black hair. What was left he wore combed straight over from the part, with sideburns. People noticed his eyes. They were pale blue, limpid, so gentle and promising that women meeting him for the first time caught their breath. Tom Bauer's eyes could narrow to shrewdness or chill to cold anger, but countryman that he was, grounded in the anchorage of the land, they usually sparkled with amusement at the world's derelict commotion. "He ain't never going to grow up," Sally had complained once to his mother when she was alive. His mother knew a blessing when she saw one. "Then he'll never grow old," she'd said.

The Bauer farm in Crevecoeur County, Missouri, an hour east of Kansas City, had been two farms before; Tom still kept them separate in his head because they carried different mortgages. The old Dixon place, east of the home farm across a section line, was the newer purchase, 110 acres sloping up the hill from Little Cebo Creek and down toward the home farm east pasture. The bottom-land along the creek had been a sour marsh when the Bauers bought the place. They'd paid to have the marsh tiled with pipe to drain it, then plowed and disked it until the soil sweetened. Now it was a fine, well-laid field. Tom had bulldozed the old house up by the road and filled in the old hand-dug well. House and well stubbornly refused to let go: bricks turned up every time Tom disked where the house had been, and the well formed a new sinkhole every spring, not so deep as to be dangerous but notice-able enough to remind him of the history that had come before. A mound nearby regularly turned up arrowheads, probably Osage— all of central Missouri had been Osage territory before the French and then the Americans crowded in—removing the history of the place even farther back into the past. The woods that shaded the creek Tom left unimproved. He'd planned to burn out the trees and brush to enlarge his tillable ground, but Brett, his sixteen-year-old son, had stopped him with a question. "Do you have to have it all, Dad?" the boy had asked. Tom had thought about the deer that sometimes crossed his fields and decided he didn't and left the woods alone.

The home farm to the west was larger, 227 acres. The Bauers' modern one-story brick farmhouse, insulated and snug, looked out over a grassy slope toward an oil-topped county road that came straight south two miles from U.S. Highway 24 and turned east just at their mailbox. South of the mailbox, down a graveled lane, Tom had installed the buildings and feeding floors of his hog operation. A southeast wind could blow a powerful stink back to the house from the sewage lagoon there. Tom would laugh then, a little embarrassed, and call the stink "the smell of money." More reliably than any other harvest, hogs paid the bills.

Due south of the house was a barn lot and a pasture where the Bauers' white-faced black cows and calves grazed. To the west, beyond the machine sheds and fuel tanks, beyond a corrugated steel grain bin nearly empty now of last year's feed corn, beyond a roofless, abandoned concrete silo that enclosed a volunteer gathering of mosses and ferns, a field rolled gently down to another reach of Little Cebo Creek. There Tom had dammed an eroding runoff channel to make a deep pond beside a well-shaded grove of oak and hackberry trees. He'd hauled an old plywood mobile home into the grove and set up a picnic table for a camp where family, friends and relatives could hunt and fish and swim, out of sight of civilization but close enough to home to run the farm.

Everything was organized and trim—the grass mown, the buildings painted, the oiled and polished machinery stored out of the weather in barns and sheds, the fields and the fencerows free of weeds.

The soil on both farms was the richest in Missouri and among the richest on the North American continent, dark brown Knox and Marshall silt loams, Blackoar or Kennebec silt loam in the bottoms, soil in places as much as ninety feet deep. Winds off the glaciers receding at the end of the Ice Age, ten thousand years ago, had blown in the dust of their grinding—fine-grained, calcareous loess. The tall-grass prairie that had evolved then across the well-drained uplands had worked the loess to richness. Sally Bauer, whose sense of humor was peppery, liked to tell people that her

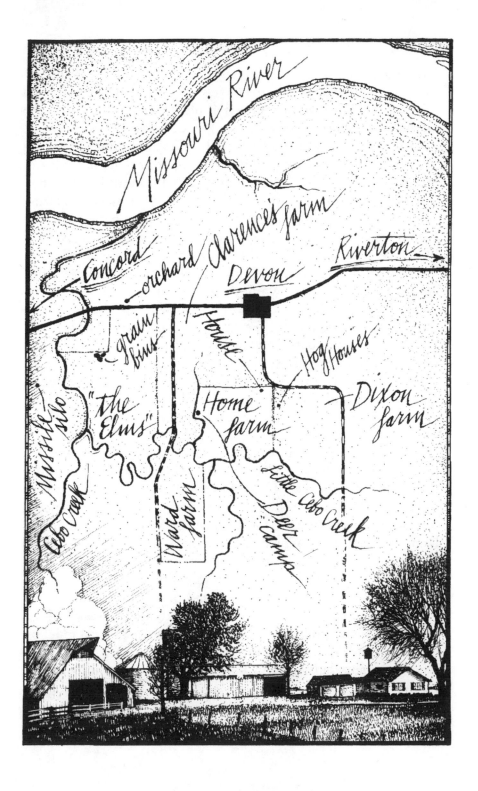

husband had bought the farm without even bothering to look at the house. It was almost true. "Give me the land and I'll build you the house," Tom would quote the old Dutchman farmers, the German neighbors of his childhood, in defense.

The harvest about to begin would be Tom's twenty-fifth since he started farming on his own. Before then, back to childhood seasons he could hardly remember anymore, he and his nine brothers and sisters had helped his father harvest rented farmland. Because William Bauer didn't believe in borrowing, there'd been no land to inherit when he died, and Sally's family was too poor for any kind of dowry. Tom and Sally had to borrow even the down payment to buy their first forty acres. They paid off that land in good time and used it in turn as down payment for a real farm.

Now, twenty years later, the Bauers owned 337 acres, more than half a square mile of the surface of the earth. They owned cattle and hogs and the equipment and buildings necessary to husband them, six tractors, four trucks, the big red combine, planters and disks and harrows, mowers and bailers and wagons, augers and feed mills and bins. They had three children, a young daughter and two sons approaching the age when they would have to decide if they wanted to follow their parents into farming. They farmed another 779 acres on shares with three landlords, the Bauers supplying the equipment and labor and sharing the harvest fifty-fifty in exchange for the use of half the land.

They had worked their way to security, and they considered themselves successful, but for all their investment of capital and labor their return amounted to less than twenty thousand dollars a year, and in the Reagan years just passing they'd seen their net worth reduced by half as rural land values plummeted. "The fat's been rendered out," Tom told a friend one day. "All those bad managers and plungers you used to hear about are *gone*." Gone and more going, probably as many as twenty-five percent more by the end of the century, and the question was, who was yet to be scourged, and what would it take to escape that winnowing, to survive?

TWO

Tom and Sally used the six o'clock farm report as an alarm clock. They listened to hog and cattle and grain prices and then planned the day's business, sometimes with a little monkey business thrown in. Except during the harvest, when he needed her to run the combine while he unloaded the trucks, Tom did the farming and Sally kept the books. They looked over each problem or plan together, held it up to the light and turned it around, tried to spy out all the angles. They usually knew before they got out of bed how they meant to run their day.

"My wife's a nervous person," Tom said once, "and she can talk a little rough sometimes, but a fellow couldn't have a better partner. I don't know what I'd do without her." Sally's nerves, which showed in her smoking and in a tendency not to let go once she started talking, were battle scars. She and Tom had worked their way to prosperity together, but she'd grown up small-town poor, and their success always felt a little precarious. She hadn't forgotten the standard Sunday dinner at her house when she was a child, chicken feet and noodles, the feet, peeled ot their scaly yellow skin, left over from her mother's work of dressing other people's chickens. "We were *poor,*" Sally emphasized when she told that story. Of the chicken feet she also said, "We *liked* them!"

She'd been a slight, tomboyish girl when she married Tom Bauer twenty-two years ago; she was heavier now, though not so heavy as many rural women over forty who'd borne three children. She wore her dark hair cut in bangs and curled. She was a good cook who was tired of cooking, her two strapping sons now nearly grown. She liked to shop garage sales and did family-treeing all over Missouri with her sister-in-law Grace, working harder at tracing the men's family name than her own since Bauer was the name passing down.

Sally was considerably more cynical than Tom, who tended to give people the benefit of a doubt. "Good old Tom," she'd say, rolling her eyes, when she heard her husband on the phone forgiving a delay in the arrival of a fertilizer truck or a mistake on an invoice, "Good old Tom."

She had strong feelings. She stood up for her children ferociously. Unfairness, real or imagined, made her flush with anger. Tenderness brought tears to her eyes. She could challenge you and then stare you down, daring you to try to weasel out of it, but she could also say something funny as hell and hold her dark eyes wide until you caught her drift and laughed. She had a good laugh.

She was generous with help. She saw her girlfriend through breast-cancer surgery and regularly drove her to the doctor in Kansas City afterward for checkups. She worked gratis most days of the week, whenever Tom didn't need her, helping one of her brothers keep his ceramics shop in order in her hometown north of the river. She enjoyed molding ceramics, glazing and firing them; she was good at it. Molded ceramic ducks, rabbits, mushrooms, pumpkins in season appeared on the peninsula of grass between the Bauer driveway and the county road, across from the mailbox. Vandals always stole her hand-painted menageries and Sally always replaced them. "They think they're getting something worth something," she'd laugh about the thefts. "They're just bolos. Pieces I didn't make right."

She said "ain't," and "don't" instead of "doesn't"—so did Tom—in the old dialect way that had come to seem illiterate to city people, though it was good enough for the English nobility two hundred years ago. She was blunt and she was smart. She didn't put on airs, but she didn't miss much, either.

*   *   *

One morning at the beginning of September Tom left the house with storage problems on his mind. The farm dogs met him at the door and followed him out. Blaze, the big, sleepy female, who was buff-colored and part Saint Bernard, calculated he was heading for his pickup and flopped down in the shade of the big oak in the yard behind the house. Molly, the small, quick female, who was black and part Labrador, cocked an ear as the pickup started and dashed ahead. At the corner of the yard where the lane that led to the farrowing house ran off from the driveway she waited to see which way Tom would turn. If he turned north toward the county road she wouldn't follow, knowing he was leaving the farm. If he turned south toward the farrowing house she would. He turned south to check on a sow and Molly raced along behind. Blaze was a twelve-year veteran, but Tom and Sally weren't sure yet if they wanted to keep Molly. She was a sweet-spirited dog, just out of puppyhood, and she worked that much harder trying to prove herself.

The biggest problem of the harvest was going to be storage. The corn and soybean crops were supposed to break records. It was anyone's guess where farmers were going to put it all. There were four billion bushels still on hand in storage from the year before. Counting commercial elevators, farm grain bins, river barges and whatever other facilities the government could turn up, the twenty-two-billion-bushel nationwide storage capacity was estimated to just match the coming harvest. But the harvest wasn't grown nationwide. It was grown in the Midwestern Corn Belt, and until it could be moved out by train and barge it would overflow the region's storage.

Tom had some ideas for temporary storage if the commercial elevators got full. He wanted to check first with the elevator that usually bought his grain, the Comstock Grain Company, ten miles east of him in Riverton. He figured a lot of guys would wait until the last minute to reserve storage. If he made arrangements early he might beat the crowd.

He parked his metallic-tan GMC pickup outside the farrowing house and looked in on the sow. She was the last holdout. The eleven other sows in the semiautomated building had already dropped their litters in the steel-barred crates where Tom had confined them. The baby pigs made a great scurrying when he came in, pigs everywhere in the darkened house, more than a hundred in all. The radio set up on a shelf on the east wall was playing country-Western music. Tom left it on twenty-four hours a day to soothe the sows. They did better with music, proven fact.

He switched on the lights and walked down the aisle. There was a strong smell of ammonia in the air. The holdout sow hadn't farrowed yet. She lay on her side, looking miserable. The day was supposed to get hot, above ninety degrees, and she'd need to be watched. With the energy of a dozen pigs inside her body to dissipate as well as her own she could easily overheat even with all the farrowing house's automatic fans kicked in. Tom milked out one of her teats—it was shaped exactly like an old-fashioned bottle nipple—without result. Sows farrow within twelve hours of letting down their milk. This one still wasn't ready. She grunted at the man examining her. "Let's go, girl," he cheered her on.

Outside again, Tom studied the sky. Haze was already building to the possibility of afternoon thundershowers. They might cool things off. He drove out onto the county road, Molly hauling up behind to watch him go.

A hand-held microphone hung from a clip on the dashboard of the GMC. It connected to a two-way FM radio, a business-band system installed in the Bauers' vehicles and at the house that allowed them to talk to each other from up to twenty miles away. Tom lifted the mike from the dash and held down the talk button.

"Mobile to base. Sally, do you copy?"

Sally didn't answer right away. She was doing laundry and had to come up from the basement. Eventually she said, "Go ahead, Tom."

"I'm going to run over to Riverton to see about storage."

"To Comstock's?"

"Yeah."

"Your dinner's in the crockpot. It'll be done at noon. You'll be back by then, won't you?" She was going to her brother's ceramics shop for the day.

"Easy," Tom said.

"Don't forget Sammi gets home at three thirty." Their nine-year-old daughter rode the bus to school in Plymouth, the county seat, ten miles west. The fall semester had just begun.

Tom kept his radio talk to a minimum. Sally would know he'd heard. He hung up the mike.

He was already at the corner where the county road intersected U.S. Highway 24. The old two-lane federal highway ran east and west paralleling the Missouri River, out of sight beyond the bluffs to the north. The corner marked the eastern limit of Devon, Missouri, a few blocks of houses and old stores. Some of the headstones in the Devon cemetery Tom had just passed recorded the deaths of men and women born in the eighteenth century. U.S. 24 followed the route of the Santa Fe Trail from St. Louis to Independence, and the town was old.

Tom turned east onto 24 toward St. Louis, putting Devon behind him, and lit a cigarette. He drove through a divided landscape: green orchards to the north of the highway with red apples ripening, fields of maturing buff-colored corn and soybeans to the south. The division marked a division in soil types as well as in venture. The Knox silt loam that prevailed closer to the river had formed under deciduous hardwoods, the Marshall, farther south, under native grass. Tom had been born in Crevecoeur County only five miles west of Devon. He knew every farm along the highway and studied each one in turn as he passed.

Uphill and downhill he drove into the morning sun, past the AT&T microwave tower, past the yard where a farmer displayed used farm machinery he'd picked up at auctions and hoped to resell, past one orchard market and then another, past the inconspicuous entrance north of the road that led back to a major complex of apartments and outbuildings owned by the Transcendental Meditation people. Tom and his friends had heard that they were studying how to levitate themselves, so they called them "carpet-fliers." Sally sometimes daydreamed of converting the fields south of the house on the home farm to a horse track, Devon Downs. She knew it was pure blue sky, but she was practical about it. She figured they could convert the vast living center the carpet-fliers had built, which appeared to be abandoned, to a weekend resort for wealthy bettors out of Kansas City. It had a big dome on top that would set the tone of the place and it looked out over the Missouri River, but with city amusements a long hour away by car it would certainly need a track to keep the gentry entertained, unless they wanted to pick apples.

Nearer Riverton the fields leveled out. Though the land was elevated well above the river, here began what Tom called the Lundbeck bottoms after the small town of Lundbeck up the road. The Lundbeck bottoms, covered at the moment with ripening beans and corn, never failed to distract him. He admired them without reservation. They occupied a place in his daydreams like the place Devon Downs occupied in Sally's. "That land's so good it makes your mouth water," he said of them, his eyes shining. "The only way you can get some is to inherit it or marry it." It was Marshall silt loam, like much of his own land. That was one important measure of its quality, but unlike his more rolling fields, which needed terraces that channeled runoff to reduce erosion, it was also open and nearly flat, sloping just enough for efficient drainage. It "laid good," farmers said. "Good soil, lays good" where farm real estate is concerned is not one valuable quality but two. The lay of the land is more important now that one man with large-scale machinery farms a thousand acres or more. Tom's father with four sons to help him farmed three hundred-some acres, his grandfather eighty. For maximum efficiency, Tom wanted an uninterrupted track across his fields and as few turnarounds as possible.

At Riverton Tom left the federal highway and drove north on the state road that led to the Riverton bridge across the Missouri River. A hundred yards this side of the bridge he turned east again onto a potholed road that cut down the face of the river bluff to bank level. Raising dust, he bounced along beside the railroad tracks that paralleled the river, crossed them and followed them to the elevators of the Comstock Grain Company, sixteen bare concrete cylinders eighty feet high set right on the bank of the river. The elevators were set at the edge of the mighty Missouri to access barges for transporting the grain Comstock bought at harvest and temporarily stored. From Riverton, hundreds of tons of corn and soybeans floated down the Missouri to St. Louis, down the Mississippi to New Orleans and from New

Orleans, transferred to oceangoing cargo ships, around the world. Bauer soybeans might well end up, six months later, on Japanese dinner tables.

In the prefabricated steel office building beside the truck scales, Tom looked up Frank Tice, the elevator manager. Tice was younger than Tom. He had thick jowls and a barrel chest and wore his jeans belted tight below his belly. Tom found him in his corner office and poked his head in the door. "I'm looking for storage," he announced with a grin.

"Ain't everybody," Tice countered. He gestured to a chair. "Set yourself down."

Tom sat. "What kind of deal you got?"

Tice leaned back and toyed with a pencil. "Everything's real short this year."

"Don't I know it," Tom said. "I'm going to start cleaning out old corncribs."

"Yeah, a lot of guys are. It may come to that." Tice got serious. "We're offering storage first of all to our fertilizer customers."

Tom nodded. "Seems fair enough." He wasn't a Comstock fertilizer customer; he spread his own fertilizer each spring to save the expense of commercial application and to make sure the job was done right.

"But customers like you who sell us grain get second call," Tice went on. "*If* there's any storage left."

"You think there will be?" Tom immediately asked.

"It's going to be a tough harvest this year. Farmers are going to have to do things they never did before. Federal soybean standards are going up. Corn standards too, probably. I've got railroad cars and barges contracted for to move it out as fast as we can when it starts coming in. But we'll be taking maximum twenty-percent-moisture corn this year."

Tom raised an eyebrow. "Oh?" He didn't approve of grain companies turning farmers away at harvesttime, whatever the excuse. Corn picked at more than fifteen-percent moisture had to be dried by blowing warm air through it to keep it from spoiling. That was an added inconvenience, and the grain companies usually compensated for it by docking—by knocking a few cents off the price they paid for the grain. With more corn expected to be harvested than elevators had space to store, Comstock's was saying they'd have to limit that courtesy.

"And we won't be accepting any lower-grade grain," Tice went on.

Tom grinned. "You never got that kind from me, Frank."

"I know I didn't."

"You hear anything about a Russian sale?" Tom asked, leaning forward and lowering his voice.

Tice sat up in his chair and tossed the pencil on his desk. "What'd you hear?"

"Hear there's cargo ships contracted for in the Gulf that don't have no designated destination. You hear that?"

Tice barely nodded. "Something like that."

"You think they're going to buy some of this grain?"

Tice wasn't prepared to commit himself. "Don't know. They're shrewd, though. Real shrewd."

"They'll wait until the price bottoms out."

"That won't be too long," Tice said.

Tom nodded and stood to go. "When do you think you'll know about storage?" he asked the elevator manager.

"We've sent out letters to all our fertilizer customers. Gave them until the seventh. That's the end of this week."

"Then you'll go with your grain customers?"

"Yeah." Tice stood to acknowledge Tom's leaving. "Why don't you give us a call Monday morning first thing? I expect we'll have some space left."

"Good enough," Tom said.

Tom ate his noontime dinner alone at the big family table in the kitchen of the farmhouse: crockpot sausage and sauerkraut, bread and butter, iced tea and apple brownies, Sally's good home cooking. The sausage came from the Bauers' own hogs, made up by German-descended butchers at a custom packing company in a nearby town. He would have liked Sally to stay home, for the company, but he knew she needed something to do besides the housework now that the kids were all in school. She'd be home soon enough, running the combine while he hauled grain to his on-farm storage bins or to Riverton.

He needed storage because he didn't want to sell all his crop at once at harvesttime. Supply overwhelmed demand then and the price bottomed out. He might decide to hold off selling some of his corn and soybeans until after the first of the year. By then enough grain had usually been moved out to improve the sale price. In the meantime he needed a place to put it all. Seventy-two hundred bushels of his own corn would fill the steel grain bin west of the house. He fed his hogs from that bin, so that corn would stay on the farm until it walked off. The corn he farmed on shares with the Landers family would go into the big 7,800-bushel bin back behind the Landers family place, the Elms, off Highway 24 two miles west of Devon. The Landerses had agreed to rent one of the two smaller 6,500-bushel bins at the Elms to Tom's other major landlord, Jack Ward, an airline pilot who was managing the family farm for his invalid mother. This year was Tom's first harvest with the Wards. But the bins wouldn't hold all the harvest. He'd have to store some of it elsewhere. Tom wouldn't harvest soybeans until after the corn was in. They'd be another problem. How much additional storage he'd need would depend also on the yield, on how many bushels he produced per acre. A bushel was about nine gallons. With soybeans, 50 to 60 bushels per acre was a good yield for him. With corn, his fields yielded up toward 160.

All in all, Tom decided, he'd better get some backup storage ready. There were old wooden bins built into the barns north of the steel bins on the Landers place. They hadn't been used in years and they'd have to be cleaned out. One of his brothers who had gotten out of farming had bin space in the barn on his spread five miles down the road.

Fixing up wooden bins didn't make Tom happy. "I wouldn't have to do it if Ward wasn't so tight," he'd told Sally. "He knew we'd need more storage this year. I started on him in June. But I couldn't get him to move. Now he wants to put in a bin but I can't get a bin. They're back-ordered. The work's all gratis, me sweeping and cleaning up and moving the grain in and out. It won't cost him anything."

"You just don't know each other well enough yet," Sally had soothed him. "It's your first year together."

"Landerses pretty much let me do what I think best."

"All Ward knows about Tom Bauer so far is what the bank told him," Sally said. "He'll learn he can trust you."

Tom went into Osage Station that afternoon to buy filters for the combine. The town of five thousand people, ten miles southwest of his home farm, was a busy commercial center with four farm implement dealers still holding on when most such towns were down to one or none. Plymouth was the same distance away to the west, a thousand people larger and the county seat. The Bauers banked in Plymouth, but Tom and a lot of folks thought the town was stuck up, more interested in its antebellum homes than in serving the needs of farmers with hog manure on their boots. Osage Station acted like it wanted your business.

Tom read a bill for a farm dispersal auction on the counter at the Case International dealer while he waited for the parts clerk to assemble his supplies. Two oil filters and one hydraulic filter cost $19.64. Air filters were on back order. He asked for one to be reserved. Across the road at Fleckmeier Implements he looked in on his big Oliver tractor. He was having it overhauled. Its diesel engine block was set crosswise on its frame, its valves and cylinders spread all over the mechanic's workbench waiting for parts to be delivered from Kansas City.

Past an old empty factory Tom turned in next at the Keller Machine Works, a tall, corrugated-steel building closer to the center of town. He needed a new set of pulleys for one of his many power augers, Archimedes' screws that moved feed and grain around. He always liked to look in at Keller's. Every kind of farm equipment was repaired there. The air inside the old building was mellow with machine oil punched with pungent ozone from the welder arcs. Circuses traveling anywhere within a five-state area sent their broken Ferris wheels and merry-go-rounds to Keller's. Tom admired the work of the Keller machinists extravagantly. There wasn't anything they couldn't fix. If he'd had time he'd have loved just to sit there and watch them. Farming was machinery, and Tom was good at it, but the boys at Keller's were in a class by themselves.

Back home in midafternoon, the sky white with haze, it was hot

enough to worry again about the sow. All four fans set in the north
and south walls of the farrowing house were running full blast.
Even with the fans, the big disk thermometer on the east wall read
above ninety degrees. The other sows were handling the heat okay.
They rested on the cool concrete slats of their crates with their pigs
sprawled around them. But the pregnant sow was overheated, still
lying heavily on her side, her mouth open now and panting, misery
in her one visible eye. Tom moved fast to the faucet on the east
wall, picked up the white plastic hose coiled underneath and hosed
the sow down. The splashing water cooled her right away and she
eased up on her panting. She rolled her eye back to see where the
water was coming from, blinked her long white eyelashes and
grunted in relief. Tom had read about a cooling system for farrowing houses that automatically dripped water onto the sows
when the temperature got high. He wanted to put one in as soon
as he could afford it, maybe next winter.

He stood in the semidarkness keeping an eye on the sow. Storage
wouldn't be a problem for some of his soybeans at least. Some of
his soybeans were already sold. He'd sold them last April, before
he even planted them, after the Russian nuclear power plant explosion at Chernobyl.

Tom and Sally had been listening to the six o'clock farm report
the morning after the news of Chernobyl broke. They noticed that
soybean futures were up thirty cents. Thirty cents was the maximum daily change, up or down, allowed by law. The second day,
beans went up another thirty cents. That got their attention. They
figured traders were speculating that the fallout from Chernobyl
might pollute the Ukraine, where the Russians grew most of their
grain. They watched the speculating. It could lock in a higher price
for their unplanted soybeans than they were likely to get at harvesttime or for months afterward. Beans went up another thirty
cents on the third day, to $5.22. That was a good price, Tom told
Sally. He'd sold beans in January, when supplies were low, for
$5.18. Sally was willing to gamble on a fourth day. Tom argued
that it could go down as fast as it went up. So that third day, April
30, Sally nervous about it, the Bauers contracted to deliver 3,000
bushels of soybeans, half their anticipated crop, in November, for
$5.22 a bushel, the first time they'd ever contracted a crop they

didn't have planted. Soybean futures dropped thirty cents the following day, thirty cents more the next. This morning, five months
later, the market price had been $4.60.

Tom called those beans his Chernobyl beans. It's an ill wind that
blows nobody good.

THREE

Tom Bauer's forebears came from central Germany, from a thousand-year-old German Catholic farming village in Hesse where half the town answered to some variation on the Bauer name. Franz Bauer, Tom's great-grandfather, arrived in the United States in 1855, when he was thirty years old, and made his way to St. Louis. He was one of some two and a half million Germans who emigrated to the United States in the first six decades of the nineteenth century, an emigration that swelled between 1848 and 1860 to a flood. The farmers among the immigrants brought with them German habits of husbandry that invested the rural American landscape with its most characteristic features, the single-family farmstead and the multipurpose barn. The midlands English who preceded them had come from a milder land where people lived crowded together in villages and walked out to farm and where cattle weren't stabled in barns in winter but fed in the fields from open haystacks.

The year after he arrived in Missouri, Franz Bauer married a twenty-six-year-old Hanover-born widow with three sons who owned a 205-acre farm. She bore him five children and died in 1870 when she was forty years old. Later the same year Franz married again at forty-five, another Hanover girl, Bernardina, twenty-three years old, Tom's great-grandmother. Ten more years,

36

four more children, and they moved to Crevecoeur County and bought a 197-acre farm from one Elliott Lackland for six thousand dollars. Franz hardly had time to develop his new farm. He died the following year in mid-December.

Franz's son Henry, Tom's grandfather, was six years old when his father died. Sally's family-treeing records didn't reveal how he grew up, but as a young man Henry found his way to Union, Missouri, nearer St. Louis downriver, and it was there, in 1903, that Tom's father, William Bauer, was born. Henry came back to Crevecoeur County in 1914 and bought land near Devon. He was the northernmost German on the road running south from Devon toward Osage Station. The people of Devon were English-descended and suspicious of Germans, especially during the years of the Great War. Some Devon men had come out to Henry's farm one night and threatened to tar and feather him. They accused him of sending money secretly to Germany to support the kaiser's war. His wife had opened the screen door and handed out a check for twenty-five dollars to give them to buy war bonds with and reluctantly Henry had signed it. The Devon people took the check and went off. Tom's grandfather always figured they spent the twenty-five dollars in a saloon somewhere laughing at him. The next day he'd gone into Osage Station, taken his war bonds out of the bank there and bought himself a .30-caliber revolver. He'd gone to Devon and shown the vigilantes the war bonds and the revolver. "If you come by my house tonight," he'd told them, "there won't be no woman to protect you." Not long after that he'd sold his farm and bought eighty acres farther south along the same road, closer in among the farms of the German community there.

Henry nearly lost his eighty acres during the Depression. "The old people he bought them from forgave the interest or he would have," Tom remembered his father telling him, one of William Bauer's cautionary tales. The farm descended to one of Tom's aunts, who still lived on the place. Tom and Sally could see its barn from their living room.

In 1929, William Bauer, Tom's father, married a schoolteacher and church organist of Prussian antecedents whose people owned a feed store in Franklin. Clara Halfen's father raised purebred hogs

and cattle as well and advertised fancy show fowls for sale—
brown leghorns, Cornish Indian game hens, white fantail and red
Jacobin pigeons. The Bauer-Halfen wedding, the Franklin newspaper reported, was an "impressive service." Though William was
twenty-six and landless, the newspaper promoted him to the status
of a "prominent farmer" for his wedding day. But if there was
money in the Halfen family, it didn't pass over as dowry.

Clara bore her husband ten children, of whom Tom, born in
1939, was the fifth son and seventh child. The Depression was
hard on the Bauers. Like the cat in Mark Twain's story who sat on
a hot stove and refused ever after to sit on any stove, even a cold
one, William learned his lessons all too well. He'd had to borrow
money for farm machinery, but he vowed that when he got out of
debt, which he finally did in 1946, he'd never borrow another
penny. As a result, he worked the same rented 335 acres from
1939 until he retired from farming the year Clara died, 1973. Sally
was part of the family by then, so her auctioneer father got the job
of auctioning off her father-in-law's farm equipment, a well-kept
but worn assortment of John Deere, Oliver, International and
Massey-Ferguson machines, hog sheds and feeders, wagons and
shop tools. William married his widowed sister-in-law in 1975.
Five years later, seriously diabetic, he died of pneumonia, leaving
each of his children savings totaling fifteen hundred dollars apiece.
"Dad thought he was rich when he had ten thousand dollars in the
bank," Tom said once bluntly. "Why, ten thousand dollars today
wouldn't even feed out a bunch of hogs."

But if there was no land to inherit, there'd been another way to
build a stake. As his sons had come of age in the 1950s and 1960s,
William Bauer had partnered those who wanted to farm into farming, sharing his equipment with them in return for help at planting
time and harvest. He'd partnered Warner first. Dale had gone into
the Air Force Reserve and then worked for the Air Force as a
civilian aircraft mechanic. He'd only taken up farming in retirement, as a supplement to his business selling seed. William's third
son, Holden, whom everyone called Cowboy, was next. Lewis
became a feed salesman and hobby-farmed eighty acres on the
side. Then came Tom. Warner was driving a semi now, Cowboy
working as a carpenter after a period of running a Lake of the

Ozarks resort, Lewis still selling feed. Only Tom had continued farming full time across the long haul.

After he'd finished high school in 1957 and had a chance to work and play around a little, Tom had joined the Army Reserve. He didn't know then if he wanted to farm. Toward the end of his six months' service, he was stationed at Fort Sill, Oklahoma, as an artillery instructor. His dad had driven down to Oklahoma to make him a proposition. "Old Drew Sauer's got a farm he wants to rent you," William told his son. "If you want to go into farming, here's your chance, and I'll help you." The Drew Sauer farm, off 24 between Plymouth and Devon, was 360 acres, big enough for a start. Tom thought it over while he finished up soldiering. Sauer had a reputation for meanness, but Tom got along with everybody and the land was too good to pass up. William loaned his youngest son nineteen hundred dollars to put out his first crops. Tom lived in Plymouth and drove out to farm. Within three years he'd paid his dad back in full.

They were harder years than Tom expected. He worked from morning to night, but he'd never minded work. He did mind mistreatment. Drew Sauer lived up to his reputation. Nothing Tom ever did was right. The old man was always hanging around second-guessing and criticizing. Tom worried himself half sick. He couldn't eat and he couldn't much sleep. William Bauer saw how his son was suffering and advised him to get out of it. "It ain't worth your health, son," he told Tom.

By then Tom and Sally had married. Neighbors had noticed how hard Tom worked. An auctioneer who owned 240 acres near Devon came to see him. "You want to rent my farm, I'd be glad to have you," he told him. Sauer couldn't understand why Tom was pulling out. "Terrible old man," Tom told Sally. "He even drove his own sons off the place." But Tom learned from the old bastard. William Bauer had been better with crops than with hogs. Sauer knew hogs cold, all the little Indian tricks. He taught Tom how to make a hog operation really go.

Two hundred forty acres wasn't enough to support a family. Along came Eli Landers next, the father of the present generation of Landerses, wanting Tom to take over the Elms. Tom and Sally added the Elms to their operations in 1969, moving out from

Plymouth to an old bungalow farmhouse on Landers land along the highway. When they bought the home place in 1972 they let the auctioneer's farm go.

Drew Sauer had been hard and mean both, but William Bauer hadn't exactly been soft. He'd raised his children hard, worked them hard, kept them spare of luxuries. They'd walked a mile each way to the one-room grade school out on the highway regardless of weather, and Tom remembered with some bitterness a blowing snowstorm one winter when his youngest sister nearly hadn't made it. Pushing against the battering of the snow, chilled and exhausted, she'd wanted to give up and lie down to sleep that day. Tom had saved her, carried and dragged her home, where he'd found his father settled in reading with his feet up beside the warm stove. "He could have come and gotten us in the car," Tom said of that incident. "He didn't have anything better to do." So gifted musically that without learning to read a score he played the piano by ear and led a band, Tom begged and begged his dad for permission to study music in high school. That would have cost the rental of an instrument, money William Bauer wouldn't spend. The only luxury Tom and his brothers and sisters were allowed was a 4-H Club membership. Neither William nor Clara Bauer attended Tom's high school graduation. Sally was shocked.

The worst time Tom remembered with his dad was once when Lewis had talked back to a neighbor who was helping them put up hay. Lewis was fifteen then, a year older than Tom. The neighbor, Nero Polotto, had been a coal miner when they were still working the veins of coal around Osage Station—there'd been forty-six coal mines in Crevecoeur County at the height of the mining earlier in the century—and then had turned to farming. Childless, Nero was like a second father to Tom, but he had an ugly mouth. He was always pushing people, giving them lip. He'd been pushing Lewis that day. Lewis had the job of raking the hay into windrows with a side-delivery rake pulled behind a tractor and Nero was harassing him about missing hay at the end of the windrow when he turned the tractor around. Lewis had finally blown and mouthed off.

"Dad didn't believe in younger talking back to older," Tom would recall. "That evening he came in to where Lewis was wash-

ing up and coldcocked him, knocked him out. No warning at all."
Tom helped his brother to his feet when he came to. They went
down to supper and William Bauer told Lewis to get on up to
Nero's and apologize. In the state he was in, and after a hard day
out in the field, Lewis had to walk a mile uphill to Nero's. The
Italian farmer was surprised and embarrassed. He knew he'd egged
Lewis on. He got up from his supper and walked all the way back
with Lewis to straighten the thing out.

Tom remembered a battering his dad gave him at sixteen. Tom
was setting a fencepost, his hand flat on the post, listening to his
dad going on about something he didn't want to hear, when all of
a sudden the old man slammed Tom's hand with his big fist. It hurt
like hell. "Goddamn it, boy," his dad had sworn at him, "quit that
pouting and act like a man."

"He didn't like you to carry a grudge," Tom said when he told
Sally that story. "Once the argument was over you was supposed
to straighten up and get on with it."

Tom took after his dad in money matters, Sally discovered.
"You helped me with that," he told her when they reminisced. "I
was just like Dad. Didn't believe in buying anything he couldn't
pay for."

"He made that old landlord rich," Sally complained of her husband's father. "All the work you boys and him put into that farm.
And the man didn't even appreciate it. The landlords used to look
down on their tenants around here. That's changed. Mr. Landers
didn't treat you that way. He appreciated what you done for him."

William Bauer didn't approve of Tom and Sally buying their
farm. Neither did Nero Polotto. Buying the Dixon farm before
they'd paid off the home farm was even worse in the older farmers'
eyes. "I didn't see that they'd done so well financially that I should
follow their advice," Tom judged levelly. "I finally had to tell
them, 'It's my money and I'll decide how to spend it.' It looked to
me like they'd passed up a golden chance back in the forties with
the war. That old man who owned the farm Dad rented wanted to
sell it any which way. Fifty-fifty, he told Dad, cash, whatever.
Fifty-fifty was just like farming on shares except Dad would have
had the whole expense and he'd have had to pay half the profits to
the landlord. When he said fifty-fifty, though, that ought to of been

Dad's signal, because it meant if there was a bad year he'd pay less against it. But Dad passed it up. So I didn't see what they had to say to me."

The time came when Tom had to tell his dad to mind his own business. Tom was off one morning trading one of his trucks for a better used truck, upgrading. His dad was helping out with the harvest. William Bauer came in and confronted his son. "You ever going to get out here in the field?" he asked him.

"I traded trucks, Dad," Tom explained, happy with the exchange.

William Bauer made a face. "I knowed that money would burn a hole in your pocket," he snapped.

"It's bought and paid for and it's my money," Tom snapped back.

His dad took off for the field then without another word. Tom decided it was damned well time to declare his independence. He waited awhile and then drove out himself. His dad was combining. Tom passed him at the end of a terrace and stuck out his tongue!

William Bauer had the good grace to quit his pouting. He laughed. Tom had made his point and the fight was over.

FOUR

A combine is a mobile factory that separates grain and seed from husk and stalk and pod. It's a tunnel that connects the natural to the human world, a cornucopia, and it comes big enough to handle the job. The Case International 1460 that Tom wheeled from the darkness of its storage shed that first week of September, diesel engine growling, exhaust stack smoking, five picker-head snouts thrust forward, was about as tall and nearly as long as a double-decker London bus and the same bright, cheerful red. To reach the big glassed-in cab that hung out over the machine body—room for two to sit there shut of dust and weather—Tom had to lower a steel stepladder locked up horizontally against the side. He climbed the stepladder to the cab porch, locked the ladder horizontal again out of the way, turned and opened a glass-windowed door and entered the cab. It was musty from winter storage. Cobwebs collected soybean chaff that had sifted up from the floor on winter drafts and there were mouse nests in the corners. Dust clouded the big tinted-glass front window. Tom worked the windshield wiper to sweep the window clean.

Looking out and down from the elevated cab, he could see the picker head like a giant open hand extended palm-up below. It was the right attachment for corn, with steel snouts to guide the rows of cornstalks into the chain-driven snappers that broke the ears loose. The attachment for soybeans and wheat, the one he'd used helping out his neighbor, was different. Called a header, it had a reel like a paddle wheel that gathered in those lighter crops. Tom had stored his bulky twenty-foot header on another farm.

A bin big enough to hold nearly two hundred bushels of grain occupied the upper level of the combine behind the cab housing. A fourteen-foot auger like a red steel stovepipe stowed horizontally against the bin. By shifting a lever, Tom could swing the dump auger out away from the combine body to unload grain from the holding bin into a truck or a grain wagon. Behind the holding bin, set crosswise, a 185-horsepower diesel engine propelled the combine and powered its machinery, its silver-painted exhaust stack pointing straight up into the air.

Below decks on this flagship of the prairie, an automated production line received whole ears of corn or pods of beans or heads of grain into its throat from the picker head or the header and separated and cleaned the grain as it passed through, augering the clean grain up into the holding bin and discharging the waste of stalks or straw out the rear. Tom would harvest corn first that autumn, soybeans next, and then, the following June, if he got any planted before winter, soft winter wheat. With the right adjustments, a combine operated by one man could harvest sunflower seeds, oats, grass seed, even rice, passing over hundreds of acres in a single season. Tom's 1460 sold new in 1979 for eighty thousand dollars. He'd bought it used three years ago, when it was worth about forty thousand dollars, for eighteen thousand dollars and the trade of his old Massey-Ferguson. He still owed about nine thousand dollars on it.

Tom drove the combine down the packed dirt lane between the fields of the Ward farm where he'd stored it and out to the county road, studying the condition of the ripening corn along the way. The combine with its picker head was fourteen feet wide and he checked the two-lane blacktop both ways before entering it and heading north toward the highway. Sometimes big semi's came roaring out of nowhere, commercial trailer trucks that belonged on the interstate highballing the back roads to avoid the weigh stations that would gig them for being over legal weight. "I thought

I was going to marry him for sure," Tom quipped once when he nearly got sideswiped. The combine had deep-treaded front tires tall as a man. It steered through its smaller rear wheels—the steering linkages reversed the direction Tom turned the wheel inside the cab. At its road speed of eighteen miles per hour it tended to wobble because the weight distribution was bad when the holding bin was empty. He kept it half on the road, half on the shoulder to allow room for cars to pass.

Back home Tom wheeled the combine around onto the yard south of the house, lowered the picker head to the ground and moved a lever to disconnect it from the combine throat. He backed away, the combine looking suddenly naked without its rank of armored snouts, wheeled again north, swung around east and parked on the concrete slab outside the workshop. Coming out of the air-conditioned cab into the heat of late morning, dust blowing on a humid wind, reminded Tom of Reagan administration budget director David Stockman's complaint against farmers and their "air-conditioned tractors." Tom and Sally would spend more than two hundred hours during the next three months driving the combine day and night through clouds of blowing chaff, mold, insects and dust, in humid ninety-degree heat and in cutting twenty-degree cold. Nothing pained him more than hearing poorly informed city types echoing Stockman's insult. "That's just ignorant," he'd say. "I used to come in at night with the dust chills. Lie there shivering and cough and cough until the middle of the night, trying to get that old dust up out of my lungs. Farmer's lung used to be near as bad as the black lung miners get. It's just like in a factory. Controlling the cab environment saves lives, that's all."

The working surface of the combine, the rotary, was a steel tube like a submarine torpedo that ran back inside the machine up a thirteen-degree incline. The engine turned it at hundreds of revolutions per minute through pulleys like manhole covers attached to its upper end. It rotated inside a fixed steel housing that was rifled to transport the dry stalks and leaves of the crop being harvested back through the machine. Bolted onto the surface of the rotary, sixteen hardened-steel rasp bars grooved like oversized files crushed stalks and ears down against concave steel gratings fixed below, breaking everything up. The loosened grain, which was

heavy, fell through the grating spaces in the concaves; the lighter
crushed stalks and cobs barber-poled onward and upward, to be
dumped at the rear of the machine onto toothed screens called
sieves that sorted out any grain the concaves missed.

Eventually augers lifted clean grain up to the top from the bottom of the combine where it fell and poured it into the holding bin
behind the cab. A litter of stalks and cobs, rocks, clumps of mud
and whatever else the combine had picked up in the field dis-
charged out the rear end, to be disked back into the soil for organic
matter at planting time. Reaping and threshing had once been
separate chores, one done in the field, one in the farmyard. The
combine combined them. Hence its name.

In the hot sun outside the workshop, Tom unbolted two red-
enameled panels from the left side of the combine, below and
behind the cab. That exposed the three steel concaves. The concaves were heavy and awkward to handle. Their near ends were
attached to long bolts that had to be cranked down to loosen
them. The bolts raised or lowered the concaves against the rotary
to adjust them for different kinds of crops. Their far ends were
hooked, the hooks catching a steel rod on the other side of the
rotary. Once he'd cranked the contours down, Tom slammed them
in toward the rotary to free the hooks, then jerked them back out
to jump the hooks over the rod. One by one he pulled them free
and set them on the ground leaning against the combine. Removing
the contours exposed the surface of the rotary. With penetrating
oil and main force he meant to unbolt the rotary's old rasp bars
and replace them. They were original parts, worn rounded by
seven years of harvests.

He worked through the morning, stopped for dinner and to
check his hogs, worked on through the afternoon cramped between one of the big tires and the side of the combine, the sun
beating down, using a compressed-air impact wrench to spin out
the bolts that held the rasp bars. The penetrating oil found its way
into the bolt threads and was supposed to loosen them, but the
nuts were seized up from years of exposure. Tom skinned the
knuckles on both his big hands trying to wrench them free. He
didn't complain—whom would he complain to?—and worked
steadily, stopping to drink from the well tap at the side of the

workshop. Molly patrolled the combine margins, hunting down
grasshoppers. She'd stepped in an oil puddle and left dark paw-
prints on the dusty concrete slab to show where she'd pounced.

The end of the afternoon and the end of the job came together,
but the last nut holding the last of the old rasp bars wouldn't give.
By now Tom had stripped the socket of his impact wrench. He
tried a pair of locking pliers. They wouldn't budge the stubborn
nut. He fetched a hand-held grinding wheel to grind it off. When
the grinder wouldn't fit into the cramped space under the rotary,
he committed the heavy artillery: wheeled out his portable acetylene rig, wetted down the chaff in the combine bed to prevent fire
and, sparks showering, burned the nut off.

Tom had found a problem when he went to check his hogs. These
were feeder pigs, the growing offspring of another group of sows.
He'd moved them from the farrowing house after eight weeks of
nursing and weaning to a feeder floor twenty yards farther down
the lane. He currently had some two hundred hogs on feed. At an
average one hundred pounds apiece they were about halfway along
to market weight. The feeder floor was a setup of eight long,
narrow pens. The back section of each pen was solid concrete
flooring sheltered under a shed roof. The open front section was
slatted concrete where the hogs could move to relieve themselves.
The waste dropped through the slats into a holding tank that Tom
flushed once a week into the sewage lagoon. Each pen contained
feeding bins filled automatically from above by augers, a flap-
valved steel waterer that the hogs worked with their snouts, some
forty hogs and a chipped bowling ball. The bowling balls were hog
play toys. They were spiraled blue and white, like the earth seen
from outer space. The hogs nosed them around when they got
bored with jockeying for position in the hog-pen pecking order.

Tom's hogs were crossbred. Most were pink, with white hair. A
few were rust red, a few black. Some had spots—large patches of
color or missing color—white on black, black on white. They were
all lean and long-sided compared to old-fashioned hogs, a modern
conformation that maximized their production of bacon and pork
chops, which come off the animals' sides. Tom and his younger
son, Brett, had castrated the males when they were only a few days

old. That made them barrows, a word that derives from an Indo-European root, *bher,* meaning "to cut." The sexually immature females among the feeder pigs were called gilts, a diminutive of an Old Norse word for "sow." Old words carry old history: people have eaten pork for thousands of years.

Most of the hogs had been flopped down in the shade of the shed roof at the back of the pen, fitted together like a jigsaw puzzle, when Tom had visited them. A few lay out in the sun around the waterer. They'd learned to splash water with their noses to cool the concrete slats. Tom could move from pen to pen along an outside aisle. In the third pen from the lane, a white gilt stood alone looking miserable, chewing on the iron pipe of the pen gate. A swollen, bluish tube of tissue, blistered and bloody, protruded from the gilt's body under its docked tail. A section of its rectum nearly a foot long had turned inside out.

"Damn," Tom had sworn. "She's prolapsed." He'd taken the problem under advisement, returned to the workshop and worked on the combine until the end of the afternoon, when Brett drove in from football practice.

"How come you're limping?" Tom asked his son when he joined him outside the workshop. At sixteen Brett was already six feet tall, muscular and solid, with light brown hair trimmed to a cap and an open, American face. He was gifted like his mother at mocking pretension.

"I tackled a guy in scrimmage and got a cleat up my butt."

"Better watch that," Tom cautioned. "You already tore up your knee."

Brett let his shoulders droop and hung his head. "I remember," he mocked. He'd had surgery the previous year on his left knee for torn cartilage, a football injury.

"Let's get on down to the feeding floor," Tom told him. "We've got a prolapse."

"Ugh."

"Yeah, it ain't pretty, but it's got to be done."

Tom never lifted anything a machine could lift and never walked when he could ride. He wasn't lazy and he wasn't naturally opposed to exercise. He just had too much to do to do it all by hand. For the hundred-yard drive to the feeding floor he wheeled out a red Kawasaki three-wheeler, straddled it and started it up. It was a saddle horse that ran on gas, an off-the-road motorcycle with wide soft tires. Brett mounted up behind, wincing. Tom toed the gearshift lever and made the gravel fly.

He stopped first at the farrowing house and fetched a disposable plastic glove. At the feeding floor at the hottest hour of the day Brett slipped into the pen and caught the gilt by the back leg and dragged it squealing out into the aisle.

Tom pulled on the glove. "We got to haul it up by its hind legs and hang it over the gate," he directed. Brett caught the other back leg. It was slippery with brown manure and hard to hold. He worked the animal around as if it were a wheelbarrow, its front legs the wheel, until its belly approached the gate to the pen. Bracing himself, his father helping with his free hand, he heaved the hog up so that it hung down with its hind legs latched over the gate, its butt in the air, the prolapse flopping to one side like a water-filled balloon.

"Hold her now," Tom told his son.

"I'm holding."

Carefully Tom began working the sore, swollen rectum back into the gilt's body. He made a blunt probe of his fingertips and thumb and used it to force the tissue through the tight anal sphincter. The gilt screamed, the scream piercing up from where its head hung below. Tom's eyes widened in sympathy.

"Gross," Brett said. He liked animals and was good with them and paid attention. "What causes that, Dad?"

"It's probably in the breeding, son."

"We've had three in the last six months."

"I know it. I'm thinking I ought to replace that old boar. He's getting wore out. When those gilts are ready to breed we'll need new blood anyway." Nearly a year ago, Tom had saved back the best twenty-five gilts from a farrowing to increase his breeding stock. Since the boars now on the farm were their sires, he'd need new boars for them to avoid inbreeding.

With half the prolapse back inside, Tom worked on easing in a blister. A grunt of pain from the gilt squirted the entire prolapse back out again. Tom dropped his gloved hand to his side in disgust and stretched his fingers to rest them. Brett hitched the animal up more comfortably over the round iron pipe and got a better grip. Man and boy were both sweating.

Tom began again. This time he worked the blister more carefully. It passed in. The rest of the replacement went easier. Brett lowered the animal to its feet. It stood for a moment blinking, finding its bearings, then scooted off to join the herd.

"Think it'll take, Dad?" Brett asked. He closed the gate and dropped in the long pin that latched it.

"It might, son." Tom moved aside and peeled off the plastic glove. "The next couple of days will tell the tale. Check it when you run feed in, okay?"

"If it comes out again will you ship it?"

Tom nodded and led the way to the three-wheeler. "Don't have much choice," he said.

At five thirty Tom pulled the combine into the barn next to the cattle lot to get it out of the weather. One thunderstorm had already blown by to the west and more were forming far to the south like a mountain range rising. He cleaned up and drove off to a combine clinic just as Sally was arriving home.

He followed the county road east around the Dixon farm and then south toward Osage Station, passing trim white farmhouses centered on green yards. The full-grown corn and soybeans squared off the fields to solid blocks. Rolling green pastures separated them where black, white-faced cattle grazed. The sky above this former prairie reached unbroken from horizon to horizon. It gave a sense of vast distance and made the land seem domed. The wind had picked up. Towering black thunderheads roiled up now to the south. At their full height they sheered out into hammerheads. Lightning stitched and splashed them. They advanced northward toward Osage Station above a broad line of slanting rain the color of seawater shot with light, so that the land where the storm worked seemed submerged.

The wind was blowing hard at the Case International dealership when Tom pulled up in front and parked. He walked around outside the building past a new red 1660 Axial-Flow combine to the shop floor. There was already a crowd on hand in the open concrete bay. The bay was as big as a school gymnasium, with a

high ceiling. Farmers were trading an hour of their time for the free supper the dealership would serve and enjoying socializing with their neighbors and friends into the bargain. Most of the men wore blue jeans or denim overalls and plain cotton shirts, but their seed caps made a show in the gray, grease-stained shop. There were blue, green, red, yellow, brown and black caps on hand, sewn with patches advertising Busch beer, hybrid corn varieties like Funk's, Jacques or O's Gold, the Missouri Farmers Association co-op in Osage Station, Comstock's or Case. Companies started out giving the caps to farmers to promote sales. By now they'd become a trademark of Corn Belt farming as distinctive as the cowboy's Stetson or the construction worker's hard hat. Tom owned a dozen seed caps. They hung on hooks around the wall of the mud room of his house, off the kitchen inside the back door. He usually selected one that went along with the business of the day. He'd worn a blue Comstock cap when he visited the elevator to talk about storage. Tonight he wore a red cap with a Case International patch.

The big hanger doors at the north end of the shop had been rolled back to show off the brand-new 1660 combine. Two men from the parts department grilled hamburgers on two tripod charcoal grills set just outside the door. Farmers loaded paper plates with hamburger buns, tomatoes, onions and chips from a red-draped picnic table, picked a can of beer or soda out of the shaved ice of a cattle-watering tank and moved on to the grills to claim their hamburgers. The Case dealer, a fleshy man in a Western shirt and cowboy boots with wavy silver hair, manned the table serving iced tea. He sponsored the clinic to show customers the new combines and to sell them on coming to him for upgrade kits and repairs. The rural hard times of the Reagan years hit dealers as much as farmers. Business wasn't good.

Tom saw his nephew Hollis sitting in the front row of the folding chairs the dealership had set up. He retrieved a Pepsi and joined him. Hollis was as broad-shouldered as his uncle but thicker through the waist and not so tall. He welcomed Tom with a nod, standard laid-back farmer style.

"How's it going, Hollis?" Tom asked, popping the top of his Pepsi can.

"Not too bad."

"You waiting out this line?"

"Yeah." Hollis pointed to a compact, muscular farmer across the room. The man needed a shave. His side-whiskers were white and he wore a greasy green cap bare of endorsement. "Old Jenkins and his boy just bought themselves a new combine," he said.

"The hell they did. They're real farmers, those two."

"They're buying up farms right and left these days. Paying cash."

"So I hear," Tom said. He swigged his Pepsi.

"They work hard, though. I don't think Jenkins has ever taken a vacation, has he?" Hollis had a Lite beer.

"Not that I ever heard of." Tom winked. "They'll eat your ass out if you get in their way, but they're good farmers." He studied the line awhile and then stood. "We better take our chances, Hollis. The way the implement business is going, these boys might run out of hamburgers."

Hollis stood with him. "Might be better for us if they did. They could always order one for you out of that parts depot they got in Kansas City. Only take a week."

"Take a week and cost a fortune," Tom piggybacked. Laughing, the two men joined the line.

The 1660 filled the entire open end of the shop. The two grills in front of it smoked like altars. The smoke blowing into the room would have made men less familiar with dust and commotion uncomfortable. As the wind picked up, the storm coming on, the smoke swirled thicker around the men in line. Finally someone complained and the two parts men moved the cookers to one side. It was the wrong side, the side from which the wind was blowing. The combine faded behind a screen of smoke then, like a magician's elephant disappearing from a stage. The room turned blue with smoke, the dealer crossed the room to swear at the parts men, the parts men scrambled the two cookers across the smoky opening to the other side and the wind blew the smoke away to reveal the looming red machine.

Abruptly the storm broke and the comedy ended. Instantly it was cold. Cold wet wind lashed through the room taming the smoke, kicking paper plates to the floor, flipping over empty beer cans. Thick lines of driving rain beat a slant across the opening and pounded the concrete deck. Lightning lit the big machine. Thunder crashed. The trees whistled in the wind.

The men finishing their suppers hardly seemed to notice. They lived with weather every day. It was harvesttime. They didn't need rain now. They needed sun.

Tom noticed. He liked all weather, all seasons, all elements, all challenge and change. The storm passed over. The rain stopped. A Case rep stepped up to introduce the new combine and point out its new features. Its bank of working lights made its enameled red surfaces glow. It and its kind would dominate their days and nights for months to come, a set of God-sized shears to trim the crop that grew like golden hair on the back of the muscular brown land. Tom nudged his nephew. They worked on and through machines. Every machine had to be serviced and adjusted before it could be used. Getting everything ready was hard work and there was pride in the accomplishment. The factory-clean machine displayed before them helped them see their way through to that end. Tom nodded at the combine and gave it an admiring wink. "She's set on *go,*" he said. So was he, for the harvest soon to begin.

FIVE

First thing every morning Tom checked his cattle and hogs. The holdout sow had farrowed during the night. Ten squeaking pigs, wrinkled and thin, climbed over each other scrapping along her teat lines, fighting to establish their claims. Two pigs had been born dead. One had died weeks earlier in the womb and was mummified, purple and shriveled. The other was a large, healthy pig that had probably smothered in the birth canal. On his way out, Tom picked both of them from the slatted floor at the back of the farrowing crate and dropped them into a five-gallon bucket that held earlier losses. "Seems like it's always the biggest pig that comes out last and gets smothered," he told Sally. Birthing as many as fourteen pigs at a farrowing, the sows tired, their contractions weakening. Once Tom would have set the alarm through the night for several nights running if necessary to midwife a sow. He had too much to do now to trade sleep for a pig. During waking hours when a sow began farrowing he injected it with oxytocin, a drug that strengthens contractions, to help the later pigs along. He'd saved a lot of pigs that way.

Except for Wayne, who was a sophomore off at college, the whole Bauer family sat down to breakfast together every morning before heading its separate ways. Sammi, the nine-year-old, still baby-plump, a child's tummy rounding her waist, was excited about the first meeting that Thursday of her special gifted class.

She had her mother's dark eyes, large in her child's open face, and wore her dark straight hair cut bobbed. Last spring she'd tested out with the highest IQ of anyone in her grade in the entire Plymouth school district. She was a champion reader and a chatterbox with a quick smile. To ask a question she imitated a character from a book setting a finger to her cheek and cocking her head. Collecting ran in the family. Her brother Wayne collected Western-style belt buckles. She collected Barbie dolls and their endless accessories, buying them up for pennies at the garage sales she and her mother liked to shop. More than sixty of the skinny, platinum-haired dolls filled an entire room in the finished basement of the house, where Wayne and Brett had their bedrooms. It looked unreal, rows of identical dolls staring from shelves and chairs and daybeds, like a congress of cheerleaders assembled somewhere beyond the twilight zone.

In the backyard, under the big oak, Sammi had built a model countryside of dirt roads and twig fences. An assortment of plastic farm animals grazed her fields—small horses and giant chickens, hogs larger than cows—and a heavy traffic of battered steel toy trucks left over from her brothers' childhoods lumbered through the dappled shade. A combine had been her cradle. She'd slept through the harvests of her infancy in the cab beside her mother as Sally worked, corn and soybeans roaring lullabies.

Sally was off again to the ceramics shop. She was packing pieces to sell at the annual show in Kansas City in October, trying to get her overworked brother organized before Tom needed her to run the combine. Brett, a junior at Plymouth High School and a popular tackle on the junior varsity, would stay after school again for football practice. "You'll need to mix some feed when you get home," his father instructed him. The feed was for the hogs.

Tom planned to start the day by moisture-testing some corn, then clean out one of those backup storage spaces before carrying on with servicing the combine. There was also a corn test plot to visit down in the river bottoms that the Young Farmers Association was picking that day. It was cooler this morning after yesterday's storms, the sky blue and clear. Tom collected a broom, a scoop shovel and his portable moisture tester and drove off in the blue International work pickup rather than the GMC. The old truck coughed and stalled its way down the lane, warming up. Toolboxes built into its side panels and a seventy-five-gallon diesel fuel tank mounted behind the cab with a pump that ran off the engine battery allowed him to service and repair his farm machinery in the field. He'd nicknamed the truck Babe after the blue ox of the Paul Bunyan tall tales. Its odometer showed 147,000 miles, well along on the second hundred thousand.

The first field Tom planned to pick was a bottomland fifteen acres on the Ward farm. Field corn varieties differ by days and even weeks in the time they need to grow from planting to harvest. The corn Tom had planted in the Ward bottomland in April was an earlier-maturing variety, so it would be ready before some of his other fields. Since bottomland didn't drain as well as upland, he also wanted to get the field picked before autumn rains turned it into a mire. Tom made it a practice, a gift of goodwill to his landlords, to harvest his share crops before his own.

Field corn wasn't the sweet corn that city people ate. The individual kernels were bigger, longer in the tooth, dented at the top when they dried, and the ears were twice as big. They grew one and sometimes two to a stalk. They were picked ripe, when the meat of the kernel, the endosperm, had turned to starch and hardened, rather than green, when it was still mostly sugar paste and soft. The husks that protected the ears from the weather ripened too, toughening to the color of raw linen from sweet corn's unripened green. You could eat field corn when it was in the sugar stage just as you could eat sweet corn, but that wasn't the stage in which it was harvested. When it was ready for harvest the kernels were flinty. You had to wait for it to dry down below twenty-percent moisture unless you wanted to dry it in the bin with propane. It needed air blown through it once it was picked and in the bin to drop it on down below ten-percent moisture for long-term storage. Otherwise it could ferment and the heat of fermentation could kill it, pockets within the bin burning to a black carbon char. Each individual corn kernel was alive, a plant embryo in a state of arrested development packed with a starter supply of nutrients. If it died, chemical changes reduced its food value. Harvesting such living fruits by the billions meant paying close attention. It was anything but routine work.

Tom parked on the same road through the Ward fields that he'd driven earlier in the week when he'd brought out the combine. The Ward farm was located a mile west and south of his own. To get there he drove north to Devon, west on U.S. 24, south on the county blacktop. The road through the fields ran east off the blacktop, dividing the bottomland of the farm from the upland. It followed the rise of a low, weathered hill to the old fallen-down homestead collapsed within a grove of big oaks that looked north from the flattened crest. Beyond the homestead on the table of upland was the converted barn where Tom stored the combine. Beyond that, more corn and soybean fields extended south up a further rise that dictated their terracing. Back at the beginning again, at the northern limit of the farm, Little Cebo Creek meandering west formed the boundary of the bottomland. Tall rows of cornstalks standing shoulder to shoulder hemmed in the road, blocking the view of the creek, but the grass and weeds growing on the hill slope and the shallow pond at the western edge of the bottomland signaled drainage problems. Tom had only farmed the Ward place for one season. He had major plans for improving it.

He left Babe on the one-lane road and pushed his way into the bottomland corn. Five rows in he snapped off an ear, rustled a few feet farther down the row and snapped off another ear. He shucked the husks, carried the ears back to the truck, found a coffee can and shelled it full. The kernels were plump and rosy yellow. Tom chewed one to test it, nodded and spit it out.

His portable moisture tester looked like a high-tech coffee can. On the open tailgate of the truck he poured it full of kernels, set its scale and pushed a button. A battery sent electricity through the corn sample and a meter measured the sample's conductivity, which depended on its moisture. A rotating scale gave Tom the number he was looking for, twenty-one percent. That was still high, but it was getting there. With the sun out, even one day would make a big difference. The blower would work more efficiently on these first loads, before the bin filled up. It wouldn't be long now.

He hadn't used his moisture tester since the previous fall. It might be off. Tom decided to check it against a big state-inspected unit at an elevator. The Missouri Farmers Association cooperative elevator in Osage Station, four miles due south on the blacktop, was closer than Riverton. From MFA he could loop around the other county road to his brother's place. He backed Babe out to the blacktop and headed south.

Periwinkle-blue chicory bloomed at roadside. The soybeans had begun to turn. The leaves yellowed before they dropped. This early, the passing fields looked as if they were laid over with dark jade veined with gold. The countryside changed color from season to season, but at transitional seasons, spring and fall, it also changed color from day to day and you could tell exactly how things were if you knew what you were looking at. When the crops were harvested it opened up; when the crops were full grown it closed in. It breathed. There was life from horizon to horizon right down to the least small organism in the soil.

Two miles along toward Osage Station Tom passed an access road marked with a No Admittance sign. It led to a locked gate and beyond the locked gate to what looked like a small fenced lot. But the lot was surfaced with smooth gray concrete with stream-lined curbs and a microwave communications antenna was mounted on the fence. Tom was used to the installation and hardly gave it a glance. It was a missile silo, blast-hardened and eighty feet deep, one of 150 punched into the central Missouri countryside on precise five-mile centers, insensible to the lay of the land. A three-stage Minuteman II missile was shock-mounted inside the silo, ready to fire, with a 1.2-megaton warhead.

In the scale room at the MFA office Tom gave the young clerk the coffee can of corn to test. The clerk weighed a 250-gram sample and poured it into his tester. The digital screen on his tester read out 23.7 percent. He poured the kernels back into the coffee can.

"How come you run that tester three percent high?" Tom asked, his voice going hard.

The clerk was surprised. "You're kidding."

"I'm serious. That old boy who used to work here said it ran high. There's a lot of talk about it."

"The state inspector always passes it," the clerk said. He turned back to the machine and ran another sample of Tom's corn. This time he got 23.9, well within tolerances.

"I don't know," Tom concluded as he picked up to leave, "it sure looks to me like it runs high." He made a mental note to send Brett to Comstock's with the coffee can to compare the two testers. Farmer against miller was a battle as old as the hills.

Tom pulled into the driveway of his older brother Warner's house and knocked on the back door. No one was home. A timid German shepherd came around from the front yard. She did her bows and Tom gave her a pat. His brother was making some changes. He'd decided to sell off most of his land. Lately he was driving a semi as an independent hauler, hauling corn down to Arkansas to the big Tyson broiler factories there. He was probably off making a run. The wife worked.

Tom crossed to the weathered gray barn behind the house and slid back the heavy door. Parked inside was his brother's silver pickup and, directly behind it, a small, open-seat New Idea tractor fitted with a scoop blade. The key was in the pickup's ignition but it wouldn't start. The battery was dead. Tom shifted into neutral, jumped down, pushed the truck out into the driveway and set the brakes. Back inside the barn he studied the two connected corn-cribs off the main aisle that he meant to clean. They'd been turned to storage, truck tires stacked in, pumps, lumber, pieces of angle iron, a quilt wadded into mouse nests on the floor, dust everywhere and cobwebs and chewed chunks of corncob. Tom counted four truck tires. They were new. He kicked one. "I bet old Warner bought these at a sale somewhere," he said. Out in the yard the German shepherd heard him and wagged her tail.

In the garage between the barn and the house Tom found an extension light. He strung it into the cribs to penetrate the gloom. Out came the junk, piece by piece. Tom loaded it into the tractor scoop. When the scoop was full he started up the tractor and drove around to the south side of the barn to an open cow shed. He stacked the junk neatly inside the cow shed by type, five-gallon oilcan with five-gallon oilcan, rags with rags, six-by-six oak beam leaned against the wall with its shorter twin. He made sure nothing metal was touching the ground where it might corrode. His brother wouldn't have to move his junk again for years.

Tom swept the cribs clean of trash, his black sideburns and

eyebrows going gray in the process, then latched together the home-made wooden ducting that would channel air through the corn to dry it. When he was finished he could count six thousand bushels more capacity than he'd had before. "I sure as hell hate to haul that corn all the way over here, though," he told his brother later. "That combine's going to be just sitting out in the field waiting."

The Young Farmers Association corn test plot was laid out on good Missouri River bottomland. The test plot was an annual deal to face off the new varieties of hybrid corn that the corn companies came up with and see how they performed under real Missouri conditions. Different farmers donated the land in exchange for the free seed. Good hybrid seed cost around fifty-five dollars a bag. A bag weighed fifty pounds and contained about eighty thousand kernels. If you planted twenty thousand seeds to the acre you used about a fourth of a bag, so free seed saved that much expense. For the test they planted six rows of a standard corn and then six rows of a test variety. When they picked it they averaged the standard's yield across the entire twenty-acre field to give the test varieties a fair comparison across better and poorer patches of ground. This year's test plot was planted on April 17 with Jacques 7700, Jacques FX21, Coker 8391, Paymaster, Funk's, Super Cross, Garst, Pioneer 3901, MFA 4115, Cargill 893 and Asgrow varieties. Herbicides were Lasso and AAtrex.

Forty was the age cutoff for membership in the Young Farmers, so Tom was too old, but they allowed members who passed the age limit to stay on as associate members. Tom had been active in the organization when he'd had a real say. He only checked in once in a while now. The younger men were running it.

He'd gone by the house and cleaned up and picked up the GMC before driving over to the test plot, which was north of Plymouth a few miles down a dirt road. It was nearly noon when he arrived. Pickups were parked fanned out in a ledge of tall weeds above the field. The broken-down weeds made the air acrid with their sap. Tom hiked down the ledge into the flat, open field—the outside rows had already been picked—and there was his older brother Dale. They grinned and shook hands, making a joke of it. "You old devil," Tom greeted his brother, "how you been?"

Like Tom, Dale was wearing a Funk's Hybrid G cap, showing the colors, the cap's light tan crown and bill set off by a good-looking patch with an ear of corn on it embroidered in green, red and gold. Dale sold Funk's seed to supplement his income from farming and his patch had an extension panel incorporating his name, address and phone. He was six feet tall, confident, heavier than Tom and balder, with cheeks like Santa Claus and a ruddy complexion. His eyes were the same blue, with the same twinkle. Anyone could tell they were brothers. He was retired after twenty years as a civilian aircraft mechanic for the Air Force, and sometimes Tom envied him that monthly retirement check. It made farming a lot less dicey proposition.

The combine picking the test corn was a Gleaner, finished in galvanized iron sheeting and angular and alien, the most insectlike of all the combine designs. The two brothers watched it make a pass-through, picking six rows at a time, then wheel off to one side of the field and dump the corn into a grain wagon, make another pass-through and wheel off to the other side and dump that corn into another grain wagon, separating the standard from the test plantings. Dale nudged Tom and they headed into the corn to look for corn borer damage, cornstalks broken at the joints and blown over where borer larvae had weakened them by eating out the pith. They found moderate damage, a stalk down every twenty or thirty plants. Out in the open again they walked up the stobble rows where the Gleaner had passed, following a trail of corn kernels the machine had failed to separate from the discharge. "He's got something out of adjustment," Tom said. "He ought to be picking that up." Dale nodded agreement.

They stopped to watch the farmer who owned the field trying to engage the gearshift on a rusty John Deere tractor hooked up to one of the loaded grain wagons. The gears wouldn't shift.

"Linkage is shot," Tom speculated.

"Hell," Dale said, "he's probably known about that for a year. Now, when he needs it, it breaks down." The Bauer boys took care of their machinery. "Then they come up to us when we're out in the field," Dale bragged, "and say, 'You're lucky, you don't have breakdowns.' "

Jeb Hurder joined them to watch the comedy, one of Tom's

neighbors, blond and handsome, another former Young Farmer. Like Tom, Jeb owned a red Case International combine. He knew Dale favored John Deere equipment, which was green. "Damn," he said, "I guess we could of brought some red paint. That would have helped that old thing." Farm machinery loyalties were always good for a laugh.

The men working on the tractor brought up a grain truck and tried to release the tractor's gears by towing it. It was seized up and wouldn't move. They unhitched the grain wagon then and hauled it away with another tractor. Behind them at the edge of the field, in the rich bottomland, sunflowers grew to twice a man's height in clumps where last year's seeds had fallen. They towered over bountiful stands of lacy marijuana. In the nineteenth century, hemp was an important Missouri crop, and volunteer marijuana grew everywhere in the state. Tom hitched a thumb in its direction. "That's probably worth more than the corn," he joked. It never would have occurred to him to smoke it. To all three men, weeds around a field, like a poorly maintained tractor, betrayed slovenly farming.

They hiked up to the barn for the free dinner. Two Plymouth banks this time had donated hamburgers and fixings. Young vice-presidents bulging from clean new blue jeans manned the charcoal grills. Forty or fifty farmers were on hand, the younger men in wash-faded jeans, the older men in grease-stained bib overalls. When they weren't Young Farmering, everyone was busy servicing machinery, getting ready to harvest.

The Gleaner worked on through dinner, eating up the rows, dumping the twenty-one- and twenty-two-percent-moisture grain into a batch drier set up at the edge of the field. The batch drier was a green cage of fine-mesh steel screen hooked up to a gas-fired blower that howled like a banshee. Below the blower's howl they could hear the deep growling of the combine. The growl changed in pitch as the machine worked toward them and away. After dinner Tom caught the Gleaner unloading, its iron auger gushing yellow grain. He climbed the ladder to the cab and rode a couple of rounds to check it out. "That booger hits into the rows, the RPMs don't drop," he told Dale afterward, a little surprised. "She can handle the corn." Gleaner made a good machine, but it wasn't a rotary. Rotaries were simpler. They wore better because they didn't have as many moving parts to get out of whack. International had a bunch of patents on the rotary design. He'd stick with them.

A couple of hours was as much time as Tom could stand hanging around watching someone else pick corn. He took off and drove back toward Devon. About half a mile west of town he turned in to a gravel driveway and followed it south past a one-story white farmhouse to a collection of weathered gray outbuildings. Parked in front on the gravel in the shade of a big elm was a rusty, four-row Gleaner F2 combine. Tom pulled up behind it.

His best friend, Clarence Galen, came sauntering out of the workshop gloom to greet him, his gray, grease-stained coveralls opened in the afternoon heat halfway to his waist. "Hey, boy," Clarence demanded, "get on over here. This old piece of crap needs that electrical expertise of yours."

"You mean you or that junk combine you bought?" Tom shot back, meeting Clarence halfway.

"Watch it, boy." They didn't shake hands; they got together nearly every day.

Tom had taught himself electrical wiring fixing up his own used machinery. Side by side on two sections of stump in the weeds outside the workshop the two men searched for the F2's wiring diagram in the shop manuals Clarence had assembled. He'd bought the old Gleaner at a bankruptcy sale for thirty-five hundred dollars. New, it would have cost sixty thousand but it wasn't nearly new. The bankrupt owner was a kid who'd inherited the family farm and run it into bankruptcy in just nineteen months. Tom didn't know how you could start with all your land paid off and run it into bankruptcy in nineteen months but the kid had managed it. The F2 was rusty because the kid had left it out in the field all year. Its electrical system was a mess because whenever the kid had an electrical problem he'd simply cut the wires.

The Galens were an old family in Crevecoeur County. Clarence's dad, Oliver Galen, owned a farm due north on the other side of the highway that ran back to the river bluffs. There were other Galens up and down the highway in orchards. Their descent was German, like Tom's family, but instead of lifelong Democrats they were solid Republicans. Clarence at sixty-three was pure gold, a lean, almost lanky man with a weathered, heavily lined face, full lips and bushy dark eyebrows. He was a Second World War infantry veteran, a tough survivor. He liked to clown as much as Tom did, but there was fatalism under the playfulness. Partly that was just his character. Partly it was the war. Partly it was circumstance. His only child, his son Gene, who operated a construction crane for a living and was running for city council in Plymouth, was fighting cancer.

Between them, Tom and Clarence couldn't find the wiring diagram. They went over to the combine and Tom climbed up into the cab and looked around. "This was all disconnected when you got it?" he asked Clarence.

"Hell, they was just tore out." Clarence pulled a pack of cigarettes from his breast pocket, set one in his teeth and cupped a Bic lighter to the tip.

"So you're just kind of having to guess at it?"

"Yeah."

Tom had brought along a pocket circuit tester, two wires forking from a glowlight. He began checking for lights and found a few still working, a utility light over the holding bin behind the cab and the rear flashers. He found the headlight wires and connected them within the cab. They worked, but the wire he hooked them to got hot.

"The two top lights should be on," he called down to Clarence.

"They are."

"Wire's getting hot. She's pulling a lot of ohms is what she's doing."

Clarence climbed the ladder and leaned into the one-man cab. "Let's see if we got a taillight." He worked a switch overhead.

"That could be the slow-moving-vehicle switch," Tom said.

Clarence clamped his cigarette between his teeth and hung off the platform. The smoke made him squint. "Nope. No taillights."

"We got to find that top wire is all," Tom said. "We ought to just run another pair of wires and bypass the problem."

Clarence looked back in. "You know why the priest wore his shorts in the shower?" he deadpanned.

Tom could deadpan too. "Reckon you'll tell me," he said.

"So's he wouldn't have to *look down* on the *unemployed*." Clarence laughed, loud and barking, and did a slow-motion parody of slapping his knee.

Tom laughed as much at Clarence's clowning as at his joke. "That the best they come up with down at the Liars' Club this morning?" The Liars' Club was their name for a diner in Devon where farmers stopped for coffee.

Clarence wiped his eyes with the bent thumb of the hand that held his cigarette. "Yeah. Sure was. Like to died when I heard it." He barked another laugh. "Wouldn't have to be looking down on that old *unemployed*."

Tom went over the wiring while Clarence tried to figure out how to take a gear assembly apart. By the end of the afternoon they had all the lights working again.

SIX

There were wasps coming and going from Tom's combine. He traced them to the opening around the fuel filler cap, six feet up the pull-down back steps beside the engine well. First there was one wasp and then as the morning sun warmed the fuel-tank housing a regular relay of them flew in and out running errands. They were yellowjackets, the meanest kind.

Tom figured he had another two or three days' work with his sons' help finishing up servicing the combine and servicing the two big grain trucks, two grain wagons and the tractors he would use for the harvest. He wasn't going to get the job done with a bunch of damned wasps around. He fetched a can of WD-40 penetrating oil from the workshop, looked sharp and sprayed a cloud of the stuff into the opening.

Watch out! Tom jumped back. Blaze saw what he was up to. She'd been there before. She tucked her tail between her legs and took off for the house. Molly panted from the edge of the concrete with a wild look in her eyes, eagerly wagging her tail. Beyond the cloud of oil spray an angry hum came out of the fuel filler opening and then yellowjackets began boiling off in every direction, looking for something to attack. The WD-40 had them buffaloed. They didn't know which way to turn.

"Hell, there must be a hundred of them in there," Tom told

Molly. The little black dog raised an eyebrow but kept her eyes on the wasps. Ducking and dodging, feinting in and out, Tom chased down first one wasp and then another and hit it with the WD-40 and sent it reeling. When he backed off in Molly's direction she backed off behind him. When he darted forward she started to move with him but halted at the edge of the concrete. That was as near as she dared to go and she whined in frustration. Like choppers hit by enemy fire the wasps turned nose up, went crazy, buzzed in wild looping tailspins and crashed to the ground.

Tom stood back to study the situation and lit a cigarette. It looked as if they were all either dead or flown the coop. Molly moved in cautiously, respectfully avoiding the wasps that still kicked and pawing the dead ones. In spring and summer the farm was alive with wasps. You got used to them. Paper wasps hung nests like gray brains from the barn rafters. Shiny black mud daubers skimmed water on the fly from the puddle under the well spigot beside the workshop. Some kind of solitary wasp laid eggs in the bolt holes in the I-beam frame of Tom's better truck and sealed the holes over with clay. There was a bumblebee nest inside the grease storage shed west of the workshop. You didn't fool around with bumblebees. They nested in the fields too. Sometimes, disking or chisel-plowing, you'd hit a bumblebee nest and all hell would break loose. Bumblebees were the worst, but yellowjackets weren't much better. It was getting on toward the end of their time or they'd have been a lot more aggressive. It was almost autumn. Fog had filled the creek bottoms that morning before the sun burned it off.

At least he'd reclaimed the combine. "That's about all of our wasp adventure for today," Tom told Molly.

He finished his cigarette and turned back to his work. The picker head would pick ears of corn and cornstalks and feed them back into the combine's throat. Bolted there to the front end of the rotary, heavy steel paddles like elephant ears forced the material up and around the outside of the rotary where the rasp bars could break it up. Wear plates protected the leading edges of the elephant ears and like the old rasp bars these were worn, worn sharp as knives. Heavy bolts with countersunk heads and square Allen sockets held them in place. Tom had sprayed the bolts with WD-

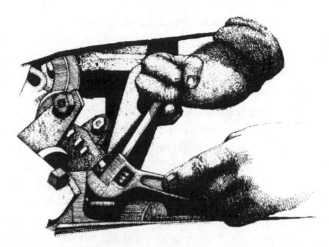

40 the night before. This morning they came out on the first try. He'd ordered new wear plates from a parts place in Illinois. They fitted perfectly.

Next the contour gratings needed to be adjusted for corn. Tom carried them into the workshop one at a time like bowed steel window gratings and clamped them into a vise. They were spotted with rust. After a few days in the field they'd be shiny as a silver dollar from the abrasion of all the tons of material that passed through them. Steel rods ran the long way through iron crossbars in the heavy frames. Tom pulled out every other rod to make the grid openings larger. He'd spaced them smaller last fall for soybeans. Clamping the rods with a pair of locking pliers and holding the pliers while he hammered on them to pull the rods free was hard on hands.

A rock or a lost piece of a farm implement had crashed through one of the contours and bent a hole in it. Tom leaned the heavy grating against the workshop door, popped a flame on his acetylene torch, heated the bent iron crosspiece cherry red and hammered it back into line with a blacksmith's hammer and a steel punch. The iron had stretched to allow the rock or whatever it was to pass. There wasn't room within the frame for it to straighten. Tom cut the weld at one end of the iron crossbar to make some room where it attached to the frame, white sparks showering when the flame cut through. He bent the crossbar the rest of the way straight, brought around the cables from the arc welder mounted

under the big workbench on the south wall of the shop and
clamped the ground clamp onto the contour. Selecting a welding
rod from an open quiver set beside the bench, he held a black
welding mask up to his face, struck an arc and welded a new bead,
the hum of the welding transformer dropping in pitch as the powerful arc pulled current, ozone spicing the air.

When the weld had cooled Tom reinstalled the three contours
under the rotary and closed up the side panels. Earlier that morning
he'd opened the combine's hydraulic lines to drain them. Now he
sealed them back up, retrieved two five-gallon plastic cans of fresh
hydraulic fluid from the grease storage shed and hauled them up
the back steps to the engine well. A few yellowjackets still patrolled
the fuel filler opening. Tom watched them warily while he slowly
filled the hydraulic system, tipping up one and then the other can.

The combine's three radiators—for its engine, hydraulic system
and air conditioner—needed hosing off. Tom hit them with the
high-powered stream from his Handy brand power washer and
sent the chaff and mud flying. He went on to change oil filters and
the big aluminum air cleaner, which had cost him forty-eight dollars and an extra trip to town. To rake free the trash from the two
sieves behind the rotary, in the back of the combine, he crawled up
into the discharge opening until only his legs were showing,
grooming the monster from inside its maw, and emerged albino
with soybean dust. He filled the big front tires with twenty pounds
of air, the air-compressor pump at the back of the workshop
kicking in to meet the large demand, and let a little air out of the
rear tires to ease the strain on the axle bouncing around in the
fields.

The combine still needed a grease gun taken to its wear points,
its chain drives tightened, its cab vacuumed and its windows
washed. He'd get to those over the weekend. To end the morning
he blasted the caked, hardened mud from the side panels where the
big tires had flung it spinning through his neighbor's muddy, half-
frozen field. When the combine dried off it was sparkling, like a
big red fire truck ready to roll.

That afternoon Tom cleaned up and drove over to Franklin, thirty
miles east of Riverton on 24, to a farm-equipment auction. If the

price was right he wanted to buy a rotary mower, a tractor-mounted machine for mowing pastures like an overgrown lawn mower with double blades big as airplane propellers. The sun was shining but the air was cool. Clouds were building here and there in the sky. The corn was drying down in the full, ripe fields south of the highway and the beans were yellowing. North of the highway red apples loaded the green orchard trees. Orchards were a good business. You had a commodity people couldn't get enough of and it was perishable. Tom had watched them process the apples at Siegelstecher's, the orchard across the road from the Elms. They ran them through a bunch of washes and sorts and sprayed them with a wax that made them shine. Fred Siegelstecher had a cold-storage building back behind the processing plant big enough to hold half the corn and beans in Crevecoeur County. If worse came to worst maybe he'd be willing to rent it. They said the apple crop this year was going to be small.

Tom pulled up at Case International in Franklin twenty minutes late. The auctioneer had already started. The auctioneer worked out of a stand loaded on a pickup like a camper shell and with his PA system you could hear him chanting all the way out to the road.

Lots of farmers had shown up for the sale. It had everything from gates, high-loaders, planters and cultivators to tractors and a whole collection of combines, all laid out in rows, ten rows at least of farm implements and machines. There were even some trucks. The auctioneer had started with the small stuff and the crowd that was following him was still fairly sparse. Most of the men were dispersed around the grounds looking things over, making up their minds how much they wanted to bid. The younger men tended to jeans and button-down shirts and a fair number of them had long hair. The older men wore bib overalls and carried a lot of weight. Or else they were thin as rails and looked as if they were made of bootstrap leather.

Jeb Hurder turned up, strolling over with his hands in his pockets. He walked with a roll, like a sailor. It didn't take the two of them long to pass on the mowers. "They're shot," Tom judged. They headed over to the combines. Farm boys in the cabs solemnly worked the steering wheels. There were Massey-Ferguson, Gleaner and John Deere machines up for bid as well as International. Most of them looked the worse for wear, but a couple of the Internationals were exceptions. They were 1480s, one size up from Jeb's and Tom's. That sparked Jeb's interest.

"How much you think they'll go for?" he asked Tom. With his farm cap concealing his baldness Jeb looked like a muscular Douglas Fairbanks, Jr.

"More than they're worth," Tom quipped.

The auctioneer's pickup stopped parallel with the two men in the next aisle over. A classy-looking woman dressed in jeans and a Western shirt crossed the open aisle. It was unusual to see a woman at a farm auction. Tom and Jeb took notice and the auctioneer interrupted his pitch to sweet-talk her:

> *Lookie lookie lookie.*
> *Here comes a cookie.*
> *Comin' down the street,*
> *Looks so neat.*
> *Ain't cheap.*

An old farmer in bib overalls, brown canvas jacket and faded red cap sat forward on the bright orange scoop of a high-loader studying his gnarled brown hands. When the woman went by he didn't even look up.

Tom and Jeb watched the auction crowd pass on down the adjacent aisle. "Them wetbacks get all the sunflowers out of your beans?" Jeb asked. Back in August they'd both hired undocumented workers waiting to pick apples to cut the weeds in their soybean fields that the herbicides they'd applied hadn't controlled. Some of the farms in Crevecoeur County went back to before the Civil War. In apple season the Mexican workers lived at the orchards in the old slave quarters.

"Yeah, they got them," Tom said. "Then after they left I noticed they was all growing back."

"Mine too," Jeb chuckled.

"They cut them off just below the top of the beans."

"Yeah. How much you give them for it?"

"Three bucks an hour."

"Same here."

"Next time I'll go out and watch them at it and check their work."

Jeb put out his cigarette. "May not be no next time. Supposed to be the feds are going to crack down."

"They always say that. The fine's so puny the orchard men just go in to Kansas City and pay it and pick up another load. Anyway, the wetbacks want to work. They got families to feed just like everybody else."

The auctioneer rounded the far end of the row. The two men noticed a friend of theirs bidding hard on a baler, then a disk, then a bale loader. "He's protecting," Tom said. Jeb nodded. Protecting was bidding up to a high minimum price arranged in advance with the owner. If the bidding went over, the protector dropped out. Otherwise he took the buy and the owner kept the merchandise.

"These old boys know it, too," Jeb said. "Look at how they're standing back."

"Nobody wants to bid if they think they're getting kited."

Even with the bidding protected, the auctioneer was knocking off one machine every two to four minutes at above ten thousand dollars each. When farmers were making money in the boom years of the 1970s and farmland prices soared, the plungers among them bought brand-new equipment—new round bailers, four-wheel-drive tractors, larger-model combines. Then land prices slumped and everyone's collateral shrank and the plungers found themselves in trouble. These days, sales of used equipment were popular because that's what everyone was buying. Hardly anyone was risking buying new.

Tom and Jeb walked up the row ahead of the crowd to look at an old Massey-Ferguson 750 combine. Jeb's son was just getting started in farming and Jeb was interested if the price was right. Tom had operated a Massey-Ferguson for years before he traded it for his International and he knew the problems Massey-Fergusons had. He pointed out patches of rust and bad belts. "Looks like it's been sitting out," he concluded. "I bet it don't bring seven thousand dollars."

The auctioneer bid the late-model John Deere and International combines last. Both men paid attention. Jeb was ready to bid.

Protectors pushed the bidding beyond what he thought he could afford and even then the machines didn't make their prices and got pulled out.

Jeb left to go home. Tom found a new disk around on the other side of the dealership that looked as if it'd spent a year or two outdoors. One of the guys who'd been protecting came around to talk to him about it. Tom could use a new disk, an implement assembled from ranks of knife-edged, cymbal-like steel disks that roll along behind a tractor chopping straw and stalks and breaking up the soil to prepare it for planting. The disks on his old one were worn down from twenty-two to twenty inches from years of use and there were fatigue cracks in the steel frame. It still worked well but one of these days it would need to be replaced.

"We got this from a dealer over in north central Kansas," the salesman said. Tom was examining it carefully, noting defects. "He wants seven or eight thousand for it. It's brand new."

"Been left out," Tom said bluntly.

"Yeah, it's been left out, but it's not been used."

"See, here," Tom said, pointing, "this paint's rusting out. Here's a rusty spring. Don't know how deep that rust goes." He looked the salesman in the eye. "I ain't one of those plungers," he told him. "Just a plain old dirt farmer. I've got a pretty good disk at home but I could always use a better one. Wonder if he'd take a trade and three thousand difference."

The salesman stuck his hands into the back pockets of his jeans and thought it over. "He said he didn't want to trade except FOB Kansas. I can call him, though, and see. You going to be around awhile?"

"I can wait awhile," Tom said.

Three thousand would've been a good price with the trade, but the salesman couldn't get the Kansas dealer on the phone. He promised Tom he'd try to reach him next week and Tom took off.

He stopped for a Pepsi at the convenience store at the bridge turnoff in Riverton. A farmer was kidding the older woman who ran the cash register. He let Tom in on the fun. "She says she's the mayor of Maywood," he told him. Maywood was an old town south of Riverton that was nearly depopulated.

Tom was in a good mood. The corn was drying down and he

was just about ready to pick it. He hadn't bought a mower or a disk today but he hadn't spent any money, either. He swooped up a can of Pepsi. "If she's the mayor of Maywood," he said happily in his deep drawl, "then I'm the Duke of Devon."

Wayne, the Bauers' firstborn son, twenty-one years old, came home from college for the weekend. Missouri State was only thirty miles away. Wayne pulled in just before dark on Friday evening. His license was restricted to daylight driving because he had limited vision. He had a condition called nystagmus. His eyes moved in a searching motion to and fro and he didn't have sharp central focus. His eyes had been damaged in an incubator when he was a baby. He was left with vision so blurred that he'd have been seriously disabled if he'd ever known anything better. What little he saw was all he knew and over the years he'd made the most of it. He was bright and hardworking, a good student. He couldn't play football so he'd played percussion in the high school band, carrying the cymbals in halftime parades and doing the marches by the numbers by counting steps. In college, where he had a scholarship, he was taking a double major in agriculture and accounting and doing well.

He was a big, solid kid, with powerful shoulders and arms and an open, honest face. Behind his thick glasses his eyes were warm brown. Their motion back and forth made him seem nervous. Sometimes he had to turn his head partly away and look out of the corners of his eyes to slow the flickering and fix his vision enough to focus on detail. That seemed a little odd at first until you got used to it.

Wayne was stubborn about his eyes. He'd taken a lot of mean kidding for them along the way and at some point he'd made up his mind never to ask for special favors. In high school one year he'd been doing well on his English homework but flunking the tests, getting scores so low it looked as if he never studied at all. Tom and Sally knew better. They went over the whole story with the English teacher two or three times from start to finish before Tom played a hunch and asked to see the tests. Sure enough, the tests were mimeographed in purple ink on glazed paper and they were hard even for Tom to read. Instead of asking for a better copy

Wayne had just marked answers more or less at random. "Don't you think you could give this boy a typed copy and give him a fair chance?" Tom had asked the English teacher sternly. The English teacher gulped and said he could. Wayne's test scores shot up to where they were supposed to be. But he'd never have complained even if he'd ended up flunking English.

He'd gone off to college and then he'd been hit with a second blow. He developed a terrible thirst and started losing weight. His doctor tested him for everything else and then as an afterthought had him tested for diabetes. It was diabetes, all right. The results were so bad that the lab called Tom all the way from Kansas City and told him to get his son to the nearest emergency room. That threw Wayne for a while. He didn't see why he had to be hit twice, first his eyes and then diabetes. It made him furious. "Why couldn't it be *Brett?*" he even raged once. But he learned to control his diet and take his insulin and eventually he was able to get off medication entirely.

Wayne was a hell of a worker. He'd already have everything fueled up and ready to go when his dad came out the back door in the morning. He'd run the tractor all day mowing or chiseling or disking and Tom would just about have to order him to quit work and come home at night. Working that many hours must have been hard on his eyes but he never complained. He was always pushing to do more. Tom could see him compensating. Hooking up the tractor to an implement involved mating the two hitches. Wayne didn't have any depth perception to judge the alignment from a distance, so he'd climb down off the tractor and measure it with his hands. How he got in and out of sheds when the tractor or the implement only had inches to spare going through the door, Tom never did figure.

He was still part boy. If he got uncomfortable talking to you he'd lapse into Donald Duck sounds. He was shy around girls, the shyness probably prolonged by his eye problems. He didn't want to eat the salads Sally made for him even though he understood that a balanced diet and weight control were important to managing his diabetes. "Oh, what the hell, pass the grass," he'd say when his mother scolded him long enough. But every month in college he was changing a little, finding a little more confidence, developing a little more dignity and reserve. He had friends. He was going to be a good man.

He wanted to farm. He worked so hard at farming to show his parents he could do it despite his handicaps. That worried Tom and Sally a lot. They didn't want to wreck his dream, but they just didn't believe he could see well enough to farm. It was too dangerous. He couldn't see the danger coming. Farming was the most dangerous occupation in the country. Even with 20/20 vision it was dangerous. What was it when someone was almost legally blind? Tom and Sally hoped their son would come to an understanding on his own. In the meantime they lived with the worry.

That weekend Brett castrated the baby pigs and Wayne changed the oil in the trucks and tractors. Their dad finished up with the combine and cleaned out the wooden grain bin at the Elms, another three thousand bushels of storage space in reserve. Tom and Wayne drove in to Fleckmeier's on Saturday afternoon to pick up the big Oliver tractor—the parts had finally arrived from Kansas City—and Wayne drove it home, its slow-moving-vehicle lights flashing. Sally did laundry, including Wayne's college laundry, and mowed the lawn. Sammi weeded the yard fence and played with her rabbits. She kept two fluffy rabbits, a white male and a black female, in a wire hutch mounted on the outside south wall of the grease storage shed west of the workshop, fed them and watered them morning and night.

The entire family went to six-o'clock Mass Saturday night in Grants, a little town east of Osage Station. The Catholic Church in Devon was closer, but the church in Grants was German and felt more comfortable.

Sunday, Wayne helped Tom set up at Landers'. They moved the big blower from the Landers bin to the smaller bin next to it that Ward was leasing. The flared cylindrical housing around the fan made the blower look like a stubby jet engine. It attached to the corrugated-steel bin at the bottom through a steel collar called a transition and plugged into a junction box mounted on the bin. The bin had a false floor made of finely perforated steel. The fan blew air into the space below the false floor and the air percolated up through the perforations, through the corn when the corn arrived and out a manhole at the peak of the bin's cone-shaped steel roof, carrying the corn's moisture away.

The manhole was covered with an enameled red cap. Tom climbed the bin's steel ladder to the peak, thirty feet up, and unbolted the cap and set it aside. Back on the ground he fetched two spades from Babe, handed one to Wayne, found the depression that marked last year's auger hole and started digging. A foot down in the gravelly dirt he struck a layer of rotten corn, sour and foul.

"Looks like I found the right spot, Wayne," Tom said.

"Sure does," Wayne agreed. "Man that stinks."

They worked together to enlarge the hole. When it was big as a bushel basket Tom set aside his spade and disappeared into the barn. Wayne heard him starting up the old International Harvester tractor he kept there, a tall, narrow machine with a sulky-style steel seat open to the weather, a 1953 model Farmall. The engine misfiring, Tom drove out of the barn and waved his son aboard. Wayne jumped onto the drawbar and they drove around behind the building. A grain auger was parked there next to the fence, a twelve-inch galvanized iron pipe slanting up fifty-two feet into the air, mounted on a light rubber-tired frame. Tom maneuvered the tractor drawbar to the tongue of the auger frame and Wayne dropped a steel pin in place to hold it.

Around in front again Tom backed the auger into position with the upper end of the big auger lined up directly over the peak of the grain bin and the lower end over the auger hole they'd redug. Wayne unpinned the auger and lowered its near end into the hole. Going forward and backing, Tom wheeled the tractor around to one side. Wayne hooked up the auger drive shaft to the power-takeoff socket at the back of the tractor, the PTO, and slid a bright-orange plastic safety shield over the connection.

"When I was a boy," Tom told his son, coming down off the tractor, "I saw a man of about fifty straddling a PTO just in bib overalls, no shirt or shorts—we was putting up hay and it was hot. Weren't no safety shields then. All of a sudden that PTO just grabbed him and the next thing he was standing there stark naked in just his shoes. And he was lucky."

Wayne had heard the story before. "Could have lost his seeds," he recited the next line. His dad glanced at him to see if he was mocking. He didn't crack a smile.

"Could have lost more than just his seeds," Tom said. He was still horrified. A full-grown man abruptly stripped naked and nearly unmanned wasn't something a boy forgot.

They took turns hand-cranking the grain auger into position, lowering its upper end until the flexible aluminum spout attached there extended down through the manhole into the grain bin. To finish the installation they lined the auger hole with pieces of an old canvas tent Tom had saved. Some farmers bought expensive plastic bins to set their augers in and dump into. If you didn't watch when you were dumping and it overflowed then you had to clean the mess off the ground anyway. Just as easy to dig a hole. "I'm glad I saved this old tent," Tom told Wayne.

"We was tired of camping anyway, Dad. It's about rotted, isn't it?"

"It'll do, son," Tom said.

They fussed for a while with the new Stiralator Tom had installed in the big Landers bin, an electrically driven system of unhoused augers that would slowly rotate through the grain and stir it to dry it more uniformly. Everything was ready. They headed home, stopping on the way to moisture-test some Landers corn. It came in at twenty-percent moisture. Back home Wayne showered, loaded his clean laundry and the freezer bags of food his mother had cooked for him and left again for college. He had studying to do.

Tom was about to call it a day when Clarence pulled up in his red pickup. After they'd kidded around for a while and Clarence had passed along the latest joke, he mentioned that the vet was coming out Monday to castrate some of his calves. Tom immediately volunteered to help. He didn't tell Clarence he'd meant to start picking corn. When a neighbor needed help you gave it unless you were just completely strapped. But he sure as hell wanted to get that Ward farm bottomland field picked before it rained.

SEVEN

A

t eight o'clock Monday morning, the hour Comstock's opened, Tom called the elevator to see if it had any storage left. A friend's sister who worked in the office answered the phone and put him through to the elevator manager. "You're the first one today," she told him.

"Hell, Tom," Frank Tice started out, "I haven't even had a chance to drink my coffee yet."

"It's the early bird gets the worm," Tom fielded the implied compliment. He had a fund of sayings, family and traditional, and used them comfortably wherever they fit.

"Which worm you fishing for? That storage we talked about?"

"That's it."

"You're just in time. We got some. How much you need?"

"Reckon you could take four thousand bushels of soybeans?" Tom figured he could store his corn on the farm, use the wooden bins if he had to, but he'd need space elsewhere for his beans.

"Don't see why not," Tice told him.

Tom was relieved. "Well, that's fine then," he said. "How much you charging?"

Tice's voice picked up some tension. "We had to set up some special terms."

"Oh?" Tom responded suspiciously. Special terms was usually code for picking a man's pocket.

"Got a lot of people wanting storage," Tice explained. "We're asking for a ten-month deposit. That's paid in advance, today."

"How come ten months? Crop loans only go nine."

"That's just the way it's set up, Tom. I don't know why they threw in that extra month. I guess it's just a hedge."

There wasn't any use arguing with the man. He held the better cards. "Okay," Tom said. "Reserve me four thousand bushels. I'll be over directly." He'd wanted to pick corn today. Between highway robbery at the elevator and helping out with Clarence's calves he wondered if he'd even get started. Brett had a football game at five o'clock he'd promised he'd watch. Things were starting to get busy.

From the desk next to the refrigerator in the big kitchen of the farmhouse he filled Sally in on what she hadn't already overheard. She just shook her head and drank her coffee. She wasn't surprised. Some people took advantage of you whenever they had the chance.

Tearing a blank check out of the check ledger, folding it and putting it into his billfold, Tom was already searching out the bright side. "I'm glad to find a home for it," he told his wife. That didn't excuse Comstock's. "When I get back I'd like to move the combine over to Ward's," he added. "Can you wait?"

The kids had already left for school. Sally had planned a morning at the ceramics shop. She made a wry face. She didn't mind helping her husband. Taking care of your own was the first thing you did. It was just life as usual screwing up plans. "Looks like I'll have to," she said drily.

Tom met Tice coming out of the elevator office building. He'd heard the tension in the manager's voice over the phone and decided to see how it played. They made a little small talk and then Tom sprang it on him. "Wonder if you could find room besides for four thousand bushels of corn."

Tice hemmed and hawed. They had a lot of other customers. Yields looked like they were going to be high. They didn't want to have to be dumping the stuff on the ground. But he was embarrassed enough about the ten months' storage deposit to give in. "I'll take a chance," he said. "You have to take a chance once in a while."

In the office Tom found out that the chance Tice was taking had another hook in it. Not only did he have to pay for an extra month's storage beyond the nine-month run of any government crop loan and pay ahead, but the count of months would start on September first, last week, when the beans and corn were still in the field and would be for weeks and even months to come. That was taking advantage and it rubbed him raw. But he'd have storage guaranteed. He wouldn't have to move grain in and out of the corncribs he'd fixed up at his brother's place and at Landers'. And he wouldn't have to spend seven or eight hundred dollars to buy a new blower for his brother's corncrib. So it wasn't all bad by a long shot.

Back home, a cigarette burning and another cup of coffee at hand, Tom called Jack Ward in Connecticut, where he lived, and let him know what he owed Comstock's for his fifty-percent share of the soybean storage. Ward said he'd send a check the same day.

Next Tom called Ed Geizhals, a retired farmer, his landlord on forty acres of good land halfway to Plymouth. It was the forty acres Tom and Sally had bought when they'd started farming. They'd sold it to old man Geizhals to raise the down payment for the home farm. Now they farmed it on shares. Geizhals wasn't home; Mrs. Geizhals answered. "I booked four thousand bushels of storage for our corn," Tom told her, "but I had to pay the bill up front. So Ed needs to send me a check for six hundred sixty dollars. That's right. They want the money right away." He paused, listening. "That's guaranteed. That's ten months' storage. They'll reimburse us for what we don't use." Another pause. "We're eligible for a government loan on it." Another pause, longer. "That was the only place I could find, Mrs. Geizhals."

The Landers family corporation was called the Elms Corporation. The Landerses had sufficient storage on the farm and tended to sell their crops out early in any case. They didn't like to carry them over to another tax year.

With Sally following in the GMC, Tom shuttled the combine to the edge of the Ward farm bottomland field, ran back in the GMC, shuttled one of his five-ton grain trucks to the road beside the combine, ran back in the GMC once more and shuttled the older of his two Oliver tractors to the Landers storage bins down the section road a quarter of a mile behind the Elms. There were two grain wagons stored in the barn at the Landers farm and he hooked them up to the tractor. Then Sally took off for the ceramics shop in the family car, a dark green Oldsmobile diesel, and Tom finished out the morning doing maintenance.

After dinner, the air warm, a moist breeze blowing, Tom drove Babe over to Clarence's to help him with his calves. The vet was due at one. It was close to that when Tom pulled in. Clarence's dad, Oliver Galen, eighty-seven years old, was already there, leaning against Clarence's pickup with his hands covering the head of a stout oak walking stick. You could see the family resemblance in his face. He was a widower and a little bent over with age, but he still ran some calves himself even though Clarence was after him to quit.

Fred Siegelstecher was there too. He must have seen Clarence and his dad out waiting and decided to kill some time. He was a bald, gravel-voiced man in his sixties with a red face and a bulbous nose. People said he hit the bottle some. He may have, but he had a hell of an orchard operation going.

"What're you going to do with all that money you're making this year, Fred?" Tom started up. He lit a cigarette and nodded to Oliver Galen, who returned the nod with slow formality.

"Hell," Fred parried, "all that pocket change is going to wear my pants out."

"I hear you're getting eighteen bucks a flatpack," Clarence put in. "Said the apple crop was short this year."

"It's already down to fifteen," Fred said.

"How come?" Tom asked.

"Apples started coming in from Washington State."

"I thought the deal was to get in on the market earlier with Missouri apples."

"Washington just ripened a little earlier this year."

"Only fifteen bucks a flatpack," Clarence said. "Damn, Fred, that breaks my heart."

"By God," Fred countered, "we used to be poor." He looked at Clarence. "You know how poor we used to be?"

"How poor'd you used to be, Fred?" Clarence played back the line, already cracking a smile.

"We was so poor our mother cut the pockets out of our pants at Christmastime so we'd have something to play with."

Oliver Galen laughed silently. Clarence's laugh was happy and loud. "Cut them pockets out of their pants," he echoed.

Tom brought up the big cold-storage building. "You're probably wanting to rent that thing out, ain't you?" he kidded Fred.

"We'll fill up that building pretty good," the orchard man said seriously.

"You will?" Clarence sounded surprised. "I thought you was short this year from that late frost last spring."

"We are," Fred agreed. "We won't fill it for long at any one time. But she does get loaded when we're at peak season." He took a last puff on his cigarette, dropped it to the gravel and ground it out with his heel.

"How much she hold?" Tom asked.

"Seventy-two thousand cubic feet."

"Stacks up pretty high with that high ceiling, don't she?" Clarence asked.

"Yeah. Costs an arm and a leg to cool her down, though."

"I was thinking about asking you if you'd rent it," Tom told Fred. "If I couldn't find anything else."

Clarence stared out across the pasture east of his weathered gray barn. "I can remember back in '48 when corn was four dollars a bushel. That's '48 prices. It'd be four times that now." Comstock's was buying corn that day for $1.92 a bushel.

Oliver Galen cleared his throat. The men waited for him to speak. He nodded acknowledgment. "It ain't over yet," he said solemnly.

"You better believe it," Tom agreed.

"There's still plenty of tall buildings on Wall Street," Clarence said. "Them boys still have plenty of windows to jump from."

"You can't take down the largest industry in America," Tom said, "without dragging the rest of it along. Agriculture's bigger than General Motors and all the rest combined—uses more steel, more chemicals, more petroleum."

"That's right," Clarence seconded. They'd been badly scared by the farm recession. Farming was more than a business to them. For Tom especially it was the only life he'd ever known, or wanted to know.

"You make your bed," Oliver Galen announced, leaning on his stick, summing up, "and then you lie in it. You make it soft, or you make it hard."

The vet was late. Tom was tense, which wasn't like him. There was a tremor in his hands. He wanted to get rolling.

Finally, at almost two, they saw Doc Mitchell's muddy pickup coming along from Devon, hauling his portable squeeze chute behind. Fred Siegelstecher took off to check up on his apple factory.

Doc turned in at Clarence's sign and pulled back to the barn. "Sorry I'm late," he told them. "I just did a real ornery bunch of calves. Took me longer than I figured it would."

Clarence had his nineteen calves—young bulls and heifers—penned in the lot south of the barn. He planned to run them into the barn to crowd them, then send them out the west door one at a time. Doc backed his squeeze chute into the little west lot, Clarence opened the door all the way against the side of the barn and they maneuvered the chute up against the door frame. Clarence unhitched it and Doc pulled his truck to one side. He levered the squeeze chute off its rubber tires down solidly onto the ground and then opened the tailgate of the truck and began setting up his medicines. He was a young man, lanky, with sinewy forearms and a broad, well-muscled back, deeply tanned, a gold caduceus decorating his green seed cap.

"We're going to vaccinate for blackleg and rednose, worm them and castrate the bulls, right?" he called over his shoulder.

"Right," Clarence confirmed, distracted. He opened the gate into the calf lot and slipped through, Tom following and latching the gate behind. The two men began herding the nervous calves into the barn. Oliver Galen stationed himself out of the calves' line of sight against the west barn wall where the squeeze chute butted against the door frame. If a calf tried to escape between the chute and the door frame he was positioned to scare it back.

Doc set up his equipment. He had a steel syringe for blackleg vaccine, a spray can to squirt rednose vaccine into the calves' nostrils, a big plastic bag of creamy green worming solution with a hose and nozzle that he hung up like a blood bag on the squeeze chute, a sharp knife for castrating, a bucket for the seeds. When everything was organized and at hand he called to Clarence and Tom, "Send one on through!"

He'd stationed himself at the end of the squeeze chute away from the door. The squeeze chute was made of iron pipe welded to form a cage large enough to hold a calf or a cow, with a narrow, cleated wooden floor and a deep V of pipe framing the exit. To a calf in the barn it looked like a narrow walkway opening onto a feedlot. But the vet was standing out of the line of sight at the exit to that walkway with both hands on a long iron lever, and as the first calf came clattering through the chute—"Heifer!" Clarence called—and arrived at the point where its neck was in the V of pipe, he abruptly hauled down on the lever, clamping the V and squeezing one side of the chute against the animal's body to hold it pinned. The calf, a two-hundred-pound roan animal that stood about waist high, kicked and struggled and then held still.

Quickly, Doc injected blackleg vaccine into the young female's shoulder, sprayed both black nostrils with rednose vaccine and hauled down the worming-solution hose. He used his thumb to force open the heifer's jaw and stuck the nozzle between the back teeth and partly down the animal's throat. The heifer swallowed a measured dose, green foam appearing at the corner of its mouth. Doc hung the hose back up, released the squeeze chute and slapped the calf on the rump. It bolted through the open V and out into the lot, stopping a ways away and turning around to puzzle at what had happened.

"Ready, Doc?" Clarence called from inside the barn.

The vet rushed to set up for the next calf. "Ready," he called back.

"Bull!" Tom shouted. A black bull calf shot from the barn. It was big for its age and had shoulders like a Spanish fighting bull. It almost dove for the V. The chute shuddered with the impact when Doc slammed the squeeze shut and the bull let out a bellow. When it realized it was pinned it rattled the cage with its kicking, snorting and tossing its head. Doc went about his business. After he'd given the vaccines and forced the worming medicine down the bull's throat he took his knife and let himself into the chute through a small side gate at the barn end. He'd parked his bucket within reach outside the chute.

Tom stepped up into the doorway. "Watch him, Doc," he said. "He ain't going to like what you're doing to him."

"Hell," Clarence spoke from inside, "I wouldn't neither."

"Wouldn't matter no more to you, would it, Clarence?" Tom called back over his shoulder.

"By God, you better believe it would."

The young vet moved the calf's tail aside, took firm hold of its bag and deftly slit it open. The bull jumped at the cut and tried to look around to see what was happening, its eyeballs straining from its head. Quickly Doc popped out a testicle—egg-shaped, blue-veined, white, big as a man's fist—and began pulling it firmly and decisively down, the muscles standing out on his forearms, the strain showing in his neck. The pulling stretched blood vessels and muscles until they tore free. Tearing rather than cutting them made them less likely to bleed. With the tearing, the bull raised its rump, going swayback, fighting the painful, relentless pull. Its neck curved down, its muzzle went up into the air, its eyeballs rolled up into its head until the whites were showing and then with the worst of the tearing its tongue came out, blue-gray and twisted, and flailed in a long, terrible bellow. When Doc had the white tube of the vas stretched to its full extent he quickly cut it through. With a flip of the wrist he tossed the testicle into the bucket. He pulled the other testicle, the bull writhing again in pain, cut the vas, sprayed the incision with antiseptic, let himself out of the chute, released the choke and slapped the bull on the rump. It bolted from the chute, ran off a few yards and stopped to shake its head, foam flying from its mouth. Then, seeming to forget its ordeal, it wandered over to join the heifer.

Castration was an old practice, probably as old as the domestication of animals. It was part of what animals endured from men, who fed them and protected them from harm in order ultimately to kill them and use them for food. Once most people raised their own food, birthing and feeding and killing, castrating too. More efficient agriculture allowed the preponderance of the population the luxury of living in cities and of paying other people to do that hard work for them. Anyone who ate meat or wore leather was equally responsible with farmers for the lives and the ultimate fate of domestic animals. The fact was, anesthesia would have been a blessing before castration, but it cost too much.

Removing a bull's testicles made him sterile, but for Clarence's purpose, which was fattening calves to market for beef, a side effect was more important: castration removed a major source of the male steroid testosterone. With reduced testosterone, males became more docile. Bulls fight. Steers don't. A steer developed more fat intermingled with muscle in its meat, which made the meat more tender. And although a steer grew more slowly than it would have as a bull, it fattened faster.

"Fabulous pair of seeds," Tom commented from the doorway.

"Anyone want them?" Doc asked him, setting up for the next calf.

Tom called into the barn. "Clarence? You going to save these seeds?"

"Let Doc have them," Clarence told him.

"Mighty good eating," Tom coaxed. Calf fries—soaked, sliced, breaded and skillet-fried—were greatly admired in Crevecoeur County. The Young Farmers usually held an invitational Nut Fry once a year with hog and turkey fries on the menu as well as calf.

"I know they is, Bauer," Clarence said. "I got a freezer full. Let Doc have them. He's just a kid. He needs to keep up his strength." He called out. "You want them, Doc?"

"I'd sure enjoy them!" the vet called back.

"They're yours," Clarence concluded. "You earned them the hard way."

One by one they ran the calves through the chute. One bull calf collapsed in the neck squeeze, dropping to its knees and gasping. Tom noticed and alerted the vet. "He's choked down, Doc," he told him. The vet quickly finished castrating and released the squeeze. Tom came around and helped him drag the calf up out of the V. The pressure wasn't to the windpipe but to the carotid arteries in the neck, the classic choke hold. The calf staggered off drunkenly. Doc kept an eye on it until it had fully recovered. Calves had been known to die that way.

Another bull calf, a white-faced Hereford cross, tried to sit down in the chute to avoid castration. Doc already had its seeds out when it made the move. Tom and Clarence were both watching from the doorway.

"Looks like he don't want to sing soprano in the feedlot choir," Tom observed.

"Hit that high C," Clarence added.

Doc hauled the calf up by its tail and finished the castration. The bucket was nearly full of seeds.

"Doc's changing their minds from ass to grass," said Clarence.

Cattle for beef production was a relatively recent luxury in the world. Even in the United States, beef consumption had been modest until the years after the Second World War, nearly doubling between 1947 and 1978 from 66 to 120 pounds per capita before beginning a gradual decline brought on by concerns about cholesterol. The traditional use of cattle had been for milk and occasional feasting. Because they converted grasses that humans found inedible to milk and succulent flesh, because they were large and long-lived, cattle counted for money before money took any other form. "Chattel," as in "chattel property," was a variant of the same Norman French root, and the English word "pecuniary" came from the Latin word for cattle, *pecus*. The Masai of East Africa still maintained the old relationship, killing their cattle wealth only as a last resort, subsisting whenever possible on milk and borrowings of blood.

Cattle throve on cellulose that humans couldn't digest. To accomplish that work they had evolved an enormous stomach of four communicating reservoirs that filled the entire left half of their abdominal cavities. In the largest of the reservoirs, the rumen, bacteria flourished that converted cellulose to volatile fatty acids. Cattle briefly chewed the pasture grasses they rolled their tongues around and plucked before swallowing them into the rumen. There the grasses mixed with saliva, up to twenty gallons per day, which supplied the waiting bacteria with the urea they needed for growth and made the environment benign with bicarbonate. The bacteria in turn fermented the grasses to acetic and propionic acid, nutrients the cattle could digest. Cattle began to ruminate as soon as their hunger was satisfied, spending about six hours a day eating and eight hours ruminating. They regurgitated semiliquid digesta from their rumens, reswallowed the liquid contents and chewed the plug of solid material for a minute or so to grind it up before swallowing it again. The rumen contents remained in the great fermenting vat of the stomach for twelve to forty-eight hours before passing on to the other stomach reservoirs for concentration and further digestion. By the time the material got to the intestine it was prepared for processing there just as in nonruminants.

The British had been the great breeders of cattle and champions of beef in modern times. They were equally well known for their cheeses, cheese a way of preserving milk in the days before refrigeration. Hereford, shorthorn and Angus were all British breeds. The Americas, with prairies and pampas and only one native ruminant, the bison, which was reduced nearly to extinction by 1864, had been a vast pasture waiting to be grazed. Texas was far and away the leading cattle state in the United States, with some 13.4 million head. Kansas in second place counted only 5.9 million head. Nebraska, Oklahoma, California, Iowa and Missouri followed in that order, Missouri supporting about 4.6 million of the hundred-million-head national herd. With an annual production of a single calf each, less frequently of twins, after a gestation of nearly nine-and-a-half months, cattle were an extravagance only uncrowded countries with ample land could afford.

Tom took his leave as soon as they'd run the last calf through the chute. It was past three o'clock and he wanted at least to get started. Clarence noticed. It wasn't like his neighbor to hurry off like that. Tom drove fast on 24, turned south onto the blacktop, followed it uphill and then down, crossed the bridge over Little Cebo Creek, turned in at the Ward farm gate and pulled up beside the combine.

It was a golden afternoon and the linen corn rustled in the breeze. Everything was set on go. Tom climbed into the 1460's cab and started her up. Closing the door quieted the engine to a purr. The lever to the Hydra-matic controlled speed and direction both. Tom studied through the windshield to get his bearings and then eased the Hydra-matic forward. The combine began to move. Shifting other levers and throwing switches, Tom started the rotary spinning at five hundred revolutions per minute directly below the cab floor. When the RPMs were up on the orange diode display he kicked in the snapper chains and the center-feed auger on the picker head. They growled over the purr of the diesel.

He came to the sparse outer rows of the field that were fed on by deer and squirrels, wheeled the big machine into line and dropped the picker head. Four rows of cornstalks ran in between its snouts. Abruptly the stalks snapped down and the ears in their shucks clunked into the center-feed auger, augered out of sight into the picker-head throat, thumped past the elephant ears, broke up between the rasp bars and the steel contours below. Corn becoming grain was the sweetest sound Tom had ever heard. He grinned, felt the sobriety of what he had just done and stopped grinning. Formally and ceremoniously he announced it. "So the harvest begins," he said aloud. He had to raise his voice over a roar of corn.

EIGHT

The next morning Tom was up early, raring to go. The tile man was coming today to lay drainage tile at the Ward farm. Tom had two grain wagons full of corn ready to unload that he'd picked yesterday before he had to quit to go to Brett's football game. Sally was going to run the combine once she'd finished doing the laundry so that he could supervise the tiling and haul grain. Things were getting busy all right.

Tom drove out to the field in his second grain truck, a white Ford with a touchy gearshift. The truck had a tilt-up cab mounted over the engine with the transmission behind it. The gearshift linkage ran out to the far right, back behind the cab and then in again to the center. It was loose as a goose and you kind of swam the gearshift around trying to find the gears. He'd bought the truck cheap, three thousand dollars, and spent three months the winter before last giving it a total overhaul. It ran fine now. It was good for Wayne to drive because with the cab set up high and no hood sticking out in front he could see the road a lot better.

Sally and Sammi had gone with Tom to the game. A lot of parents turned out to show support for the team. They were playing Osage Station, old rivals, and Brett made two great tackles and the Plymouth JV won. Brett's teammates carried him off the field on their shoulders. Sammi was so happy she giggled the whole way home. Brett could use some wins. He was having trouble in school.

He always had trouble getting started studying in the fall after he'd been on his own all summer. But this year he was going around saying he was dumb. Tom would have to have a talk with the boy. He needed an attitude adjustment.

Tom lubricated the combine, hitting the grease fittings a few licks with the grease gun. He'd filled its ninety-two-gallon fuel tank from Babe last night before he drove home. The morning was cool and moist, around sixty degrees. It was partly cloudy and the forecast had said a chance of rain. He wanted to finish picking before it rained. In the summer, when the crops were growing, rain on a field wasn't usually a problem. You wanted as much rain as you could get short of flood. The sun evaporated it and the plants sucked it up and used some of it and put the excess into the air. But once the crop matured and began drying out it didn't draw water anymore. The air cooled off and there was less evaporation. About the only place the water had to go then was into the ground. That meant mud and the crop left standing in the field until the ground either dried out or froze enough to get a combine in.

Since the tile man hadn't showed up yet, Tom started combining. Yesterday afternoon he'd opened up the field. He always planted twelve rows around the outside of his fields and picked those first. That made a wide space where he could turn the combine around. Some farmers edged their fields with only eight turn rows. Tom couldn't figure out how they maneuvered their machinery. Since Sally wasn't as confident driving the combine as he was, opening up a field also meant picking its hard-to-get parts so that she could run straight through from one end to the other. In the case of this particular Ward field there was a little two-acre piece down by the creek that a creek meander partly surrounded. He'd already cleaned that land out.

Sally called Tom on the radio to tell him she was on her way. The rosy yellow grain was mounding high in the combine's holding bin when she pulled up in the GMC. She waited there, finishing her cigarette upwind from the blow of dust and chaff, while Tom wheeled over to the Ford, swung the dump auger out at right angles to the bin and dumped the load in the front half of the truck's grain bed. Lightweight chains held the wooden sides of the grain bed together against the onslaught. The front chain parted the flow of grain from the auger into two piles that slowly settled into a single pile with a crease across the top. The clouds were opening to the sun and the grain glowed in the light. It would take two full dumps to fill the truck.

Sally had Tom ride with her for the first couple of rounds to make sure she remembered how to run the combine. Coming back from the second pass, they saw the tile crew pulling up on the gravel road above the field and Sally let Tom off to go meet them. There was a pickup truck in front, a flatbed truck next with a rubber-tired bulldozer loaded on and a dump truck last with a flatbed trailer. The monster yellow tiling machine was chained down on the trailer. Coils of black plastic pipe ballooned from the pickup bed. Years ago, and back into ancient history, drainage tiles had been real tile, either cylindrical or rectangular red brick tubes, and the trench they were laid in was dug by hand. That durable but cumbersome system had been replaced in recent years by machine-dug and -filled trenches and lengths of slotted, ribbed four-inch plastic pipe.

It turned out Jack Ward wasn't so tight after all. Tom had convinced him in a long weekend phone call that it was worth the sixty-two cents per foot—several thousand dollars in total—it would cost to tile the bottomland field to enlarge it. Between the bottomland and the upland, on the slope of the hill that rose up south of the corn Sally was picking, a wide strip of disked land lay fallow, overgrown with weeds. It wasn't fallow land set aside to meet the requirements of a government program, as many such patches were in the country these days. It was land that under-ground drainage from the hill kept too wet to farm. A stand of sunflowers in the middle of the strip marked the site of an old spring. Ward had also agreed to tile and drain the shallow pond and its weedy surrounds to the west of the field. But the disked strip below the hill came first. With any luck they'd get fifteen acres of new land dried out enough to plant next spring.

Fenton, the tile man, burly and white-haired, had the dozer off the truck and had started knocking down weeds even before Tom caught up with him, wading through the tall grass from the com-bine. Tom climbed up onto the dozer fender and they rode along together in the soft morning air discussing the drainage.

"I wish I had a lot more land that was as rich and laid as good as this," Tom told Fenton, deepening his voice to be heard over the noise of the dozer's diesel. Yesterday Tom had asked Clarence's dad about the land's history. It was native prairie back sixty years, Oliver Galen had said, until two years ago when the previous tenant had plowed it up. Mr. Galen had remembered the spring at the foot of the hill. There'd been a fence once, running north and south, that partly divided the hillside. In the summer you could tell the difference between the part that'd been cropped and the part that'd been prairie grass by the color of the plants. Even with fertilizer the cropped part didn't turn as deep a green. That showed what erosion could do. The cropped part had lost precious inches of original topsoil, eroded into the creek in the days before terraces slowed down the wash of rain. People used to plant corn straight up and down the hill. That just washed the topsoil away. "Every row is a little terrace," was one of Tom's sayings. If you planted straight up and down the hill, every row was a little gully and the rainwater ran thick and brown with fertile topsoil that had been a thousand years in the making.

Where the dozer tore away the weeds it launched insects. Swallows darted and dived around the machine on their scissor wings, gliding and swooping like hawks, feeding on the windfall.

Tom wanted a line of drainage running along the base of the hill to intercept the water coming down underground. That should dry up the strip he'd had to leave fallow. Another lateral line crossing it to the west would start to drain the pond surround. Next spring, once he'd seen if the lateral was working, he'd cut the pond dam and drain it. Eventually the whole sweep of bottomland ought to be all one well-laid field.

Fenton radioed back to the pickup. His crew hauled out a long aluminum pole mounted on a tripod, found a place above the trench line on the hillside and began setting it up. Strapped onto the pole was the video-camera-like box of a laser. It pointed up into a spinning mirror that reflected its red beam out at right angles to form a level sheet of light sweeping the air above the field. The massive tiling machine carried a photodetector mounted on a short flagpole. When the tiling machine was running, the detector locked onto the sheet of laser light and signaled its ele-

vation. The working surface of the tiling machine was a chain of
heavy, toothed-steel buckets like a ferocious tank tread that dug in
at an angle to the ground. The operator sat in an outrigger chair
off to the side. At the rear, a coil of black tile set up on a rack fed
under the bucket chain into the trench the machine dug. An on-
board computer used the elevation from the detector to adjust the
trench depth. It built in a continual fall so that soil water that
found its way into the tile would drain by gravity. At its lowest
point the pipe would jut out from the bank above Little Cebo
Creek, where it would dump the water.

While the tile crew got started, Tom drove his second-best tractor, a green Oliver with an enclosed cab, up to the converted barn
behind the Ward farmhouse where the combine had wintered over.
He once again hitched on the two grain wagons he'd parked there
the night before, each loaded now with three hundred bushels of
corn, seventeen thousand pounds, and hauled them out to the
blacktop and east on 24 to Landers' to dump them. Going back
behind the Elms on the dirt section road to the grain bins was
tricky. The Landers farm was steep and hilly compared to the
other farms he managed and terraces crossed the section road. He
had to slow down to ease the high, narrow grain wagons over the
terraces. Once, the Landers family had owned most of the ten
miles of land on both sides of the highway between Devon and
Plymouth. That was a couple of generations ago. This generation
was professional people and only 509 acres of the worst land was
left. They were good people to work with but he wished they
hadn't sold off all the good land.

Tom lined up the first grain wagon beside the auger hole. The
wagon was an open box set on rubber tires with a sloped floor. A
vertical door was cut into the side on the lower slope with a wheel
like a steering wheel that cranked the door up and a fold-down
spout. By adjusting the size of the door opening Tom could control
the flow of grain. He cranked the door up two inches and the corn,
still warm from its afternoon harvest, began to flow into the auger
hole.

Quickly Tom climbed up and started the Farmall. Back on the
ground he pushed in the tractor clutch by hand and pulled out
the ring-handled rod that engaged the power takeoff. That started

the big fifty-two-foot grain auger, the corn beginning its journey to the top of the grain bin. He crossed to the bin, found a fluorescent-orange length of extension cord that hung down from the roof and plugged it in at the junction box. It connected to a spreader mounted inside the bin below the manhole, motor-driven paddles that deflected the fall of corn to spread it uniformly around the bin. When the corn in the auger began dumping into the bin, the spreader flung it wide, crashing it against the bin's steel sides. Last of all Tom switched on the blower, adding that banshee wail to the noise.

Back at the auger hole, Tom watched the grain flowing from the wagon and adjusted the wheel to keep the hole full. There was a guard of rusty iron reinforcing rods welded over the auger intake where the screw that gathered the grain was exposed. He'd bought the grain auger in 1972, when his dad was still living. The old man was always leaning down cleaning trash out of the grain and Tom had welded on the guard to keep him from losing a hand.

As the corn flowed from the wagon, the morning breeze threshed away a stream of pale red chaff. Wings, Tom called the flakes of translucent scale that blew off the corn. One on each side of a corn kernel nested it into its socket on the cob. Wings had reddened the stream of chaff that had blown off the dump auger on the combine before. Each handling blew more wings away and cleaned the corn further. If the kernels of corn Tom had grown counted in the billions, then more billions blew off of pale red wings. Eventually their fluffy pink drifts would bury the concrete footings of the grain bins.

While Tom was cleaning out the second grain wagon, reaching his arm around through the door to scoop the last handfuls of grain from the corners, along came Clarence in his old grain truck loaded with corn. Tom was surprised to see Clarence. He had corn of his own to pick and he wasn't yet finished fixing up the sec-ondhand Gleaner F2 he'd bought. Tom figured he must be feeling guilty for keeping him from the field yesterday with his calves.

Grinning, with a cigarette clamped in his teeth, Clarence stuck his head out the truck window. "How's it going there, Clem?" he called. They both thought Clem was a funny name. "Brung you some corn."

"Hey, Clem," Tom returned, "you don't have to be hauling corn for me. You got your own work to do."

Clarence shrugged, happy to have his purpose understood. "Figured you could use a little help with all you got going today."

"How're those calves?"

"Doing okay. They was all eating this morning."

"Let me get these wagons out of the way so you can dump." Tom started up the tractor and moved the wagons across the lot.

The grain trucks dumped from the rear, their entire beds hoisted by hydraulic pistons. With the wagons out of the way, Clarence backed to the auger hole, nicely gauging the spacing, set his air brakes and engaged the hoist. He gave her some gas and the grain bed began to tilt. Tom levered up the bed's grain door and corn flowed out in a wide, flat stream.

Leaving the truck bed to hoist at idle speed on its own, Clarence came back to stand beside Tom watching the streaming corn and the blowing wings. Both men smoked.

"Boy, look at that corn," Tom broke the silence. "It's so big and plump, it could be candy corn."

"How's your moisture?" Clarence asked.

"Eighteen, nineteen percent."

"She's coming down."

"Yeah."

Clarence cocked his head. "Blower sounds a little ragged, don't she?"

Tom listened. "I believe she does, Clem. I better give her an oiling."

"Oil her one for me," Clarence said. "Say, Clem, you know how an old maid's like paint?"

"No I don't, Clem. How?"

"Stir either one of them up and you can't get them off your hand." Clarence barked and slapped his thigh. Tom chuckled. "Thought of that coming over here from your field," Clarence added. "Passing Miz Carpenter's."

"Ain't she a tough one, though," Tom said. "Sure wouldn't want her for a landlord." He tapped the grain door lever with the heel of his hand, adjusting the flow. There was an art to dumping grain, fine adjustments of the grain door so that the flow kept the auger intake full without overflowing the hole. He listened to the blower. The Landerses rented the bungalow farmhouse north of the grain bin yard to a retired couple from the city. Tom hooked his thumb in its direction. "Them folks are going to get awful tired of hearing this blower before they're through," he told Clarence. "They wanted to move out into the country to be peaceful. Ain't going to be very peaceful." Tom would run the blower night and day for weeks to come so long as the humidity remained below fifty percent. Above that percentage it would add moisture to the grain rather than dry it.

"Ain't going to be very peaceful," Clarence agreed. "Looks like a damned good yield this year, though, don't it?"

Tom left the tractor and grain wagons at Landers' and rode back to the Ward farm with Clarence. Now that he knew the bottom-land was dry enough, he could use the trucks to do the hauling.

The tiling machine had dug halfway along the fallow strip, starting from the creek and working gradually uphill. A foot-wide trench edged with a parallel mound of rich brown dirt extended all the way back to the creek. Clarence parked behind Tom's trucks in the turn rows on the south side of the fifteen acres and the two men walked over to study the trench.

On their way they came across deer tracks, cloven impressions in the soft dirt of the fallow strip. "Mmmm, don't that make your mouth water?" Clarence paid his respects. Both men hunted deer in season. Venison steaks and sausage were delicacies even finer than calf fries.

"Long way to deer season," Tom said. The season in Missouri opened November 15.

"A fellow can dream, though, can't he?"

"No law against it."

The trench was five feet deep, narrow, with firm vertical sides. The black plastic tiling lay in the bottom ready to be covered over, work that Fenton was beginning with his dozer down at the creek end. From top to bottom the soil was the same color, a five-foot depth of rich brown loam.

"Ain't she pretty," Tom said proudly.

"Looks good enough to eat," Clarence agreed.

The combine coming through the corn sounded like a commercial jet roaring in the distance. Sally finished four rows and headed toward the trucks to dump, leaving a square block of standing corn behind. Tom went over to see how she was doing and Clarence followed.

The tiling machine crawled slowly up the slope. The dozer worked toward it from the creek bank, filling in the tear it had made. The red combine dumped yellow grain into a white truck. Under a fleecy sky patched now with blue, the wide field separated the sounds of each machine. Nothing returned them. The breeze took them. The swallows had gone their way, emptying the lower air, but now a red-tailed hawk circled high above the standing corn. The hawk was using the combine as the swallows had used the dozer, putting the brutes to work. Rabbits and mice nested in the corn. The combine progressively reduced their cover. When Sally finished dumping and dropped the picker head on the next four rows a rabbit flushed farther down, streaking for the trees. When she came back along she saw blood splashing the stobble behind a rag of brown fur.

NINE

The corn that Sally picked was a Native American invention, domesticated in Central America some five thousand years ago, the grain upon which the great Mayan, Aztec and Incan civilizations were built. The last Aztec emperor, Montezuma, collected a tax of three hundred thousand bushels of corn per year from the twenty provinces of his empire. Columbus carried corn to Europe, the Portuguese to Africa. Farmers throughout the world today harvested it to the extent of some fourteen billion bushels per year. The Corn Belt states produced forty percent of that volume—by order of production, Iowa, Illinois, Nebraska, Minnesota, Indiana, Ohio, Wisconsin, Michigan, Missouri, South Dakota, Kentucky and Kansas. Corn was a semitropical plant, but summer in the Mississippi Valley in any case was hot as tropical summer, sometimes hotter.

A grass distorted to biological monstrosity, the most prolific of all cereals in converting solar energy to food, corn was nearly three times as productive acre for acre as wheat. Across a long four-month growing season, it dug in a dense system of roots four feet deep, grew a thick, sectioned stalk six feet tall, leafed out in two dozen alternative wavy-edged blades. Male flowers appeared at the top of the stalk on tassels, female flowers halfway down as ear shoots, one or two per plant. Two months along, in midsummer, on a fixed schedule run by an internal biological clock, the ear

shoots extended a hollow filament of corn silk from the site of each potential kernel out through the upper end of their green husks. The flower tassels rained down millions of grains of pollen. If a silk caught a pollen grain, the grain extended a tube through the silk to the site of its attachment and fertilized it and a kernel of corn developed, five hundred to fifteen hundred kernels per ear. But the ears that this reproduction plumped and filled were too densely populated to propagate naturally. Without humans to shell and disperse the kernels, the thousand seedlings growing from a fallen ear would crowd each other to eventual extinction. People depended on corn and corn depended on people.

It was less than a perfect food, low in tryptophan and lysine, two of the eight amino acids essential to human nutrition, deficient in niacin. A diet exclusively of corn caused pellagra, a vitamin-deficiency disease that used to plague the rural South, which lived on corn bread and hominy, and still plagued Africa. Industrially corn made cornstarch, corn oil, corn syrup, dextrose and ethanol, but more than ninety percent of the corn consumed in the United States was fed to animals. People ate it indirectly as meat, milk and eggs.

Pre-Columbian Native Americans developed more than two hundred corn varieties, including red corn, blue corn, yellow corn, field corn, sweet corn, dent corn, flint corn, flour corn, pod corn and popcorn. Twentieth-century American agronomists studied Darwin and Mendel and learned to crossbreed inbred strains of

corn to produce vigorous hybrids. Yields increased even as acreage
planted declined, though twenty-four percent of the principal crop
acreage in the United States was still devoted to corn, more than
double the acreage of any other plant. The hybrid yellow dent corn
that Sally picked and Tom hauled to the bin and the elevator was
a harvest few city people could have identified, but it was the
foundation of their diet, the principal food plant of the Western
world.

Sally Bauer had been a small-town girl, not a farmer's daughter.
Tom's sisters hadn't been sure she'd take to farming. She'd worked
at Tom's side off and on for more than twenty years now and long
ago earned his sisters' respect. She'd started out driving the big
grain trucks back and forth to the storage bins or the elevator to
dump the grain. The combine was a complicated machine to operate and skillful operation made a difference. If you didn't stay on
it you could leave a lot of crop in the field. But waiting in line at
Comstock's with a bunch of men she mostly didn't know got old.
A few years of that and she'd asked Tom to let her combine
instead. Now she handled the combine like a pro, though she never
learned to interpret the machine sounds the way he could and
broke down more often than he would have. Tom never got mad
at her about it. They were a team and they worked as a team. Most
farmers' wives wouldn't get near a combine. Most farmers
wouldn't let them. Tom was glad for the help.

She liked it best when she knew the field, knew how the rows
ran and where the terraces came out. They were harvesting the
Ward bottomland field for the first time this year, but she knew it
from having disked it, especially one corner down near the creek
that was so waterlogged—"sour," Tom had called it—that he'd
had her disk it four or five times on sunny days to open up the soil
and dry it out. It was easier too when Tom told her how he'd
planted the rows. He worked it all out ahead of time. Sometimes
it was like a jigsaw puzzle and the boys would kid him, get him to
explain why he planted the way he did. He tried to make sure all
the rows laid like little terraces to slow down runoff and reduce
erosion and he tried to plant as few point rows as possible so
there'd be less backing the combine and turning around. Point

rows were short rows you had to plant between long rows that
followed the contours of the terraces and so came together at less
than a ninety-degree angle. Point rows got shorter and shorter and
finally came to a point. She didn't like picking the corners and the
point rows. She didn't think she did a good enough job. Usually
he'd clean those up for her ahead of time and let her pick the
middle. She still couldn't go through as fast as he did, but he'd
been handling machinery all his life.

When they were first married and she was working for a wholesale nut and bolt company in Kansas City she used to bring his
supper home from the city and carry it to the field. She'd see him
combining and drive to where she thought the rows came out and
he'd turn up somewhere else entirely. She hadn't spied out the lay
of the terraces. He'd pulled a trick on her once when she'd been
combining at night. She'd lost track of where she'd started from.
He'd just sat there in the truck with the lights off and watched.
Finally he'd called her on the radio.

"You lost?" he'd asked her.

"You're damned right I am," she'd told him. "Where *are* you?"

He'd turned on his lights then but she still couldn't see him.
He'd let her go on like that for a while. He was a cute one, he was.
"Look behind you," he'd finally said. Then she'd found him.

She'd learned bookkeeping at the nut and bolt supply, keeping
the books for the owner. Mr. Jenkins hadn't wanted her to leave,
but when the kids came along she came home. They'd meant to
have Wayne and Brett. Sammi was a surprise. Tom didn't believe
in birth control. He said it wasn't natural. Sally hadn't wanted any
more children but she was glad to have a little girl. That was it as
far as she was concerned. She liked kids but she didn't like babies.
Crying and crying and you didn't know what was wrong. She
hadn't even played with dolls when she was a girl. Dolls made her
brothers jealous and they took them away from her and tore them
up. Babies were for the birds. The more the merrier as far as Tom
was concerned.

She'd never expected she would marry Tom. She hadn't even
liked him at first. He'd dated one after another of her girlfriends
and she'd had to be the shoulder they cried on when he broke their
hearts. A big country boy on a big motorcycle. He'd had a band.

He was singing and playing guitar all over Missouri and up into
Iowa and Nebraska. Then one of her girlfriends who'd been in
love with Tom had to go away one summer. She'd asked Sally to
look after him while she was gone. Sally had said she would. She
hadn't liked him for what he'd done to her friends, jilting them one
after another, and she'd decided she'd show him one girl who
could see right through him, one heart he couldn't break. But
along the way they got to be friends. She hadn't fallen in love with
him. She told her mother once she'd never been in love in her life
and her mother said that was good, being in love made you crazy.
Sally hadn't fallen in love with Tom but they came to be best
friends, sharing dreams. That was another kind of love. It was a lot
steadier. So they got married. Wayne's eye trouble brought them
closer together. There wasn't any room for distance between them
when that came along. She thought it might even have saved their
marriage.

Her heart wasn't in combining the way it used to be. They'd
both worked so hard when they were starting out. Tom's dad
didn't approve of her running the combine. "A woman's place is
in the home," he'd told Tom. After Tom's mother died, his dad
had bought a house in Plymouth. Sally had gone in to help him
clean it up. They'd work together side by side and Sally would
come home exhausted. She was determined to prove that she was
a hard worker who could hold up her end. Tom's dad would work
along slow and steady from morning to night and hardly ever stop,
so she wouldn't stop either. He had big hands. He'd hurt people
shaking their hands and not even know it. His hands were so big
he was embarrassed about them. He'd tuck them under him when
he sat or fold his arms and hide them in his armpits when he was
standing. He and Sally finished cleaning up the house and she still
didn't know what he thought of her work. After he was settled in,
he came out to the farm to putter, cutting weeds in the fencerows
and odd jobs like that. One day when he was alone with Tom he
told him, "That little woman of yours is a hell of a worker. She just
about wore me out. Start first thing in the morning and work
straight through till night. Never would stop. I had to jump to
keep up with her." Tom thought that was funny. His dad never
said anything more about her driving the combine.

They all worked hard. If her heart wasn't in combining the way it used to be, maybe it was because they'd gotten a little bit ahead. Tom's dad had a harder time. He had ten children to feed and that was part of it. But the boys were also extra hands to help with the work. His refusing to borrow money to buy land was the real difference. Tom had been almost as bad. He hadn't wanted to borrow a penny. Sally'd had to talk him into it, show him where the land they bought would generate the return to pay for itself. It made her nervous, though. She couldn't wait until everything was paid off. They never fought about money but they talked hard sometimes. These days, when they got something paid down, Tom would want to get started on something else. He was never a plunger and he always had a plan but she wanted to pro and con his plans every which way to make sure they were solid.

He'd seen the hard times coming, starting back in 1979. He talked it over with her. He was even thinking about getting out of farming. The interest rates shot up to eighteen percent and worse. The grain embargo Jimmy Carter slapped on when the Russians invaded Afghanistan worried him. It meant farmers couldn't count on exports the way old Earl Butz, Nixon's secretary of agriculture, used to preach to them they could. "Plant your fields from fencerow to fencerow," Butz would say. "You can't ever grow too much crop. American farmers are going to feed the world!"

Reagan worried Tom more. There was a bumper corn crop in 1981, which meant corn prices were way down and farmers were hurting—wasn't it a crime when doing a good job meant you lost money?—and Reagan's comment was, "We ought to keep the grain and export the farmers." Even more than the interest rates and the grain embargo, that got to Tom.

"A man talks like that," he told Sally, "you don't have to look around to find out what he thinks of you. Hard times is coming and we ought to put our house in order, not buy new cars and trucks and tractors. Tighten our belts, not buy anything we don't need. We got to get rid of that debt."

The most debt they ever had was about twenty thousand dollars. But they decided not to borrow any further. Sally worked for a couple of years for the gas company in Plymouth. They operated on cash and paid down their debts as fast as they could. People they knew went under. If they hadn't tightened up they wouldn't have made it. As it was, their net worth was just about cut in half from the $450,000 they'd built up to by 1980. Most of the loss was the drop in land values. Land that had been selling for up to fifteen hundred dollars an acre all of a sudden wasn't worth more than five hundred. That was the extreme. Theirs kept more of its value. But they felt the loss. "You ask our city cousins and bankers," Tom said once, "if they could take a fifty- to sixty-percent cut in pay and still meet their commitments. That's it in a nutshell."

The hardest she'd ever worked combining was the year Tom had surgery on his tailbone for a pilonidal cyst. The doctor told Tom he'd be up in three days but the cyst was a lot deeper than he expected. He cut out a lot more and left in a drain. Tom couldn't sit but he could stand. A neighbor who had a new John Deere combine had come over to help Sally pick corn and the two combines had chased each other all over the field. The neighbor brought his hired hand and two trucks to add to theirs. The hired hand moved the four trucks. He'd take one to the bin, leave it and bring another one down. Tom ran the grain auger because he could do that standing up. Sally was driving their old Massey-Ferguson. It had a gearshift instead of a Hydra-matic with a whole slew of gears. Tom told her just to open it up and not worry if she missed some corn. She wasn't sure she could keep up, but she did. They got both their fields picked in one day.

Tom's voice came over the radio. "How you doing, hon?" he asked. He and Clarence had taken the first truck in line to Landers' and dumped it.

She plucked the mike down from the combine overhead. "The Ford's full," she told him. "I'm starting on Clarence's truck. Where are you?"

"I'm over here at Siegelstecher's," he said. "We'll be right along."

"Ten-four," Sally said. "These tile people look like they're about ready to finish up."

"You missing me, hon?" Tom said with amusement in his voice. "They still got that lateral to do over west."

Clarence took over the two-way. "Hey, Sally," he radioed.

"Go ahead, Clarence," she said drily, knowing some foolery was coming.

"You know what the difference is between a widow and a wife?"

"You sure you ought to be putting that out over the radio?" Sally asked.

"Sure I'm sure. This is one of my clean ones."

"Well, go ahead."

"The widow knows where her husband is." Clarence didn't leave his mike open, so Sally couldn't hear him laughing, but she knew he was.

Tom turned into the field off the blacktop a few minutes later. By then Sally was dumping on Clarence's truck. The men had bought half a peck of apples. She climbed down and joined them beside the truck. They took a break and munched apples. There were two varieties. Clarence didn't care about the variety. An apple was an apple as far as he was concerned. Tom liked Red Delicious because they were sweet. Jonathans were Sally's favorite, the best apples Missouri grew. Tom claimed Jonathans were sour. They weren't sour, Sally defended them, they were just tart. Everything didn't have to be sweet.

TEN

The harvest was rolling now. The tile crew loaded its machines and moved on, leaving a line of dark, freshly turned earth like a seam striking diagonally across the field. Tom and Sally finished picking the Ward farm corn, moved the combine and the trucks and started on Landers'. Toward the end of the week it rained.

There was more to the week than combining. The animals still had to be chored twice a day. By and large they took care of themselves, sows caring for pigs, cows for calves, the adult animals seeking out feed and water and using what they needed, but injury and disease and breakdowns of the semiautomatic machinery of their housing were always risks. When his parents worked in the fields, Brett husbanded the animals, Molly and Blaze following along. Sammi gave him his marching orders. She got home from school earlier than he did and took messages from her parents over the two-way radio in the house where she played with her dolls. If she didn't want to join them combining she was safe at home, Tom and Sally never more than a radio call away.

Four PIK certificates arrived in the mail one day. Monopoly money, some farmers called the baby-blue federal certificates. Ronald Reagan's first secretary of agriculture, John R. Block, had pushed the Payment-in-Kind program through Congress in the early 1980s. It was supposed to reduce government commodity

surpluses, encourage farmers to grow less and boost prices on the
open market, all at the same time. It was also supposed to be a
one-year program, but like most government programs it kept
getting renewed. And maybe it did some good.

The government came to own surplus commodities in the first
place because it loaned farmers money against the value of their
crops, one way their city cousins helped farmers survive. The crop
loans were based on a loan rate the government set each year that
was supposed to give a farmer a reasonable return on his investment. Sometimes the loan rate turned out to be lower than the
market price. Usually it was higher. If the market price for the
Bauers' corn didn't come up to the loan rate within nine months
after they borrowed against their crop, they could default on the
loan and the government would forgive the interest and take the
corn. The corn might be stored at Comstock's or even in one of
the farm grain bins Tom used. With his loan default it became
government property, which had the effect of paying him the loan
rate for the grain he'd grown.

To qualify to participate in the government programs in the first
place he'd had to agree not to plant a certain number of acres of
his land. He left the land fallow through the growing season and
lost its use, so the safety net built into the government loan program wasn't a handout, wasn't farmer welfare. It was a trade-off.
The Bauers didn't grow all the corn they might have grown if
they'd had the use of all their land. They were also required to
institute extensive conservation measures such as terracing and
pond-making to prevent soil erosion, not that they wouldn't have
done so anyway. The government, in return, arranged indirectly to
buy the corn they did grow at a price higher than they would have
gotten on the open market.

A second program established a target price for corn and other
commodities in exchange for setting aside cropland. If the market
price of corn didn't come up to the target price, then the government paid Tom the difference directly. That was called a deficiency
payment.

The PIK program worked another angle. Farmers who agreed to
hold an additional percentage of their land out of production
would be paid not only directly in deficiency payments and indi-

rectly through defaulted loans but also directly in kind, corn for corn, wheat for wheat, rice for rice, cotton for cotton. How much they got depended on how many acres they'd planted to those crops in previous years, a base figure against which all of the United States Department of Agriculture's support programs were figured. "It goes to show that in this particular game it's important to keep your corn base up," Tom explained the requirement as it applied to him, meaning that it was important to plant as many acres in corn every year as USDA regulations allowed. If he didn't, his base would decrease, and that would decrease his participation in future programs. Once your base went down, there was no way on a particular farm that you could increase it again except to get out of the government program for a few years.

The PIK commodities came from government surpluses and the baby-blue certificates officially conferred on their holders owner-ship of a certain number of bushels. In practice the certificates were generic, redeemable in corn/wheat/rice/cotton or in cash, and showed a face value in dollars. Since commodity prices varied from day to day, the number of bushels a PIK would redeem fluctuated with the market. Once bought with a PIK, the commod-ities could be held or resold. As a result, farmers, grain companies and other riverboat gamblers quickly learned to speculate with PIKs. They were issued at harvesttime and began losing face value on a graduated scale a few months later, which made the gamble that much more interesting. Old farmers who didn't understand what PIKs were for and didn't read the fine print sometimes held onto them while they dropped to eighty-five percent of face value, then to fifty percent, and eventually became void. This year, with a four-billion-bushel holdover on hand in storage, the grain com-panies were buying PIKs at a premium immediately upon issue. Comstock's was currently offering $1.10 to the dollar. Buying PIKs, Comstock's bought a portion of the loan corn that farmers had stored the previous year in its elevators that had defaulted to government corn. With ownership, the grain company could move the corn out on railroad cars and barges. That was why it was willing to pay a ten-percent premium. It needed the storage space for the new crop.

Tom and Sally figured corn prices weren't going to get much

better three months down the road. If the harvest broke records the way everyone was expecting, they might even get worse. The ten-percent Comstock premium looked good, money in the bank, so the day after the PIKs arrived, Tom drove over to the elevator and sold them for $1,587. He'd had to leave land fallow to buy into the PIK program. It was land on which he'd otherwise have planted corn or soybeans, and PIKs were compensation for that loss. The set-aside land reduced surpluses the government would otherwise be committed to buy. The return from government programs averaged out to about eleven dollars per acre more than a farmer could make on his own. That eleven dollars didn't count a farmer's labor, though. Government economists considered a farmer's labor to be of nominal value. As far as government economists were concerned, farmers who wanted to earn money for their labor could always work in town.

From Riverton, watching the corn roll by, Tom drove west across the county to Plymouth to deposit the Comstock check. The president of his bank noticed him in the lobby and called him into his office to talk. Luke Cage was a native Plymouthian and retired Army officer, an older man with a boyish shock of gray hair that fell over his forehead on one side. He'd been bank president for about five years, since his retirement from the Army as a lieutenant colonel after two tours of duty in Vietnam. The bank was a small branch of a big Kansas City bank. Tom left on his seed cap and lounged in one of the leather chairs at Luke's big desk, one work boot crossed on the other knee. The two men respected each other. Luke had loaned Tom the down payment on the Dixon farm and would have been glad to loan him money for new machinery or buildings if he'd had a mind to buy any. The banker believed that management made the difference between success and failure in farming. Since he often asked Tom's opinion before he bought or sold a farm he must have thought Tom managed things better than most.

Sally had gone in one day to lock in the interest rate on a loan. Luke tried to convince her she ought to let it float. "I just do what Tom tells me." Sally dug in her heels. "I think you better too. He's bigger than you and me both put together." But what if the interest rate goes down? Luke pressed her. "Then we'll borrow the money

from you to pay off the loan," Sally explained. Luke saw her point
and locked in the interest rate. As the Bauers figured it would, it
went up, not down.

Today Luke had a farm to sell. First he asked Tom the standard
harvesttime opener, "How's your moisture?" Then they went over
the storage shortage. Then he got around to the farm. It was just
east of Devon on U.S. 24, 110 acres of good terraced land. Tom
recognized it when Luke pointed it out on the county plat map. It
was part of the farm that the kid who'd previously owned Clarence's Gleaner F2 had inherited from his parents and run through
to bankruptcy in nineteen months. Since Luke didn't volunteer the
details of that disaster Tom didn't pry. People would tell you their
business if they wanted to.

"What kind of price you think you'll put on it?" Tom asked.

"We've got it down for seventy thousand dollars," Luke told
him.

That was a good price, $636 per acre for fine Crevecoeur County
farmland right on a federal highway. Tom and Sally had bought
the Dixon place nine years ago, in the late 1970s. Land prices had
ballooned at the end of the seventies because farmers were making
money for a change and bidding them up and the Bauers had paid
$1,200 an acre. They'd known that was high even then but had
decided it was worth it because the land was adjacent to the home
farm and had potential, especially the boggy bottomland along
Little Cebo Creek. But Tom still thought buying it so high was the
biggest mistake they'd made during the boom years. They were
stuck now with paying off the mortgage at the old price when land
values had been cut just about in half.

But land was one thing, what you could grow on it another.
"What's the grain base?" Tom asked Luke about the sale farm.

The banker looked surprised. "Why, I don't recall." He waved
at the thick file squared away on his blotter. "It's in here somewhere."

"Make all the difference," Tom said.

"I'll look it up." Tom waited while Luke set his reading glasses
on his nose and shuffled through the papers. Three-quarters of the
way down the pile he found the sheet he was hunting. "Seven point
two acres wheat," he said, frowning. "And nine acres corn."

Tom raised an eyebrow. That was a pitiful grain base. The kid must have let it slip. "Reckon it would make good pasture," he drawled.

Luke took off his glasses. "That bad?"

"Can't make a living growing corn and selling it at market when the other guy's got a government price. I guess a fellow could feed it to his hogs."

"If he didn't already have enough corn land for his hogs," Luke finished the thought.

"That's about the size of it."

"So it doesn't look like a good deal to you."

"Might be for someone who wanted to raise hogs," Tom said politely. "Hog prices are high. Everybody's getting in."

"When you bought that farrowing house you told me the time to get in was when hog prices were low and everyone else was getting out."

"Well, sure," Tom grinned, "but not everybody believes that."

A young farmer in the neighborhood named Cort McAntire was working as a seed salesman to make ends meet. He came by one morning to pitch Tom a new hybrid wheat. Cort was built like Doc Mitchell, lean and muscular, and tanned nearly the color of mahogany down to the collar line. In the farmhouse kitchen Tom poured him some coffee and they reminisced about seed salesmen they'd known. "He could talk the pants off an old widow woman," Cort summed up one man's talents.

Hybrid wheat was new. It came from Europe, where small farms and a shortage of farmland made increasing yields even more important than it was in America. The seed company Cort worked for was German, but the seed he was selling had been grown in Missouri to acclimate it to local conditions. Hybrid wheat could yield twice as many bushels to the acre as ordinary wheat, he told Tom. It took a lot more fertilizer, though, especially nitrogen, and intensive management.

Tom ended up ordering twenty bushels. That was enough to seed thirteen acres, a good test. Cort would schedule delivery at the beginning of October. Tom wouldn't begin planting soft red winter wheat until after the Hessian fly-free date for central Missouri, October 6. The Hessian fly first turned up in New York back in 1779 near a camp of Hessian soldiers. It wasn't much bigger than a gnat. It emerged on warm days in the fall and laid its eggs on the young blades of fall-seeded wheat. The maggots that hatched at night from the eggs crawled down the stems of the wheat seedlings and sucked out the sap. Once they hatched there was no way to eradicate them and they could destroy an entire crop. Wheat was the only grain Tom needed to plant in the fall. It was always touch and go. It had to germinate and put down roots in the narrow window between the October Hessian fly-free date and the hard freezes that usually began in late November. If it made deep enough roots it wintered over under the snow green as a rich man's lawn, then put up stalks and headed out in the spring, to be harvested in June.

The day it looked like rain, Tom decided to work in his shop. There was so much fog in the morning that the world faded out at the far fence of the cattle lot south of the house. The sky hung low and gray until the sun got well up. Then it swirled with light.

Sally went off to the ceramics shop. Tom brought in the Ford truck to fix the driver's window, Molly greeting him at the turnoff and chasing the truck up the driveway. Blaze as usual slept on the patio behind the house, under the eave up against the wall. The mechanism that rolled the truck window up and down was broken. Tom unscrewed the door panel and found the culprit. A little plastic bearing supported the entire window glass. Some sharp engineer made the whole operation depend on a flimsy little plastic bearing not much bigger than a toothpaste cap. That meant a trip to Osage Station to find a replacement, five miles each way through the morning fog. Tom tried a body shop first but they couldn't help him. Luckily the Ford dealership had the part. After he installed the new bearing he cleaned the Ford's cab and the windows, parked the truck south of the house and raised its grain bed to a thirty-degree angle so that any rainwater would drain away.

The rain approached across the cornfield south of the house, rushing on the dry blades like traffic on a distant highway. The sky darkened and as the wind picked up Tom rolled the big shop doors partly closed. Molly slipped into the shop through the narrowed opening, wagging her tail, found the cat chow Sammi put out for the one farm cat and settled down frowning with seriousness to crunch it in her back teeth. Like Blaze, who came to full attention when Tom moved machinery that might scare up a nesting mouse, Molly got scraps but no store-bought food and lived off the land.

Rain rattled the shop's tin roof. Tom turned up the radio when Paul Harvey came on. For the next hour, listening to the farm news and the rain, thinking about the harvest, he puttered.

He usually had a shop project in mind for off days. It was either that or dig into the pile of honey-do's Sally had accumulated for him, repair jobs around the house. "Honey, do this," the slang encoded, "honey, do that." Tom preferred farm work to housework and when the rain had blown past he shouldered the shop doors open to the fresh, cool air, Molly bursting out to inspect the morning of the new world, and strolled around to his scrap pile west of the grease shed to see if he could find a length of steel ladder. Raindrops sparkled on pipes and fence posts and reinforcing rods but he didn't find a ladder. He wanted to bolt one permanently to the side of the grain bed on his International truck to make it easier to climb in and out.

He remembered a galvanized iron ladder on an old windmill at Landers', just the ticket. He'd need a ladder to fetch it. There was a wooden ladder in the shed where the International was parked. He lifted it down, loaded it into the back of Babe and drove off, leaving Molly behind.

He caught up with the rain at Devon but left it again when he turned south into the Elms. Half a mile in on the dirt section road that roller-coastered over the Landers terraces, on beyond the grain bins, a bean field began. At that point a dirt lane branched off to the west. The old metal windmill was set halfway along toward the western edge of the field. Tom turned into the lane.

Like everything else on the farm the windmill had a history. It was stove in on the near side. Years ago he'd been coming back up the lane with the combine, the old Massey-Ferguson combine, and he'd forgotten to stow the dump auger. It still stuck out sideways. He'd been thinking about how he was going to start in on the next field, a million things running through his head, and all of a sudden he'd heard a big crash and the combine just spun around the

windmill. He'd put himself out of business for two weeks with that
stunt. He'd had to haul all the way to Memphis to get a new dump
auger. They were going to ship it. He'd waited and waited and
waited. Two weeks he'd waited in the middle of the harvest season.
He was about sick. Finally he took the matter into his own hands,
took a grain truck and drove down across the Ozarks and the
Missouri boot heel, across the Mississippi into Tennessee and
picked up the new dump auger himself at Massey-Ferguson's main
parts depot.

There was more rain coming, clouds blowing up from the southwest. That could mean lightning. The ladder ran up the bent leg of
the windmill. Tom checked a bolt for size, found a three-eighth-
inch wrench in Babe's toolbox, leaned the wooden ladder against
the windmill and hauled himself up. He had to reach above his
head to loosen the top bolts on the windmill ladder. He gave them
a shot of penetrating oil. One came easy but the next two he tried
stayed frozen. He didn't like hanging out on the windmill with a
storm blowing up. He let himself down and rethought the project.
There was a straight, perfectly good section of steel ladder right at
ground level. He sprayed penetrating oil on the bolts that held it to
the windmill, unscrewed them easily one by one, worked the bottom legs of the ladder out of the ground and threw it into the back
of the truck. Lighting a cigarette, he drove off.

On the way back he swung through the Landers pasture to
check the cattle, a herd he raised just as he raised the crops on
fifty-fifty shares. The pasture extended half a mile along the southern end of the farm, wider than it was deep, sloping south to a
stretch of fenced woods that sheltered the westward-flowing me-
anders of Little Cebo Creek. A few old oaks left standing in the
pasture gave shade but most of it was cleared, lush in autumn with
pasture grasses and still green.

The cattle saw Babe and came running, cows first with their
udders flapping, calves following behind. They remembered that
Tom fed them out of the back of the truck in the winter. The two
bulls that served as herd sires, warier, kept their distance. Tom
drove slowly among the black and roan cows looking for problems. He noticed one cow with cancer eye, a developing tumor.
The condition was incurable and he reminded himself to ship her.

The rust-red, fifty-pound mineral blocks he'd set out during the summer had been licked down to irregular lumps like melting blocks of ice and needed replacing. Frost would end the fly season, so he wouldn't need fly blocks this time. Besides vitamin A, vitamin D, calcium, phosphorus, soybean meal, salt, iron, potassium, cobalt, copper, mineral oil, molasses, manganese, iodine, selenium and zinc, the fly blocks contained methoprene, an insect growth regulator. It passed through the cattle when they licked the blocks for their salt and stunted the growth of horn-fly larvae that hatched from eggs the flies laid in the manure.

Tom drove on toward the middle of the pasture, leaving the cattle behind. He braked to a quiet halt on the slope of the hill above an old, half-drained pond. A great blue heron perched there on the bone-white branch of a tree that the pond had drowned. As Tom watched, warm with pleasure, the big, dark bird swung its head around on its graceful neck to study the truck, looked again toward the pond, considered the intrusion for a time and then folded its head back on its shoulders and launched itself flying, skimming low over the water and westward, black legs trailing behind, beating its wide wings.

In the workshop, Tom cut the ladder to size with his acetylene torch, the galvanized iron uprights popping and sputtering and showering his boots with sparks. Around the other side of the shop wall, in the equipment shed, he bolted the ladder to the International's grain-bed side and spray-painted it bright red to match.

On his way to the commercial meat locker at noontime that day to pick up beef for the home freezer, pulling honey-do duty after all, Tom stopped for dinner at a country café in Grants, a small town along the railroad line east of Osage Station. Salisbury steak, mashed potatoes and gravy and canned corn cost $2.95 with margarine and two slices of white bread, real iced tea fifty cents more. The fire chief, a feed salesman by trade, was eating at the next table and they got to talking seed corn deals until the man finally moved his plate over near Tom's. A retired farmer joined them, a trim, dignified old man, carefully shaved, in overalls and a plaid shirt with a buttoned-up collar loose on his thin neck. They talked about fire fighting. Tom was a volunteer fireman in Devon, which shared fire district responsibilities with Grants. Devon had just built a new fire station and acquired a hand-me-down Grants fire truck.

"Took fifteen years to get that station," Tom told the fire chief. "Grants had more people on the board and took care of itself first, which I can understand. But you all still haven't put together a map of water sources. I've got a structure on my place with a lot of water in it, ain't on anybody's map. Tankers, hell, you can empty one of those things out pretty fast."

The fire chief nodded. "We need someone who hasn't got anything else to do."

"Like you," the old farmer kidded Tom. He didn't say too much. He let the younger men do most of the talking.

"We all work for a living," the fire chief finished.

Tom grinned. "I got too much to do already."

The old farmer couldn't resist a summary. "Like they say," he threw in, " 'Do more and you got more.' "

ELEVEN

S aturday the weather changed. When Tom came out at seven it was gray and foggy. The wind was picking up out of the east. It soon got colder, the air drier, and Tom had to put on his red nylon windbreaker. Big brown sycamore leaves rolled through the yard like tumbleweeds. Suddenly it was fall.

The wind would help dry the fields. The Bauers were back to combining. No stopping for weekends during the harvest season. Stopping for the weather was bad enough. The moisture in the corn was down now to 16.5 percent. They were picking one of their own fields, over the hill west of the house. The landlords' fields left to do were muddy.

Molly had barked at the tractors and grain wagons parked west of the house that morning until Tom told her to shush. The machines weren't usually left there. She thought they were intruders. Tom hauled the fifty-two-foot grain auger over from Landers' behind the old Farmall and set it up in the farmyard at the grain bin out of which he fed his hogs. He'd emptied that bin of last year's grain just a few days ago, grinding the corn for feed and storing the meal in the two six-ton bulk bins down at the hog operation.

Tom and Sally rode around together in the big cab of the combine to open up the twenty-acre field. It was north-and-south rectangular and it had long terraces that started at the east fence, ran

123

to the southwest corner, then swung around ninety degrees and continued on nearly to the northwest corner. The terraces stopped at the waterway that fed the pond Tom called a "structure." Beyond the waterway in the grove of oaks that shaded the northwest corner of the field were the trailer bunkhouse and picnic benches of Camp Kookamunga, where in less than a month Tom and his brothers and their boys would camp out to hunt deer. There was still plenty of mud in the terrace channels that took deep impressions of the combine treads, but the terraces themselves were fairly dry. You couldn't have gotten a truck into the field, though.

Picking corn was a comedy sometimes. From inside the cab the tall stalks of corn looked like ranks of marching Scarecrows out of *The Wizard of Oz*. When they passed between the snouts of the picker head they'd shudder and flail and then suddenly go wobbly as if their legs had given way. The snapping rollers caught them then and jerked them straight down into perdition. That's how it looked. In fact they were chopped into pieces, their heavy, solid ears knocked loose and shucked just like that, all of a sudden, the Scarecrows abruptly gone and nothing left but buff-colored chop and yellow ears tumbling along the big transverse feed auger toward the mouth of the picker throat. The ears thumped against the sheet-metal snouts as they were torn loose. Tom and Sally could hear them inside the cab. The crop was knocking on the door and it felt good. After years of combining, Tom could almost estimate his yield per acre from the vigor of that knocking.

"Harvest's my favorite season," he told Sally happily, adjusting the rotary RPMs. He was doing the picking. Sally was sitting to his left on a padded storage compartment.

"You like the achievement."

"Every farmer wants a crop. He can complain about the prices, but if he hasn't got a crop he hasn't got anything to show. The bad time is when hail or drought destroys it."

"Don't say it out loud," Sally cautioned. "You'll bring it on."

"It just kind of takes you down."

"We're okay so far."

Tom smiled. "Yield's been great, ain't it?"

Sally gestured ahead. "Sounds pretty thin along these outside rows."

"Deer and squirrels been at it, hon. I don't grudge them. Some guys raise hell about it. The animals have a right to live too. You can't have it all."

"Just so *they* can't have it all neither."

"It always gets to me when they come right out and feed in plain sight."

"Me too," Sally agreed. "You seen any deer yet this season?"

"Not yet. Ought to be some come out once we open up that bottomland down along the creek."

"You think you can get through there with the mud?"

"If I gun her through I think she'll go. Skate right across."

"I'm glad you're driving it, not me."

And around they went, picking corn the deer and squirrels had left them, opening up the field.

Tom was dumping on one of the grain wagons parked along the lane, rosy yellow corn pouring, a drift of wings pink against the gray sky. He nearly had a load. He'd left his moisture tester in the workshop, so he'd radioed in to Sammi to bring it out. All the children helped with farm work, ever since they were small. "Sammi's little arm," Tom remembered. "She'd reach up into a machine for me where I couldn't reach." Here she came down the lane bouncing along on the red Kawasaki three-wheeler, arms raised high to span the handlebars, round-faced and grinning, dark hair blowing, Molly running ahead stretched out like a sleek black midget racehorse.

In late afternoon the sun broke through, streaking from the cloud margins, and Sally had an accident with the combine. Sammi was riding with her at the time. The big front window of the cab was so covered with dust that Sally couldn't see where she was going against the glare. She scraped the picker head on a terrace. It ate dirt faster than she could shut it down and packed the throat solid. There was nothing to do but start digging. Sammi helped. Tom was in at the house, dumping the grain wagons. Sally didn't call him. She hoped she'd get the mess cleaned up before he got back. But the dirt was packed tighter into the picker throat than she'd thought it would be, wedged with cornstalks and big yellow ears like aboriginal relics. She and Sammi were still digging away with big and little screwdrivers when Tom came down the lane on the tractor.

He strolled over and assessed the damage. He looked at Sally and she looked at him. Sammi watched them both. Finally Sally couldn't stand it. "Go ahead," she broke the tension. "Say it. It was just plain *dumb*."

"Mom," Sammi began to defend her mother.

"Shush," Sally warned her.

Tom just winked. He'd seen worse. "You're getting ahead of yourself, hon," he drawled. "I was going to plow up them terraces later this fall."

Sally shook the screwdriver at him. *"Ooooo,* Tom Bauer, why don't you just get *mad?"*

Tom joined them on his hands and knees and began throwing dirt off the picker head. "Could of happened to anybody," he answered his wife reasonably. "No sense in wasting energy blowing off about it."

They worked side by side for an hour clearing the picker throat, the combine idling before them. All three of them were dirty with dark loam, the soil moist on their hands and arms and faces but drying to gray on the front of their clothes. Tom unclipped a big red wrench from its brackets on the housing of the picker head to work the auger back and forth to free it. The wrench was four feet long and fit a heavy steel nut as big around as a spray-can top. It took all Tom's strength, bending his powerful back, to work the auger, doing slowly by hand what required a 185-horsepower engine to do full throttle.

Once the dirt was clear the combine worked fine. Sally and Sammi went home. Tom kept on combining until after nine, when the dew came down and made the ground slick. First thing Sunday morning, Sally brought a roll of paper towels and a big pump bottle of Windex out with her to the field and cleaned the combine's windows.

Clarence came by on Sunday when Tom was dumping grain. Raising his voice over the roar of the tractor and the rattle of the auger, he announced he'd picked six acres of corn yesterday and averaged 182 bushels to the acre. Tom raised an eyebrow at that.

He usually averaged around 160 and didn't see how Clarence could have beaten him by that much, but he wasn't saying anything.

"Them ears just crowded in that auger," Clarence crowed, "just flowed in."

Tom picked up the chant. "Just full out that pipe, solid."

"Just yellow, pure yellow." It was a hymn to corn and they repeated it like a chorus.

"You sure know how to hurt a fellow," Tom kidded Clarence then about his corn yield. "Ruin his day. I'll have to do you better. You shouldn't tell the other guy first. Then he comes up with better."

"I don't know. I just couldn't believe it." Clarence remembered something and frowned. "Bunch of trucks backed up all the way out onto the Riverton bridge yesterday," he reported, "waiting to dump at Comstock's. Why would they do that, stop traffic on a federal highway, block a bridge?"

"Just don't give a damn, I guess," Tom said.

Clarence bit a cigarette from his pack and lit up, watching Tom adjust the grain wagon door to feed more grain to the auger. "Makes us farmers look bad," he concluded, exhaling. "Them people trying to get home from work and all. They oughtn't to do that." He brightened and smiled. "You heard about the new John Deere tractor they're making?"

Tom didn't see it coming and took the question seriously. "No. New model?"

"Yeah, it's got no seat nor steering wheel."

Tom caught on. "Aw, hell," he said.

"Yeah," Clarence drew it out. "It's for guys who've lost their ass and don't know where to turn." Both men laughed, Clarence all the harder for having suckered Tom into it, but the laughter was a little rueful. They knew plenty of farmers who were in just that state.

When the wagons were empty and the grain auger shut off, Tom climbed the ladder that went up the side of the grain bin, took out his pocket knife and tapped the bin up near its conical roof to see how full it was. Clarence watched with interest. "My bin holds fifty-six hundred bushels heaped," he said. "That ain't going to be more than thirty, thirty-five acres. I don't know where I'm going to put it all."

"I don't neither," Tom agreed, climbing down. He petted the bin with one big hand the way he'd pet the rump of a fine hog. "Hell, this bin's nearly full and I've got two more fields to go."

That Sunday, Brett drove the combine for the first time, not in the terraced field, which they'd finished picking by midafternoon, but in the bottomland field to the south along Little Cebo Creek where the rows ran straight and a novice could concentrate on the corn. The field had been brush when Tom and Sally had bought the farm. They'd had it tiled and the creek rechanneled to pick up a piece of their land isolated on the other side by a meander. Now it laid as good as any land they owned.

The sight of his son running the combine brought tears to Tom's eyes. He remembered his own dad sitting on the tractor watching him run the corn picker, the predecessor to the combine that picked the ears and dumped them into a wagon for later shelling. You stood up to steer and watch the corn and it'd made him nervous at first. Farmers had been pitched over into the picker many a time. His dad watching him made him nervous, too, but it also made him proud. Here it went again from father to son and father to son.

Times change, though. He'd sure rather be combining than picking. He'd learned not to be too nostalgic for the past. He'd gone with his dad to a threshing show once. Big, self-propelled steam engines like small locomotives ran the old stationary threshers. They boiled out black, sulfurous coal smoke and steam, hot as hell on a hot summer afternoon. Merrit and Kellogg, G. and C. Cooper, Nichols and Shepard, J. I. Case were some of the makes of steam engines, black machines that weighed tons with hand-forged plates and fancy hand-painted striping. For all that they hardly had any horsepower. "I seen my dad was getting to remembering," Tom told Brett that story, "and I said, 'Dad, you ever wish you could just hitch up a team and run it again?' He said, 'No, son, a tractor beats a team all to hell. I smelled enough of them old oat farts for a lifetime.' "

Then a drive chain broke and before Brett could shut the com-

bine down it was jammed with corn. Father and son cleaned out the picker throat together and fixed the chain.

"I can't believe you aren't mad," Brett told him along the way.

"No reason to be mad," Tom said. "It could happen to anyone."

Back at the house that evening Brett repeated his amazement to his mother. She said what Tom had said, adding, "It could have happened to him."

Tom looked up from the couch, where he was reading a farm magazine. "I would have caught it sooner," he said, "but it sure could."

Later, watching television, Brett brought up farming. "You think I could start when I finish high school," he asked his dad, "or will it be too bad by then? Everybody says there ain't no money in it these days."

"Lots of times when everybody else is getting out of something is a good time to get in, son," Tom told him. "This could be the best time to get in. You could use your old man's equipment and just run it longer hours."

"But what's that for you?"

"You help me out on my land. I get your labor in exchange for the wear and tear. Then you rent two hundred acres of your own, go to the bank for a loan on the seed and chemicals and fertilizer. The money you make after you pay off the bank you put back first for your next year's seed so you don't have to borrow. You don't buy four-wheel-drive pickups or a new car. If you have any left you buy equipment to supplement what your old man's got. Like, we need a disk. You never buy anything new. You let the other guy have that expense. That's the biggest one."

"That makes sense," Brett said, turning back to television.

Maybe he was getting interested in farming. He told his mother he'd like to run the combine all the time. "But I don't know," she questioned Tom. "Brett gets bored."

"We'll just have to wait and see," Tom said. Farming going the way it'd been going, he didn't know whether to encourage the boy or not.

TWELVE

Then the rains came. Later, when the damage was done, Clarence would say that Mother Nature had a way of taking care of surpluses.

Tom woke at four to a light rain starting. By eight the clear plastic funnel of the rain gauge nailed to a fence post south of the house had collected three-tenths of an inch and the rain was steady and cold. There'd be no combining that day.

It was time in any case to wean the pigs. With modern feed mixes, pigs could be weaned at almost any age, but Tom favored three weeks. That way his sows could farrow a fraction more than two litters a year for an annual average per sow of maybe twenty or twenty-two pigs. At three weeks the pigs averaged about twelve pounds each, muscular little shoulders and rumps filled out from the skinny two-and-a-half-pounders they'd been at birth. They were ready to go on water and feed.

Slipping from the birth canal like an egg yolk from a bowl, they'd crawled wet and wrinkled across the mountain of their mother's four hundred pounds seeking a first meal, their squeaks prompting from her a comforting of soft, reassuring grunts. They'd worked their way between her hind legs as she lay laboring on her side or, desperate and reckless, they'd gone the long way around, following the ridge of her back, past her snout where she sniffed them, to push urgently through her forelegs to the courtyard of udders where their brothers and sisters already squirmed. Hunger drove their first struggle for rank order. They competed for a teat among the two erect rows that lined the sow's belly and among those dozen teats they competed for the three or four that delivered the most milk. The teats on a sow's lower belly, a young sow's especially, tended to produce less milk than those farther forward. Within days the more dominant pigs had won superior teats all their own while the subordinate pigs shared the leftovers. "Sucking hind teat" was more than a phrase to country people.

Farrowing pigs in a crate that limited the sow's movement saved one or two pigs more than farrowing them in a pen. The crate bars forced the sow to lower herself more carefully to the floor, giving the pigs time to escape to the nursery areas outside the sow's confinement and preventing crushing. But the crowding of the crate made the pigs' struggle for dominance more acute. They were born with sharp, arguing eyeteeth. Those Brett had snipped in the first day of life with a pair of side-cutting pliers dipped before each operation in iodine. Pigs in confinement would chew each other's curlicue tails and sometimes learn cannibalism, so Brett had docked their tails to harmless stubs with the same disinfected pliers. Sow milk was low in iron because pigs in the wild met their needs by rooting in the earth. There was no iron to be found rooting a concrete floor or a rubber heating mat. To make up for the dearth, Brett had injected each pig with a hundred milligrams of iron dextran. Since then, Tom had sprinkled a rich, loamy supplement, Rootin' Iron, the length of the nursery compartment three times a week. He'd also arranged adoptions, moving a pig or two from a sow that wasn't milking adequately to another that was. You could only play God in the first two or three days of a pig's life. Any later and the foster sow would read its scent as foreign and kill it.

Brett and Tom had also castrated the boar pigs. Since the pigs were small and their seeds still inside their bodies, that was a far easier operation than Doc Mitchell's work on Clarence's calves had been. They held a pig by its hind legs, belly up, made an incision in the midline of the belly between the hams, popped out a seed, pulled it to stretch the cord, cut off the cord close to the incision with a razor blade, popped out the other seed and repeated. There was very little bleeding. The incision didn't need closing and healed by weaning time. The pigs, barrows now, never developed the boar's powerful shoulders, deadly tusks, rank meat and dangerous disposition.

A door at the west end of the farrowing-crate section of Tom's farrowing house opened to a second, smaller room, the nursery. Since the pigs' nursing days were done, the room was more a preschool than a nursery. Within its full shelter the newly weaned barrows and gilts would prepare for life on the semienclosed feeding floor next down the road. The nursery was divided into four pens with a central aisle and supplied with small-scale auger-fed feed bins and automatic waterers. To wean his new batch of pigs Tom simply moved them into the nursery, along the way sorting them by size. They would struggle for dominance all over again in their new, larger groupings, then settle down to their destined work of transmuting corn and soybean meal into pork.

Having moved the pigs, Tom carefully, one by one, let out the complaining sows. They were wobbly from their month of confinement but they relished the escape outdoors even into the rain. Until they toned their muscles again with walking they'd be sore. At the moment they were hungry. They nosed the wet autumn grass as soon as they passed through the big red steel gate into the pasture. Tom had reduced their rations across the past week by fully a third to shrink their udders against the end of nursing. Better hunger than swollen, painful udders. Weaning would bring the sows into heat within four to seven days. They'd be ready then to breed again. The three boars in the next pasture, hearing them released, rushed grunting to the fence, flirtatiously gnashing their teeth.

Wild pigs once roamed the length and breadth of Europe and Asia, living on windfalls of acorns and fruit, digging roots with their tough, perceptive snouts, grazing fresh grass. Since they were omnivores, like man, competing for the same food, they were probably not the first animals domesticated. Sheep and goats, or possibly the dog, probably came before them. But with the invention of agriculture a need arose for an animal that could convert spoiled grain and garbage to succulent meat. The pig filled the bill. Its domesticated remains had turned up in southwestern Asia in excavations dating back eighty-five hundred years.

Hogs could live on waste, but they needed high-energy feed for rapid growth, which was why their production today was concentrated in the Corn Belt. They consumed about half of the domestic corn crop, grain that otherwise would have gone begging. On corn supplemented with protein they grew more rapidly than any other class of farm animal in relation to their weight, reaching market weights of 225 to 250 pounds in just six months from farrowing and consuming about fifteen to twenty bushels of corn, eight hundred to one thousand pounds, and another hundred pounds of soybean meal along the way. Only dairy cattle returned more profit. One sow in an average lifetime could produce forty to sixty pigs that would yield between seven and eleven thousand pounds of pork and a thousand to two thousand pounds of lard. Americans no longer ate much lard, except unwittingly in commercial cookies and pies, but the rest of the world did. American farmers had marketed about eighty-seven million hogs last year.

Tom had bought his farrowing house used at a north Missouri farm bankruptcy sale. New, it'd set back some unlucky farmer fifty thousand dollars. With its crates and fans and nursery Tom got it for five thousand dollars, delivered, money he borrowed from Luke Cage at the Plymouth bank. He invested two thousand dollars more and a winter of his labor in its concrete waste pit, floors, sewers, wiring and water supply. By now he had his debt on it down to three thousand dollars. The finishing floor, the nursery pigs' next stop, he'd built himself. He'd posted a hand-painted sign

over the farrowing house door. PIG FACTORY, it announced in bright red letters.

Up the lane toward the house, just outside the fence to the sow pasture, a corrugated-steel shed the size of a guardhouse protected a supply of hog feed. Tom drove the short distance in Babe, retrieved a fifty-pound bag of swine wafers from the shed for the sows and scattered the shiny brown protein-rich soybean sticks the length of a concrete trough just inside the fence. "Sou, girls!" Tom called the sows. "Sou-ee! Sou-ee!" Wheezing a little, their hooves imprinting the muddy ground, they came running.

A car turned in at the mailbox. Tom recognized Pete, his feed salesman, a weekly visitor. He waved him toward the house and followed in Babe. Leaving their vehicles, the two men ducked out of the rain into the workshop.

Pete was stocky, with a paunch that bellied his checkered shirt over his jeans. When he took off his green Square Deal seed cap to reset it on his head, a gesture he had, you could see he was well along toward being bald. He was a few years older than Tom or looked it, his face weathered and lined, his voice gravelly, a farmer with a gold watch for twenty years' service selling Square Deal feeds, an Iowa outfit, a division of W. R. Grace.

The two men got to talking about the farm situation, Tom leaning against the shop bench with his long legs scissored and his arms folded across his chest. The price of hogs had dropped another dollar that morning. It'd been down three dollars at the end of last week. That was okay with him, Tom told Pete. He was still making money. If the price dropped a little it'd discourage other farmers from getting into hog farming.

Pete turned the talk to bankers. He didn't say so, but Tom had heard that he was struggling to keep his farm. Bankers don't know a damned thing about farming, Pete complained. "They read about it in the farm magazines and it's already three months out of date."

"Yeah," Tom agreed. "It's history."

Pete's sales territory had enlarged and thinned as farmers had gone out of the livestock business. "Used to be a lot more hogs raised around here," he told Tom. "Over in Franklin County especially. You can have too good of land. They buried themselves in their own grain over there."

"Put all their eggs in one basket," Tom interpreted. Spreading the risk was one of his basic strategies. It'd saved him from disaster in the hard times of the Reagan years.

"The river did 'em and foreign investments," Pete went on. He meant the enticement of easy barge transport from the elevators along the river and the boom days of the 1970s when grain sales abroad were high. "They thought they'd get more efficient if they got out of livestock and just grew grain, but now grain's in surplus and they can't make a living."

"They never did think much of hog farming over in Franklin," Tom recited an old grievance. "They had it too good. Looked down on us plain old hog farmers."

"Yeah, they don't want that hog stink in their combine cabs," Pete agreed. "I've seen it a lot worse than over in Franklin, though. Crevecoeur, for that matter. That mess up around Chillicothe." Northern Missouri, where the land was poorer, was a disaster area for farmers. Pete shook his head.

Finally they got down to business. Tom needed protein pellets for his hogs, Pete told him. Tom asked about discounts and got one, the fall special, and ordered a thousand pounds. "You wasn't going to give me that unless I asked, was you," Tom said with a grin.

Pete grinned back and reset his cap. "Sure I was. I always let you in on the discounts. I was just seeing if you was on your toes."

After his feed salesman left, Tom drove back to the farrowing house. The farrowing floor needed a thorough cleaning and airing now that the sows were clear. The waste pit was full and the first thing Tom did was to pull the steel extension that opened the sewer line that drained the waste into the sewage lagoon in the pasture back of the finishing floor. While the pit was draining he started up his portable propane-fired steam cleaner, hooked it to the farrowing-house water line and steam-cleaned the crates, blasting the accumulated dirt and dried manure through the floor slats into the pit. There was plenty of splash-back. It was a hot, stinking job. "I was so ashamed of myself at dinner," Tom told Sally that evening, "I changed clothes."

"You don't never need to apologize for coming into my kitchen smelling of hog manure," she said. "That's what pays the bills."

"I know that. I just couldn't stand my own stink."

He didn't finish until after dark. He stripped his second set of clothes in the mud room and headed straight for the shower, but it would take more than one shower to get the stink of hog manure out of his nostrils, even if it was the smell of money. He was so tired after supper he just fell asleep.

By the middle of the week Tom had poured four inches of rain out of his rain gauge, Clarence three and a half. Farther south a neighbor reported six inches in one night. Tom drove one morning to the big Landers bin behind the Elms, climbed the ladder to the hatch that was set near the rim of the conical roof, opened the hatch and lowered himself inside. A whitish crust of mold had formed on the surface of the corn. He marched around in concentric circles, driving his work boots through it to break it up. The corn was starting to smell sweetish and Tom was beginning to get nervous about the crop left in the field. The ground was like a sponge, but it could only soak up so much rain. The subsoil was dry. That was a help. Too much rain like they'd been having, though, and his mood was going to change. Harvest was when things got stressful. He had a lot of money standing out in those fields.

Today he wished he had propane to dry his corn. He'd never hooked up the propane ring on the big Landers blower, never needed to since he'd bought it new thirteen years ago. After he closed the hatch and climbed down from the bin he kicked on the blower even though the humidity was high. The corn needed air or it was going to ferment.

He spent the morning at the farrowing house working on an improvement. The growing pigs chewed on the electric wires that ran up from the rubber heating mats that kept them warm in winter. He could have bought new wire armored in steel but he had a collection of old black plastic water pipe that ought to do the trick. He cut lengths of pipe with a hacksaw, threaded the mat wires through them and tied them to the crate bars so the pigs couldn't nose them out of the way. Sometimes it felt as if protecting the property from the endless curiosity of hogs was just about a full-time job. An old sow could destruct a ball bearing in a grease pit.

Tom's propane man turned up that morning, stopping his white tank truck in the lane outside the farrowing house. After years of delivering propane for one of the big companies, Joe had his own business now. He was short and muscular, with a round, ruddy face, a shy and modest man. He kept a plug of snuff tucked under his lower lip on the right side. You could be around Joe for a long time and never find out that he'd raised sons who'd won appointment to West Point and the Air Force Academy. Tom thought the world of him. He charged a penny or two more per gallon for his propane, but he knew propane equipment well enough to be called as a consultant to factories as far away as Kansas City and he repaired his customers' broken equipment free. Without even being asked, he went to work cleaning the big propane heaters in the farrowing house while Tom worked on protecting the heater mat wires and the two men talked.

The question was drying corn with propane. Joe told Tom how to do it on the cheap. "Just stick a thermometer inside that transition," he said, meaning the galvanized tunnel that connected the blower to the bin, "and keep the flame low, about ninety degrees. Then you don't need no humidistat or automatic control." Humidistats were pretty shoddy. They couldn't handle much weather. "You'd just as well put it under your bed. That's how good it is. It's just horsehair. Camel hair. Or else a piece of wood. Anything that's going to soak up some moisture and lengthen or twist. It probably won't even last one season. Just use one of them indoor-outdoor thermometers instead."

Outside, after they'd finished their work, Joe wondered if Tom wanted him to fill the thousand-gallon farrowing-house propane tank and the tank up at the house to get him ready for cold weather. Gas might be cheaper next week, Joe said. He didn't know for sure. "Hell, you're already here," Tom decided, figuring that Joe wouldn't have driven all the way out if he didn't think the price was okay. "Go ahead and fill them." Even if gas got cheaper, he didn't see that he'd save enough to make a difference and with a fill now he'd be ready if a cold wave came through. Better safe than sorry. Joe hauled a heavy black hose from his truck to the tank, locked on the nozzle, opened the tank's bleeder valve, returned to his truck and sent the compressed liquid gas surging through the line. The truck ran on propane too, like a sow sucking its own teat.

Just about the time Tom was finishing dinner, Clarence pulled up. The two men wandered out to the workshop, little Molly sauntering along behind them wagging her tail. For a change it wasn't raining. Clouds scudded across a windy, hazy sky and it was humid enough to trickle an occasional drop of sweat down Tom's back. He'd ended the morning by hauling his fifty-two-foot grain auger onto the concrete outside the workshop where he could work on it. He thought it'd thrown a flighting, a section of the steel screw that spiraled inside the long pipe, and he'd loosened a pillow bearing at the top end and pulled the screw almost out of the pipe to get it ready, supporting it off the ground by chaining it to the loader scoop of his older International utility tractor. He and Clarence gave it a good looking over, but all they found was wear, the edges on the polished flighting getting sharp with the years as the elephant ears on Tom's combine had done. The big auger had been around for fourteen years. His dad had still been alive and helping out with the harvest when he'd bought it.

He'd have to order some more flighting before he could replace the sections that were worn. He and Clarence went to work sliding the long, flexing screw back into the pipe and tightening the bearings again. All that was left to do was to patch a pencil-sized hole that the screw had worn through the pipe about ten feet down from the top. It'd already been patched once before.

They were cutting a patch and hauling out the acetylene stand when a neighbor pulled up in a rusty pickup, a younger man wearing jeans and a pale blue work shirt, Clark, blond and ruddy, thin, a plug of snuff darkening his lower front teeth. The three of them stood around shooting the breeze. They'd all rather have been combining but it was too wet to combine.

The subject was bankers. Whenever it looked as if the crop was in trouble, farmers got bankers on the brain. "The ones that burn me," Tom complained, "is the ones that repossess a man's animals. Hell, his herd's the only way he's got to make more money to pay the bank."

"Hell of a note," Clark agreed.

"Don't them bankers know nothing?" Clarence denounced them, a burning cigarette dangling from his hand. He shook his head slowly and formally from side to side to show he knew the answer.

"Or the ones who tell a man to sell his corn in the fall," Clark picked up the theme, "and then he has to buy corn the next spring at a higher price to feed his hogs."

"Just ignorant," Tom said. "You'd think they'd learn and get to see the point."

Corn and feed and beating out bankers reminded them of stories they'd heard about people beating the government with false bottoms in their corncribs, illegally selling off their loan corn. They didn't approve of crime, but they couldn't help admiring the ingenuity.

"You hear about the IRS collecting taxes from bankruptcies?" Clark asked them.

"Yeah, I heard," Tom said.

"How's that deal work?" Clarence asked.

"On the debt that's forgiven when a man reorganizes. They claim that's the same as income."

"Jesus H. Christ," Clarence swore. He ground out his cigarette in disgust. "Why don't they just take a few quarts of his blood while they're at it?" He looked out over the yard. "It's going to get a whole lot worse before it gets better, ain't it?" he asked them. "Four years farther down the road and everyone's going to be feeling it. Not just the farmer. He's just the canary. He's just the miner's canary." Tom and the other man nodded. "See," Clarence went on, "I remember the Great Depression. You young bucks is too young to remember that. You was still just a gleam in your daddy's eye. Hell, the sunsets was red with the dust of Kansas and you about choked bringing in the cows, it was so thick on the ground. My dad give eighteen dollars a cow for milk cows and we lived on the cash from the milk we sold. Corn was fifteen cents a bushel. Hogs was three cents a pound. People was hurting. I mean people was *hurting*."

Tom got busy making a patch for the auger. With a length of pipe for a form they hammered and pounded to shape the patch to the auger pipe's curve. "That thing's stiff as a bridegroom's tool,"

Clarence celebrated the stubborn patch, but finally they had it properly curved and in position.

"Better light up your fire wrench, Tom," Clark joked. Tom flamed the acetylene torch and began the delicate work of welding, the galvanized sheeting popping and shooting sparks.

Clarence started grinning. "This teacher is testing different kinds of meat, see," he said, "seeing which ones the kids recognize."

"Oh-oh," Tom said. "Here it goes."

"This another one of your dumb jokes, Galen?" Clark asked Clarence.

"Just shut up and listen," Clarence said. "Teacher put out some beef, and they all tasted it. 'That's beef,' they said. She put out some pork and they all tasted that. 'That's pork,' they said. So then she puts out some venison. They all taste it and they look kind of puzzled. Teacher asks what it is. They don't know. So she asks them, 'Well, what does your Mommy call your Daddy?' This one little boy gets all excited. 'Spit it out! Spit it out!' he says. 'That's bum!' "

"Oh, Christ," Clark groaned.

Then the patch job was finished and Tom was coiling the acetylene hose around the tanks. "Comstock's is really gigging for moisture this year," Clark mentioned.

"How much?" Tom asked. "I ain't hauled no grain over there yet."

"Two and a half points for every half-percent moisture."

"The hell you say."

"Yeah," Clarence confirmed. "It's true. They got a sweet little deal going on government corn, too. Supposed to be the government wants the corn at fourteen-percent moisture, but there's a range. But the grain companies is taking loan corn at fifteen-and-a-half moisture and docking it for drying it down to fourteen percent even though the government says fifteen and a half is acceptable."

"By God," Tom said, "it makes your blood boil how they've taken advantage of the farmers this year. I bet you're going to hear about some fistfights. I guess any man will fight when he's got his back to the wall. I guess someone's got a debt load, can't get his crop out, can't get it in at the elevator, he's got to be mad about it."

"Mad as hell," Clarence agreed.

"I looked for a bastard this fall," Tom went on, "and it looks like there's going to be one. Elevators gigging you, weather going bad. Glad I got that Chernobyl contract for my beans. That sure looks good right now."

Tom's home grain bin was full and he still had two fields of corn to pick. There was half a load of corn on his combine and no bin space left to dump it. Should he unload two thousand bushels of corn out of the bin, sell them to Comstock's and take a heavy dock for moisture? Or should he leave the corn in the field to dry down and hope the weather improved and allowed him to get it out later, moving on now to combining soybeans even though he'd have all the extra work of converting over the combine? If he could combine out enough beans he could get his fields ready for wheat and go ahead and drill wheat, but it was still too wet to combine beans.

The fall was a bastard, all right, despite the bumper crops. And it just kept on raining.

THIRTEEN

"Yeah, I seen old Patton," Clarence was saying, reminiscing about his infantry days in the Second World War, blowing smoke. "Boy, wasn't he a hot dog. I swear he'd do just about anything. Got away with it, too. But his men loved him. Never wanted to say nothing against him when they was around."

Another day of rain had driven Tom and Clarence indoors in the late afternoon and then Brett had come home from school and joined them. Gray dusk darkened early below a dark sky. They sat around the big kitchen table in their shirtsleeves with their seed caps on, smoking and drinking coffee Tom had brewed. Sammi watched television with the sound turned low and did homework on the couch that divided the living room from the bright kitchen. Sally was working at her brother's.

"We came over at Havre in March of '45, went through Aachen, crossed the Saar and the Rhine and ended up in Czechoslovakia," Clarence went on, finishing his cigarette and stubbing it into the ashtray, a last wisp of smoke winding up from it like a river on a map. "That Sudetenland, the Germans was just streaming out, trying to get away from the Russians. Hell, they *wanted* us to capture them. You'd see them on the road and ask them, '*Was ist los mit die Luftwaffe?*' '*Keine Benzine,*' they'd say." Imitating,

Clarence lowered his head and his voice as if in shame. " '*Keine Benzine.*' " The memory made him chuckle.

"How do you say that in American?" Tom teased. He'd heard all Clarence's war stories before. He enjoyed them. He wasn't much for fiction. Fiction books were just one man's opinion. But he liked reading history, particularly war history, strategy especially and especially in the winter when the days got long. Clarence had lived through a big piece of history and come back to tell the tale.

Clarence translated. " 'What's wrong with your air force?' " He gave the lines the same emphasis he'd given them in German before and chuckled again at the end. " 'No gasoline,' " he told Tom. "They didn't have no gas. They was running on alcohol made out of potatoes and crap like that before they was finally beat. Hauling their artillery around with Belgian draft horses. We had a lot of French DPs we was sending home." Brett frowned. "Displaced persons," Clarence explained. "They was just skeletons. Starving. About too weak to walk. So we'd mount these French DPs up on these big Belgian draft horses and send them on their way. When they got home they could use the horses to start farming again, grow some food. If we'd left them with the Germans they'd of just ate them."

"Wasn't you in on some shooting before that?" Tom prompted.

"Yeah, we had to fight our way through. You'd lie there in your foxhole in the damned cold with this hellacious artillery barrage going by over your head all night long and the terrible thing was, you knew you'd have to move out in the A.M. to wherever it was they'd been pounding.

"But mostly it was snipers. We was securing these little villages as we went along. Dug in out in a field one time, we had a German woman sniper across the way in a shell crater firing at us. Wasn't even a soldier, just a woman, some kind of civilian. Damned Germans was fanatics. We kind of put up with it for a while—we was dug in a little higher than her and she wasn't hitting nothing—but after a while it got kind of annoying, you know, having to keep our heads down. We'd had plenty of people shooting at us already. We didn't need no more. So finally someone brought up his rifle and just rolled her over." Clarence stared past Tom and Brett out the window, his gray eyes opaque.

"We was ordered to go into the villages and break up all the weapons. Tear out a whole caseful of some old burgher's shotguns and hunting rifles, shotguns all gold-chased, break the stocks and bend the barrels. Just like that case you got over there." Clarence pointed to Tom's gun rack in its glass display case set against the living-room north wall. "I hated to do that. Destroy a man's gun collection. All them villagers would come out waving white handkerchiefs and pillowcases when we showed up—by God, they was in a *hurry* to surrender—but you couldn't trust them. They was waving the white flag, but they'd built tank traps in every goddamned village. We had to protect ourselves."

Tom remembered another detail. "You told me one time the Germans had some kind of little remote-controlled tank."

Clarence nodded. "Yeah, little bastard of a tank not much bigger than a kid's wagon. I don't know if it was remote-controlled or not. I think they just aimed it in our general direction and sent it off. Sounded like a little putt-putt motorcycle. You'd be dug in and you'd hear one coming toward you across the field. You didn't want one dropping into your foxhole with you. They was loaded with high explosives and you wanted to be out of the way and hunkered well down when one went off. Once we'd had a few go through we got to where we knew how they worked. The Germans was holed up back in the woods. They couldn't see where these damned contraptions was going. If one came in we'd jump up and a couple of us would catch the thing on the wing and just haul it around facing in the other direction. They was heavy suckers, tank treads and all. The treads would keep on spinning whilst we hauled the thing around and then it'd just set off the other way. Off it'd go back into the woods, out of sight, and then we'd hear it explode. That was a gas. After a while they stopped sending us any of those." Clarence grinned. "One of them secret Revenge weapons Hitler was going to win the war with. Sure he was."

"You saw them V-2's, though," Brett joined in. "You said they blew up."

"Yeah, that was later, back in Nuremberg, when we was guarding the SS men for the war trials. They was piling up all the German weapons so's they could burn them. I never in my life saw so many weapons piled up in one place. The artillery was set out in rows, just rows and rows of artillery all lined up in these open fields. The small-arms pile looked like a big old hill."

"How big a hill?" Brett asked.

"Big as that hill down yonder," Clarence said, pointing out the south kitchen windows to the hill of the next farm that rose beyond Little Cebo Creek.

"Huh," Brett said, cocking his head. "*That* big?" When he said *"That"* his voice cracked.

"That big," Clarence repeated.

Brett looked to his father. "That's a hundred and twenty acres, isn't it, Dad?"

Tom nodded. "Let Clarence tell his story, son."

"I ain't stopping him," Brett said defensively, his voice cracking again. "I just wondered how big a hill all those guns made." He looked back to Clarence. "That's *big.*"

"They went on as far as the eye could see, boy," Clarence added firmly. "That's how big that pile was."

"I *said* that was big, Clarence," Brett kidded him. "You don't have to make it bigger yet." Brett lowered his head and thought for a moment. "This ain't a fish story, you know," he added, looking up.

"Hush, son," Tom said.

"But the V-2's were the ball-busters." Clarence ignored the kidding and went on. "Humongous pile of those, too. They'd brought them in just like the other stuff and stockpiled them and they was blowing them up. Someway the V-2 dump caught on fire. Burned for days. You'd be standing there, pulling guard duty, and one of them V-2's would go off and the blast would just paste your fatigues back against your body, pull your pants leg back. Just like someone reached from behind you and pulled on your pants leg.

"We met up with the Russians before we got posted back to Nuremberg for guard duty. We had to hold up there in Czechoslovakia to wait for them to advance. Let them take over the country we'd already secured. Hell, they'd already had a parade for us in Prague. Here we was ragtag and bobtail and when they came up they had brand-new Studebaker trucks and tommy guns. We had old beat-up M-1's and they had slick new tommy guns. They traveled with their women, too. It was American lend-lease got them all those goodies. Stuff we was shipping them. Lend-lease took good care of them, better than the Army took care of us. Let me tell you, a lot of guys was bitter about *that*."

"Uh-huh," Brett said. "You want some more coffee, Clarence?"

Clarence inspected his cup. "Don't mind if I do."

Brett pushed back his chair. "I'll make some."

"Thank you, son," Tom said.

"It's okay, Dad," Brett clowned. "I knowed you'd do the same for me."

"The worst, though," Clarence said, "was when we got to Nuremberg." He looked at Tom keenly. "There ain't nothing someone won't do, you know? Damned people who ain't never fought don't know, but there ain't nothing someone won't do."

"You saw all the bigwigs, didn't you Clarence?" Tom asked his friend gently.

"I saw them all," Clarence brightened. "Göring, Goebbels, all them big Nazis lined up there at the war trials. We had guards on them twenty-four hours a day so they wouldn't knock themselves off. The guards rotated around—American, English, Russian and French. We had a bar set up at Nuremberg for the guards. When the Russian guards was off duty they always drank up all the liquor. The only time there was liquor was when the Russians pulled guard duty.

"We had barbed-wire compounds with an aisle down the middle for the guards. All them SS men in the compounds, thousands of them. There was a staked-out area inside the wire that made a no-man's-land. We'd walk down that aisle smoking cigarettes and them old krauts would follow along. Some guys would throw their butts into no-man's-land just for sheer meanness and when the krauts dived for them they'd shoot them. Kill them."

"Shoot them for cigarette butts," Tom said, shaking his head.

"Just when the krauts dived for them," Clarence repeated. His stare was fixed now behind his thick bifocals, his eyes widened. "And that wasn't the worst of it neither. Hell, the Poles was baking the bread we fed them. Fed the SS men. No particular reason, we just had the bread bought in town and they was Poles running the bakery. They brought it out by truck, big old round loaves of dark bread.

"They brought out a load one day and distributed it just like they always did. Pretty soon here come a man out of the barracks vomiting. Then another one his buddies was dragging between them. By God, before long we had *hundreds* of them out there vomiting and dying. It was a damned mess is what it was. The Poles had poisoned their bread. They dusted the loaves with arsenic instead of flour."

"Gross," Brett commented from the counter.

"We got orders another time to load a bunch of boxcars with SS men for Tito. Just ordinary old cattle cars. Just like what the Germans had been using to ship all them Jews. They came with a list of names and we marched them out and loaded them up. We had orders to seal the cars. No food, no water, nothing. It was four days down to Yugoslavia." Finishing his story, Clarence took out his cigarette pack and lighter, extracted a cigarette and studied it. "They traveled that way for four days and we turned them over to Tito still sealed up. We never heard from them again."

Clarence drew hard on the cigarette to light it and forced out the smoke in relief.

"You seen a lot of history," Tom consoled him.

Clarence nodded. "People talk about man's inhumanity to man. I tell you, it was *brutal*. It wasn't none of it no damned joke."

"Nobody's laughing, Clarence," Brett teased from beside the counter in the bright kitchen. "You see anybody laughing?"

Sammi popped her head above the couch then like Kilroy Was Here, miming laughter. Her gold loop earrings caught the light. "You can see me laughing," she said. "I'm laughing, see?"

Clarence winked at Tom to let him know the clowning was okay.

FOURTEEN

Tom opted to haul corn to Comstock's to make room in his bin for the rest of his crop. The bin had built-in augers, one that fed grain under the false floor out to ground level, the other outside like a spout on a teapot that carried the grain to truck-bed height. He ran them one morning to load the International. For a change it wasn't raining.

The truck had five forward gears and high and low axles, giving ten gear ratios Tom could shift to. It had brakes powered by compressed air. The big steering wheel, set nearly as flat as a platter on a table, took a lot more turning than a car steering wheel. It went around twice to turn a corner and you fed the rim from one hand to the other like a hose.

Driving fifteen or twenty thousand pounds of grain to the elevator was different from driving a car. Once the load was moving it wasn't easy to stop. Air brakes would burn out if you used them to control your speed going down a hill. You had to anticipate hills both ways, building speed to roll uphill and figuring out the optimum place to downshift to a lower gear when you needed the extra push, downshifting on the descent to use the engine compression instead of the brakes to hold you back. Switching from high to low axle was especially tricky on a hill. You pulled out the axle switch, let up on the accelerator, gave the axles time to shift with a clunk you could feel and hear, then pumped the accelerator once to engage the new arrangement, and while that shifting was going on the truck was rolling in neutral. Tom knew the eleven miles from his farm to Comstock's well. He knew where the curves were and the steepness of the hills. He knew to watch particularly for a side road about halfway there, down a steep hill and around a curve, where drivers who didn't understand that a loaded truck couldn't stop on a dime sometimes pulled out slowly onto the highway. Trucks had mashed a few over the years who didn't get out of the way fast enough.

Going down the road cut into the river-bluff face just west of Comstock's was touchy. It was the steepest descent of the entire drive. Tom stopped and shifted to low-low at the top. The engine whined going down, holding back the load. At the bottom Tom shifted the axle and then the gears, rolling along beside the railroad tracks, over a low bridge, cutting left to cross the tracks then and following the road past the elevator to a turnaround. That headed him back toward the space between the office and the elevator silos themselves. A heavy steel grating was set in concrete and roofed over between the two structures. Immediately beyond the grating shed was a truck scale mounted within a massive hydraulic lift. At the moment the lift was tilted at a thirty-degree angle, lifting the front end of a forty-two-foot semitrailer high into the air to dump the trailer's load of corn into the grating. Under the grating, augers carried the grain to a fan of other augers high above ground that led to the various elevator silos. Pipes extended from the silos for dumping into railroad cars and, on the opposite side, into barges. From the dust the semi was raising, Tom concluded that the load must be last year's grain, someone cleaning out his bins to make room for the harvest.

There was three other trucks in line to dump, farm trucks like Tom's. He stayed in his truck smoking a cigarette and waiting his turn. When the man in front of him finished and pulled away, he drove through the grating shed and onto the scale and set his air brake. The scale room looked out over the scale through a big picture window. Tom watched in the rearview mirror as a muscular kid in a T-shirt, jeans and cowboy boots came out from the scale room onto the catwalk alongside the truck carrying a long brass sampling tube. He nodded to Tom as he went by. The kid's

blond hair stuck out from under his blue Comstock seed cap like
straw and he was powdered with grain dust. Back beside the grain
bed he raised the tube high into the air, plunged it deep into the
load, rotated it to close its chamber over a measured sample of
Tom's corn, extracted it from the load and carried it back inside to
test the sample for moisture and inspect it for grade. In the meantime, the scale operator had recorded the truck's loaded weight.

An operator in the grating shed behind Tom called him to raise
the truck bed. He pulled out the red-knobbed plunger below the
dash to the left of the steering wheel that engaged the truck's
hydraulic lift and gave her the gas. With a whine the truck bed
began to tip and Tom heard the grain door in the back levered
open and then the hiss of falling grain. Eventually the hydraulics
reached their full extension and Tom let the engine idle. When the
operator behind him slammed the grain door shut, Tom pushed
the plunger back in. The bed came down slowly and seated itself
with a bang. Tom watched through the rearview mirror again
while the scale man weighed the empty truck. The difference between the two weights would be the weight of the grain. A hand
stuck out the scale-room window then and waved. Tom popped
the air brake, drove off the scale, the empty bed banging, parked
out of the way in the lot west of the office building and loped back
to pick up his receipt.

The moisture on that 16,660 pounds of grain was 16.3. That
meant a serious dock. There was nothing he could do about it, but
he didn't like it much. He stopped to talk to Frank Tice. Tom told
the elevator manager he'd heard that the elevators were threaten-
ing to treat moldy soybeans as foreign matter. With the rain, mold
was a real possibility. Tice was morose. "That's all I need," he
said, "more rumors." Tom didn't let up on him. He told him he
was getting a reputation as a bad man. Charging a man for storage
when his beans weren't even out of the field, he said bluntly, was
a bad deal. Tice just hung his head.

The Dirty Five, the farmers called the five big grain companies.
American grain was going begging on international markets because it arrived so dirty—twice as much foreign matter as Cana-
dian grain, two and a half times as much as Australian. Most
farmers didn't deliver it that way. The grain companies took first-

quality grain and mixed it with grain full of fines and dirt to bring it down to grade. Tom had heard they even mixed in dirt and gravel directly. No way the Japanese were going to put up with that kind of nonsense when they could buy elsewhere. Losing out on exports was one of the big reasons for the turnaround in farm prosperity in the Reagan years. It wasn't any wonder farmers didn't think much of the grain companies. Not that the Dirty Five gave a damn. They were big multinationals. They'd cut off their nose to spite their face. It didn't make a damned bit of difference to them whether they delivered foreign grain or American so long as they got their profit out of the deal.

It was hard enough to earn a living farming without having obstacles deliberately put in your way. Hell, the weather was bad enough. Tom drove home steaming over injustice. But injustice or not, he had more loads to deliver, more grain to sell, to free up room for the rest of his crop.

Joe, Tom's propane man, had poked around in the control box on the Landers blower and decided that hooking up the heater was doable. The old transformer that ran the spark plug that ignited the gas had rotted out from exposure even though it'd never been used and Tom had driven over to Franklin one morning in the pouring rain to pick up a new one. It was heavy and black as a car battery and it cost sixty dollars but it was either that or likely lose the corn. Joe met Tom at Landers' after dinner the next afternoon. They'd had rain in the early morning but there was only a little drizzle later in the day. The air was cool and the sky was gray. Orange-and-black woolly caterpillars crawled on the big galvanized-steel bin and underfoot in the fall grass made lush by the rains. Foxtail and wild marijuana grew thickly behind the bins, screening the hillside cornfield beyond that still needed picking.

The two men had trouble removing the old transformer from the control box. Tom fetched a set of ratchet-driven extension socket wrenches from Babe to deal with the problem. Joe had picked up a special waterproof solenoid coil for Tom in Osage Station, saving him a trip. Neither man knew the particular unit they were repairing. The operating manual and wiring diagram had been lost long ago. They talked over the wiring and worked together hooking up wires.

Joe started to remove the front panel to rewire it. Some of the wires had lost their insulation and might short out.

"You that brave?" Tom asked him.

"I just don't want to get bit," Joe said.

"That electricity bite you?"

"Did the other day."

"The housing?"

"Bare wire."

Spindly daddy longlegs high-stepped the housing of the bright red blower as the two men worked. Fighter jets from the air base nearby that guarded the mid-Missouri missile field crackled above the clouds.

Joe plugged in the big 220-volt plug and tried the push button that was supposed to light the burner. Nothing happened. He unplugged and reopened the front panel and switched a wire. Tom unscrewed a plate from the blower housing so that they could see inside. Joe pushed the starter button again. The spark plug clicked and fired.

"I see it," Tom said. Joe switched on the blower and the fan started its banshee wail, sending the daddy longlegs scurrying. When he opened the propane valve, a blast of heat and the sweetish smell of burning propane came out the hole Tom had exposed. "Great," Tom said. "She's working."

Joe turned down the flame, peering into the hole to watch the burning ring. "Don't want to make popcorn," he said. He took up hammer and screwdriver and punched a hole into the side of the bin near the point where the transition connected. He'd brought a weather thermometer sealed in a glass tube. He slipped it into the hole he'd made and the two men stood around watching the temperature of the grain slowly climb toward ninety degrees.

The burner was going to save more than seven thousand bushels of corn and the propane wasn't likely to cost more than a hundred dollars for the season. It was a good job. Tom wondered why he hadn't done it years ago, but propane hadn't always been so cheap. He measured Joe with an admiring eye. "You're just as handy as a pocket on a shirt," he told him.

*   *   *

There was more fixing to do back home that afternoon. The combine's Hydra-matic system had sprung a leak. Tom had run it
anyway to keep the corn harvest going, feeding it two gallons of
hydraulic fluid a day against the leakage, but it wasn't getting any
better. Clarence came over to help. Tom had him lie down under
the combine, between the two big front wheels, and drove the
machine back and forth over his neighbor until Clarence spotted
the leak. It turned out to be easier to fix than Tom had expected.
The seals at the joints in the hydraulic lines were soft lead dough-
nuts. A groove had worn its way into one of them. Tom called up
Case in Osage Station and talked to a mechanic. He said just to file
the groove smooth. Tom filed and sanded both, worried he might
be making it worse, but when he reassembled it, it worked.

In the midst of the Hydra-matic project, an old farmer drove up
in a muddy pickup. He got out and announced he'd lost eight
calves through a broken-down fence. He'd been looking for them
everywhere. Had anyone seen them? His shirt was split at the
shoulder seam, the belt on his pants was patched together with
baling wire, but Tom and Clarence stopped their work and mis-
tered him. He was one of the wealthiest farmers in the county. He
owned fifty-two percent of the Bank of Grants. Tom had dated his
daughter once upon a time and daydreamed sometimes what it
might have meant to have married her and have stood to inherit all
the old man's farms. A pain in the rear, he usually concluded to
temper his longing for the land. She'd gone to a private women's
college and taken on society airs since high school days, married a
dentist and been divorced. She wasn't the sort of woman who'd
help out with driving the combine, but Lord, she'd own seven
Crevecoeur County farms one of these days.

After the man left, Tom and Clarence swapped stories about
him. He was a plunger, always was. He'd bought a flock of sheep
once. No one in the county raised sheep, but he'd turned the sheep
into his young cornfields. They'd eaten the weeds and the lower
blades of the cornstalks and he'd sold them at a profit.

Another time he'd bought a bunch of razorback Mississippi
hogs for next to nothing. He was a sucker for a bargain and they'd
come cheap. The very night of the day they were delivered, crude

oil leaking from an oil pipeline had contaminated the spring they drank from. The oil poisoned the razorbacks. The next morning they were all dead. When he collected from the pipeline company, the old man put in for a herd of fat hogs. The oil boys paid up. They didn't know the difference. He had that kind of luck.

The old man's bank connection reminded Tom of how some of the early German settlers who came to Crevecoeur County got rich. Back before the First World War they'd borrowed money in Germany at one percent and loaned it out over here at three percent. Two old Dutchmen he knew about in particular had taken exactly opposite routes. They'd sold mortgages with the money they'd borrowed from the old country. One was a hard-nosed bastard who foreclosed the first time a farmer missed a mortgage payment and then turned around and sold the farm on mortgage again and made his profit that way. The other was a good man who helped his debtors and supported them in hard times. Both men got rich, but the son-of-a-bitch eventually got stomach cancer and starved to death. "I thought my money could buy anything," Tom had heard he'd told his doctor, "but it couldn't buy health." The decent man had died in his bed at a ripe old age.

"There's justice in that," Tom concluded his parable.

"You're damned right there is," Clarence agreed.

The sows had come into heat. Reabsorbing their milk had triggered ovulation. Tom had turned the three boars into the pasture with them so that the animals could breed.

A branch of Little Cebo Creek edged the pasture. The trees that lined the branch gave the sows shelter in winter and shade in summer. The creek gave them water to cool themselves, running water that didn't freeze, and it was all free.

After he'd checked the pigs in the nursery one morning, Tom stood outside watching the breeding. The dominant boar, a hairy gray animal that weighed six hundred pounds, was covering one of the sows, the other two boars standing nearby somberly waiting their turn and an attendance of sows observing. Even the sow the boar was covering was expressionless. It looked more like a funeral than a conception.

The boar's head was big and deep-jowled as a beer keg. Mean-

looking tusks jutted from its lower jaw. At the other end, the lobes of its scrotum inflated from the space between its hams like balloons. Boars had a tool like a corkscrew. Once they'd connected there wasn't much thrusting. They stayed up long and slow.

The other sows nuzzled at the copulating pair's genitals. Tom had heard they'd chew a boar's tool sometimes when the male was covering a competitor and ruin it. Occasionally one of the animals would grunt, but mostly the proceedings were silent. Tom thought the dominant boar must be getting a little wore down by now. Boars looked tough as Teamster presidents, but they couldn't breed as often as other farm animals. Bulls and rams could be ejaculated artificially as many as twenty to forty times in twenty-four hours and still produce useful quantities of sperm. A boar wasn't good for more than two breedings a day and even then the books recommended giving the animal a day or two of rest. If it was wore out it wouldn't cover. You needed more boar power when a herd of sows all came into heat at once after weaning. Three boars worked fine for a herd the size of Tom's. They had a lot of pigs to make. It kept them humping. Makin' bacon.

Tom walked out one gray afternoon to the field to the west of the house to inspect his soybeans. The knee-high plants had dropped their leaves, exposing spindly central stalks hung down their length with clustered flares of narrow, hairy, sickle-shaped brown pods like the pupae of some wildly prolific butterfly. Underfoot, the ground was hidden beneath a yellow-brown layer of dead and fallen soybean leaves. Tom's work boots planed greasily sideways as he pushed through the soybean stalks, polishing skids of dark brown mud.

Usually by now the beans would have dried down enough to rattle when a man walked through them. These didn't rattle much. Tom picked a pod in one place, another in another, until he had a handful. Each flattened pod bulged with the three and sometimes four beans it enclosed. Tom split one pod open, picked a bean, carried it to his mouth and bit it. "Butter beans," he said, spitting the bite out. That soft consistency would have been normal for the end of September, a stage in the drying process, but the bean Tom had bitten was larger than it should be, swollen with moisture, and he could imagine it shriveling and cracking when the sun came out. Shriveled beans took a dock. So did moldy beans, which he found in the next pod he shucked. So did sprouted beans.

There was damage all right. Even if the rain let up there'd be damage, maybe ten or fifteen percent. If the rain didn't let up it could be a disaster. "Looks to me like Murphy's law is operating out here this year," Tom said aloud. Depressed, he headed back toward the house.

FIFTEEN

I t was time for Sally to do the books. She saved receipts and bills in a manila folder and posted them at the end of each month into a big, old-fashioned ledger. The ledger, covered with green cloth, burgundy leather tips bracing its corners, opened along the kitchen table nearly a yard wide, giving her plenty of room to break out expenses by categories. She'd typed the categories along the top of the pale green columns: WATER, ELECTRICITY (FARM & HOME), PHONE, INSURANCE, FEED FOR LIVESTOCK, LABOR (HIRED & MACHINE), INTEREST, TAXES on the left-hand page, and across on the right-hand page VETERINARIAN, SEEDS, FERTILIZER & CHEMICALS, DUES & SUBSCRIPTIONS, FUEL (FARM USE), TRUCK EXPENSES, CAR, DONATIONS, DOCTOR & RX, MISC., REPAIRS, SUPPLIES, LIVESTOCK, MACHINERY & MISC. DEPRECIATION.

For September Sally posted first of all a $108.67 telephone bill, shaking her head as she always did at the size of it. The Bauers lived halfway between Osage Station and Plymouth and did business in both places. Calls to either town were long-distance. Sally had paid the Missouri Public Service company $215.38 for electricity. In her open but strongly vertical handwriting she broke that figure out at forty-five percent for the farm and fifty-five percent for the home, $96.92 and $118.46 respectively. Interest on their equipment loan at the bank came to $369.64. The vet got $19.50. Insurance on the two farm trucks totaled $177.80.

Crevecoeur County Truck and Tractor had collected $31.98 for supplies and $249.55 for repairs. Sally listed each charge separately. The bill from Fleckmeier Implements for the tractor overhaul had arrived, but Sally hadn't paid it yet. She posted a bill for supplies Tom had bought at Fleckmeier's, $15.64, and set aside the tractor overhaul bill to talk to Tom about over dinner.

Her boys worked for their allowances. Sally had paid Wayne $100 for his weekend labor during September and Brett $50. Six dollars went to the Franklin Clinic for a prescription. A farm hardware store got $10.52, a tire repair shop $64.94, an auto repair shop $75.54. Water had cost them $15.92, a bill they kept low by using water from their old well for farm purposes and drawing on city water only for the house. The propane Joe had sold them came to $679.16. They'd given $40 to their church.

The big expenses that month were animal feed, as always, and the fast one Comstock's had pulled on grain storage. Square Deal feeds got $1,899.52. Sally posted that expense under FEED FOR LIVESTOCK. Most of it paid for soybean meal and protein sticks for the hogs. Comstock's got $2,293.50 up front for storage with the harvest still standing in the field. There might be a partial refund on that later—with a nine-month crop loan and a ten-month charge, there'd damned well better be—but in the meantime the elevator would have the interest.

Sally recorded income separately in another part of the ledger, and now she leafed over the long green pages to that file. By the end of August, 321 hogs they'd sold so far that year had grossed $34,823, an average of $108 per hog. Selling off their old sows had brought that average down. Prices for market hogs were good and getting better. In April they'd sold 21 hogs to Wilson & Company for $115 a head, but 22 hogs in mid-August had brought an average of $153 each. Tom expected to ship again in November. The only income they'd had during September was the PIK certificate sale, $1,587. Their gross income for the year so far with that addition came to $109,199.98, most of which they'd paid back out in expenses. Barring surprises, Sally kept enough cash reserved in their NOW account and in short-term certificates of deposit to even out their cash flow. The grain storage deal was a surprise Sally didn't need, thank you very much.

Between postings, Sally fixed dinner. When Tom came in, a little after noon, she served him pot roast, carrots, potatoes with dark gravy and a salad of lettuce with Italian dressing. He had bread and jelly as well and over the meal they discussed finances.

"Can you get by without writing any checks for a while here?" Sally started out after they'd talked over the morning.

"Sure," Tom agreed. "Why?"

"The bill for the tractor came in."

"How much was it?"

"Three thousand, three hundred ninety-four dollars and fifty-six cents. I'd like to pay it before the tenth to save paying interest."

Tom nodded. "That's about what I told you it'd be. How come it's making us short?"

Sally grimaced to show how she felt about it. "Well, it wouldn't of made us short if Comstock's hadn't thrown in that twenty-three hundred dollars up front for storage. I've got the money to cover it, but it's in CDs and I hate to pull them out early. We lose the interest."

Tom thought it over, caging a slice of bread easily in his big hand and spreading it with jelly. "I've got warehouse receipts to pick up," he said finally. "Then we can sell that Ward corn we stored as government corn." That would bring in some cash. He mulled over the transaction. "They took it at fifteen-and-a-half moisture. They'll shrink it to fourteen moisture before they buy it and we get to absorb the loss. Plus, warehouse receipts is twenty dollars this year."

"They was only ten last year."

"I know it. Damned if I can see what that's for."

Sally got up to clear the table and offer Tom dessert, ice cream or banana nut bread. He chose the ice cream and she dished him a bowl. "Well," she said, "if you can do that to carry us over, I'll go ahead and pay Fleckmeier's."

Tom was still thinking about the elevator arrangements. "Looks to me like the government and the elevators is in collusion," he grumbled. He registered Sally's request then and looked up from his ice cream. "Oughtn't to be no problem," he said.

They'd had fifteen inches of rain in September. No wonder the beans were molding. Sammi had decided she wanted to be a scientist when she grew up. For a science experiment she was sprouting a handful of soybeans between layers of wet paper towels on the warm kitchen counter. Tom doted on his daughter but the same thing was happening in his fields. He didn't even like to look at Sammi's beans.

One morning before dawn Sally had gotten up to make coffee and heard the auger going in the corn bin west of the house. She looked out the kitchen window through the fog and rain. There the auger was, running when nobody had turned it on and with corn piling up on the ground. "I thought I was dreaming," she told Tom later. It scared her. She hooted two or three times for Tom to come running. He thought they had a cattle rustler. She set him straight. He couldn't figure it out at first. He jumped into his clothes and went out to see. The auger that pulled grain from the bin, the teapot spout, had started up on its own. The rain had shorted out a switch. Lucky for them the auger gate was nearly closed, otherwise all the corn in the bin might have been dumped out on the ground. The corn was wet, 100, maybe 150 bushels of it. Tom scooped it into the bed of the Ford truck, spread it out and pulled the truck back in under the shed. The rain stopped at dawn. After they'd had coffee, Tom loaded the truck with dry corn from the bin and drove it to the elevator. He told them about the wet grain on the bottom. He knew the boys at the scales from way back. They didn't dock him for it.

Donald Landers, the president of the Elms family corporation, lived in Plymouth in one of the antebellum homes there. A small, trim man, Clarence's age, he'd grown up on the Landers place. He and Clarence had been schoolmates, but he'd gone off then and become a chemist and taught college. When his father died, old Eli Landers, Donald and the other members of his family on the Elms board took over as landlords.

There'd been a little mistrust about Tom at first. Donald and his sister Elizabeth, who'd also taught college, didn't know much about farming, so they couldn't be sure Tom was treating them fairly. The time Tom remembered that he and Donald both laughed about now was when they were walking in a field one April and Donald stopped and toed the young plants growing there and asked Tom if it wasn't about time he planted their soybeans. "Them's soybeans you got your toe on," Tom had said, sucking in his cheeks to keep a straight face. Since then the Landerses had read some books and listened and learned and they accepted Tom with trust, just as old Eli had.

Donald came out from Plymouth that day and he and Tom walked out together under a gray sky into the bean field back behind the Elms. It was muddy and the fallen soybean leaves made the ground slick. Both men had worn their boots. Donald had on a heavy sweater. Tom was wearing his red windbreaker and a green Square Deal seed cap. He'd switched from his summer seed caps to his winter. The back halves of the crowns on the summer caps were made of open nylon mesh. The winter caps were solid canvas front and back and lined with foam for warmth.

Each man chose a random path across the rows of beans and picked a handful of pods. They came back together and shelled the pods out. The beans looked terrible. Some were moldy. Some had sprouted in the pod, little pointed pigtails of white shoots curling out from between the split halves. Some were swollen twice their normal size and would shrivel and crack when the sun came out and dried them, if it ever did. The beans at the top of the plants were worse than the ones at the bottom. That was unusual. Usually it was the other way around, the sun between rains drying out the top beans better. There hadn't been any sun between rains lately.

They estimated fifteen-, twenty-percent damage. Donald just hung down his head. "It's depressing to put so much money and effort into raising a crop," he told Tom, "and then have it damaged."

Tom agreed. "This was going to be such a fine crop." He looked out over the field. "We wasn't supposed to have enough room to store it all."

"If it rains just a few more days we'll have to write it off," Donald said unhappily. "That's how bad it is."

"We've about had our share of rain," Tom countered. "It could still come out all right." They headed back to their vehicles. "Reminds me of what Clarence said the other day, though."

Donald looked up at his tenant. "What was that?"

"He said Mother Nature has a way of taking care of surpluses."

*   *   *

Nothing to do now that it was October but wait for the rains to quit. It was a race against time for the corn. The rain didn't bother the corn in the field, protected in its waterproof shucks, but Tom needed to get it harvested. He needed to plant wheat before the month was out, and who knew what the beans would do?

The next morning, gray and chilly again with a serious threat of rain, he drove to Comstock's for warehouse receipts and then into Osage Station to the ASCS office to arrange a government loan on his and Ward's corn, the arrangement he'd discussed with Sally. The Agricultural Stabilization and Conservation Service was started back in the Great Depression under Franklin D. Roosevelt. It ran set-asides, deficiency payments, crop loans, disaster relief and a bunch of other federal programs. Each county had its own office and each office was governed by a county committee made up of local farmers elected by their neighbors. Tom was on the Crevecoeur County committee and had a say that way in how things were done. There was still plenty of bureaucracy from Washington. The Gramm-Rudman law that automatically took a percentage off their payments, supposedly to reduce the federal deficit, was the latest twist. But most farmers thought they had fair input into the ASCS operation.

The office was around on a side street off the main drag in Osage Station, a one-story building painted pastel green. You entered off the parking lot. The ASCS office was first in the row and then the Soil Conservation Service, where you went if you had to do any pond or waterway building.

A nice-looking woman, wiry and blonde, came out of the ASCS office just as Tom was about to go in. He knew her from the office and said hello. She had a long brass sampling tool she was carrying. Tom asked her how she liked working outdoors. It was a lot better than being a desk jockey, she said. She'd put in a couple of years at the ASCS office. Then she'd transferred to checking farmers' corn bins to be sure they had as much corn stored on government loan as they claimed they did. That's what the sampling tool was for. She drove all over the county. She'd made a name for herself for being tough but fair.

Inside there was a counter the width of the room with chairs this side of the counter where you sat to wait. Tom found two old boys in line ahead of him, a father and son who farmed together, the younger man Tom's age. Behind the counter was a pool of desks. Most of the women who worked in the office were farmers' wives. The office door over beyond the pool was open and Tom could see Rowland Howell, the ASCS director, in there talking to someone. Rowland waved at him. The pool desks all had new computer terminals. The cables were still just taped down on the floor. ASCS was converting to a completely computerized operation. Rowland had told the committee it would cost about $250,000—the money came from Washington—but in the long run it was going to be worth it. They'd have better records and they'd get the job done faster.

One of the best things about ASCS was that the county committee hired and fired the director. They'd had the sharpest director in the country for years and years, someone who really cared about the farmer. When he got ready to retire he helped them find his successor, lured him down from an ASCS office in northern Missouri, and then personally trained him for a year. Rowland Howell was originally from Franklin. He'd been a captain in the Air Force before he came back to Missouri to work for the ASCS. With all the problems up in northern Missouri he'd done all right but he was really starting to shine in Crevecoeur County. Until just a year or two ago, when some county in Kentucky caught up, Crevecoeur County had more total miles of farm terraces than any other county in the entire United States.

They were slow today, still getting used to the new computer system. Eventually one of the women got Tom signed up. They needed Jack Ward's signature as well as Tom's on the loan. They couldn't take a signature by mail. They needed Ward actually to come into the office and sign. A real bureaucrat would have put everything on hold at that point. Rowland arranged for them to go ahead with the loan. Ward could stop by next time he was in the neighborhood. Gramm-Rudman still kicked in, though, and dropped the proceeds by five percent. Someone had to pay off the national debt. Might as well be the American farmer.

Wayne was home from college for the day and after dinner he and his dad did some work on the combine. Instead of rain the sky was opening up, sunlight patching through. Clark, the Bauers' young neighbor, came by in his rusty pickup. He'd been trying to get a hog operation started that fall and he was still hot on bankers. He banked at the same bank in Plymouth as Tom but he dealt with a new young vice-president out of Kansas City who was still wet behind the ears.

"I don't let up on him," Clark told them, hands in his pockets outside the workshop door. His jeans were tucked into black rubber boots that came up above the calf, a sure sign he was a hog man. "That banker got murdered in Minnesota? I said to Jones, 'See, I told you they'd be shooting bankers before it was over.' Jones said, 'I've got on my bullet-proof vest.' I said, 'Jones, I think that old boy shot that banker in the head.'"

Tom and Wayne cracked up and after a while Clark told the story over again. Tom remembered Clarence's latest bank tale. "You know what Clarence told Jones?" he asked Clark.

"No, what?"

"He told him, 'They say every farmer feeds seventy people, Jones, and I'm getting damned tired of feeding you for free.'"

Clark howled. "Another time," he said after he'd caught his breath, "I told Jones I'd rather have my job than his. 'I only have to do what I do,' I told him. 'You have to do what you do and worry about me.'"

"What'd he say?" Wayne asked.

"Just looked at me like I was stupid."

They talked awhile about Clark's hog operation. He'd built it in a former milking shed in the old barn on his place, due west of the Elms on Highway 24. Tom had seen it last in late August when it was still under construction. Since he couldn't afford to dig and pour a waste pit, Clark had raised the farrowing cages off the floor on concrete pedestals to make channels for the waste. That meant he'd have to scoop the waste by hand, but at least he'd have a warm farrowing house instead of farrowing the pigs out in the pasture in unheated individual hog houses. He'd insulated the walls with fiberglass bats. Then, to help hold down disease, he'd covered the insulation with paneling he'd bought at an auction somewhere. It was damaged Formica bathroom paneling finished to look like marble, and it really dressed the place up. His sows had just farrowed for the first time and they'd farrowed large litters. He had two with thirteen pigs.

Tom was pleased for him. Clark worked as hard as anyone he knew. "What are you going to do with all that money?" he kidded him.

Clark made a face. "Pay off the goddamned bank," he said.

One of the few things wrong with the design of Tom's combine was the exhaust stack. It didn't have a rain cap, the hinged metal cap that the exhaust kept open when the engine was running but that flapped down when the engine was shut off to keep out the rain. Even without a cap, the stack was a couple of inches too tall to clear the crossbeam of the shed west of the house where Tom sometimes parked the combine out of the weather.

With Wayne's help, he decided to cut the stack down like a sawed-off shotgun so he could add a rain cap and still get it into the shed. They took a hacksaw to it. It was sheet iron and easy to cut but they discovered there were two pipes, one inside the other, sealed over at the top. Tom figured it was some kind of back-pressure deal and they needed to seal together the two pipe ends just the way they'd been before. He wasn't sure how to go about it. Wayne saw a way and did a little drawing on the lid of the box the rain cap came in, a flat doughnut of sheet iron that they could weld into place. They made a cardboard template and cut the doughnut out of sheet iron with the acetylene torch. Then Tom welded the doughnut onto the exhaust stack. After the weld had cooled, he ground off the weld bead, orange sparks spraying across a blue and white sky. Wayne clamped on the rain cap and tightened it down.

The combine went right in under the crossbeam with about an inch to spare. Down on the ground, looking up to admire the new rain cap, Tom noticed the blacksnake. He'd been wondering where it'd gotten to. It was folded back on itself on a loft beam, its chin resting on the loop its five-foot body made. It was waiting for the birds to roost.

On a farm, pigeons, sparrows and starlings could be dangerous pests. They carried disease. Leptospirosis was one of the worst, a water-borne pestilence that caused fever, hemorrhaging and abortions. Birds would get around some farmer's hog operation and pick up lepto on their feet. Then they'd fly to the next farm and pretty soon that farmer's hogs would start to sicken.

Tom encouraged the blacksnake even though Sally and Sammi wouldn't go near the shed. It helped scare the birds away. Brett's approach was more direct. His Future Farmers of America chapter at school gave awards for pest control. Brett led the list. He'd go after the birds at night. He called it bird hunting. He'd take an old tennis racquet and climb up into the barn lofts and bat the birds down. To prove he'd done the job he was supposed to collect the heads. He'd go to school after a night of bird hunting with his coat pockets full of bird heads. They weren't bloody, just little balls of feathers. A man could lose his entire hog herd in a week and his livelihood with it from the disease birds carried. Wayne liked animals, but so far as he was concerned, barn birds were fair game. He and the blacksnake saw eye to eye on that.

II

CREATURES

ONE

Tom was right. They'd had their share of rain for a while. It finally did seem to want to stop. One clear, dry day came along and then another. Tom checked his fields daily and after three days of sun he found them risky but possible. He might be able to get his corn in and save his soybeans after all. What the beans would do would depend on how badly damaged they'd been. He'd have to wait and see about that.

The next day, after dinner, Tom drove the combine out on the highway to the Elms to start picking Landers corn again. Along the way he stopped at the bins to rearrange the grain auger. He'd reversed it to move Landers grain out of the big bin into his trucks. Now he wanted to load corn into the bin from the field.

Before he moved the auger he took up the scoop shovel he kept at hand beside the grain bins and scooped out the auger hole. It was bottomed with corn the rain had rotted, a sour vomit smell, and he was careful to pile the waste downwind. Around the hole the rain had started a patch of young corn. The shoots were pale where they entered the ground but the blades were emerald-green. In the gray and brown of fall they popped out at you like 3-D.

Tom cranked the fifty-two-foot auger until it towered over the bin. By then the crank was above his head. It would've been out of reach for a shorter man. Backing up the auger with the Farmall, he accidentally broke off the lower half of the flexible aluminum spout against the steel bin roof. It dangled by one of its rings, a repair job for a rainy day he hoped he wouldn't get too soon. With the auger in place over the manhole Tom climbed the ladder up the thirty-foot side and then farther up the cone of the roof. He worked loose the enameled yellow cover and hung it off the manhole like a French beret, bent the broken spout piece until it broke free and threw it off the bin. Climbing back down, he cranked what was left of the auger spout into position over the manhole. Then he stood back and surveyed his work. With the auger installed he was set on go, he decided, if the mud would just cooperate. It was a fine clear day.

He'd already greased up the combine, checked its fluids and belts and chains and filled it with diesel fuel. He drove on down the grassy lane south of the Landers bins to the long, steep-sided field he and Sally had opened up weeks ago. Rain and wind had knocked down considerable corn since then, the upper stalks with their heavy ears broken over midway as if they'd been jungle-hacked. Tom found a place to enter the field and by one forty-five he was combining. He couldn't begin to say how good it felt to see the stalks parading in between the picker-head snouts and hear the ears clunking back through the combine throat again.

There was still plenty of mud. The field was partly level upland with a hillside sloping down west, three parallel terraces grading the hillside. Tom had started in on four rows on the lower side of the second terrace. Driving on the slope, he had to work to hold the combine from skidding sideways, keeping the back steering wheels turned uphill. The combine hit slick spots where even its big forward wheels began to skid. When Tom saw a low place ahead he'd gun the machine through. Halfway out he decided the rows he was picking were as far down the hill as he dared to go. He moved up and picked the crest of the terrace coming back, then picked the eight rows above the terrace on his next round back and forth. That opened up a safe lane for the grain wagon and tractor to use without risking getting stuck. Sally came along in the big green Oliver hauling a grain wagon and he dumped on her.

When she got to the bins she called him on the radio. The Farmall wouldn't start and she couldn't run the auger. The Farmall was old. Tom figured the starter had come out of gear. He told Sally to turn off the ignition, put the tractor in sixth gear and rock one of the wheels until the starter clicked back in.

She tried it and called him back. She couldn't move the wheel enough. Tom would have to do it himself. He picked on out to the end of the rows. Sally ran down the quarter-mile from the bins in the GMC to meet him. He'd have to turn the pickup around in the field. Rather than risk miring it he kicked in the four-wheel drive. Off they went to the bins, leaving the combine running. The starter was out of gear all right, easy to fix. Tom rocked the wheel and she clicked right back in.

Sally had stopped for some apples at Siegelstecher's. They usually ate fruit or bought soda pop at the little general store in Devon rather than carrying water to the field. Tom ate a Delicious on the ride back. At the bins he'd noticed that the wasps were active, a sign there was a cold spell coming despite the balmy day. Monarchs fed on the milkweed that thickened the fence that edged the lane, orange and black pulses riding the pale green pods. "This field's going to look like a patchwork quilt before we're through with it," Tom told Sally as she let him off.

It did. In the rain and warmth of the wet fall, the kernels of corn they'd lost through the combine when they'd opened up the field had sprouted patches of 3-D green like the corn spilled around the auger hole. The green patches contrasted with the buff standing corn, with the darker patches of shadow where the corn was down, with the brown-black dirt exposed in the new rows of stobble Tom had stripped that afternoon and with the shining litter of stalks. Ivy-colored morning glory figured the ground in the picked-over rows. The passing combine, a block of moving red, released a smell of garlic sometimes from the rows. Poison ivy turned sumac red blotched the lush grass on the lower waterway, below the unpicked lower hill. And always at the red grain wagons there was the rosy-yellow flow of corn against the blue sky and pink wings blowing.

Tom noticed it all because it all meant something to him. The spilled corn reminded him to check the combine discharge to see if the contours or the rear screens needed adjusting. The downed stalks probably referred to the rain but might signal corn borer damage, something else to check. Morning glories growing meant the combine's tires had broken the seal of herbicide in the soil and might give him a problem next summer, since he'd normally plant soybeans after corn and a herbicide that killed broad-leafed weeds wasn't safe with soybeans, a broad-leafed plant itself. He kept track of the domestic plants and the weeds at the same time that he kept track of the combine, the field conditions, the lay of the land, the location of the grain wagons and trucks, the fuel levels in all the various vehicles and their state of operation, the time of day, the weather, how the rows ran and how best to open them up and pick them. Even turning the combine around made a difference, a tight inside turn saving time and fuel over a turn where you had to stop and back up and jockey. Making that tight turn at the end of a swath, with all that on his mind, he still didn't miss a V-racked flight of snow geese high overhead winging oddly west, toward Kansas.

Sammi arrived home from school and called them on the radio. She wanted to ask her mother a question, she said, but Sally was unloading grain and wasn't near the business-band portable in the tractor. "I'll holler at her when she heads back out," Tom told his daughter.

Sally called in on the portable and Tom gave her the message.

"Where are you?" Sammi asked her mother when Sally called home. The microphone in the house was a table mike with crackled enamel finish and a permanent base that stood on the desk beside the refrigerator.

Sally told her and Sammi asked how long they'd be out in the field.

"We just got started good," Sally said. It was close to four o'clock. "Do you want to come on out with us or stay there?"

"Stay here."

"Then you call us every once in a while so we'll know you're okay. What're you going to do?"

"Nothing, really."

"Pick up that stuff in the living room. You remember you were supposed to do that?"

"I already did," Sammi said.

Tom's deep voice cut in from the combine. "Sammi," he ordered affectionately, "tell Brett when he gets home he's supposed to feed *all* the hogs."

"Okay."

"If you want to come on out here after a while," Sally coaxed her, "just call us, okay?"

"Okay," Sammi agreed.

When he'd picked all around the edges of the level upland, Tom dumped on a grain wagon one last time and turned the combine over to Sally. He wanted a good look at the grain. Up at the bin, running the auger, he caught a handful of the corn flowing from the grain wagon to study the quality, smoothed away successive layers carefully with the heel of his other hand, caught a second handful and another and another after that. Finally he was satisfied. It was okay. Despite the rain it was good corn. He'd found a sprouted kernel every other handful, not enough to worry about. They probably wouldn't even dock him. A few kernels here and there showed a gray mottling. That was a virus, ear rot. The virus had only one critical day across the entire growing season when it could enter into the corn kernels, so it was showing up this year only in this one variety with its particular maturity date.

But it was good corn. "I'm well pleased," Tom told Sally later. "Now if only the beans would look that good." He'd put on the propane to the bin while he'd unloaded. The heat blew the smell of warm corn into the air. Pink wings like sparks sprayed up from the manhole and caught the sunlight of late afternoon. A jet going east, out of sight overhead, drew a line of thick contrail that divided the spray.

After he'd finished feeding the hogs, Brett drove out in Babe to help. Sammi rode along with him and climbed up into the combine with her mother. She'd broken up with her boyfriend, she told Sally, and wondered if she'd handled it right. That was her question. Sally didn't think nine-year-olds ought to be dating in the first place but actually they weren't. It was some kind of nine-year-old pretend dating. A boy asked a girl if she wanted to be his girlfriend and if she said yes then she was. They didn't spend time together. If they had they wouldn't have known what to do. The boys still stuck with the boys and the girls with the girls. Sooner or later one of them would decide to break up. The boys were usually too chicken to deliver the Dear John themselves. Sammi's boyfriend at least had the guts to tell her in person. She hadn't batted an eye. "That's okay," she'd answered him. "There's other fish in the sea." But Sally could tell it hurt her feelings. Some of the kids in town looked down on farm kids. There was one mother who wouldn't let her little girl play with Sammi. She didn't even want her out on a farm.

In early evening, Tom took over the combine. Sally and Sammi drove home in the GMC to fix a supper of sandwiches to bring back out to the field. Brett wanted to go bird hunting but dumped grain instead. Crossing the field, or even following the smooth waterway, the tractor and grain wagon hit resonances that made them buck. Brett had to slow down then to break the resonance and smooth out the ride. The bouncing wasn't so much a problem for the driver as it was for the hitches. The tractor seat was cushioned and mounted on hydraulics, but bucking could fatigue the steel tongue that connected the wagon to the tractor. Too much stress and eventually it'd break. "You don't need to drive a tractor like you was driving a hot rod," Tom always told his boys. He didn't have much use for tractor jockeys.

Sally and Sammi parked along the waterway and set out ham-and-cheese sandwiches, more apples, potato chips, brownies and cans of Pepsi on the tailgate of the pickup. There were mosquitoes in the air now, big from all the rain. "We ought to put out some *blood*," Brett said with a bite of sandwich in his cheek, slapping one dead. "Look here, Dad," he went on, displaying a smear of blood on his hand. "It's a vampire."

"Eat your supper, son," Tom soothed him.

They left Tom combining and drove home in the GMC. He wanted to pick another load before it got completely dark. He ran on until nine under a waxing moon with a visible terminator and a planet or a star keeping it company close by. Tom saw other combines in the distance working other fields. In the country darkness the ranks of headlights on the combines made them look like steamboats working a wide, dark river.

Tom parked his 1460 in the grass waterway along the edge of the field, shut it down, started up the tractor and hauled the loaded grain wagon up to the Landers bins. He parked the wagon on the grass there to unload in the morning and drove Babe home. He'd staged the vehicles before hand so he wouldn't have to walk.

The morning was cool again and sunny but the forecast called for a thirty-percent chance of rain the next day. The question was whether to risk the wet lower third of the field in the hopes of beating the rain. Tom loaded Babe with chains and cables. Out in the field he transferred them to the tractor and the combine against the possibility of getting stuck.

Greasing up the combine, Tom saw three deer—two does and a yearling buck—slip out from the woods onto the lower waterway. They crossed the waterway, watching alertly, and disappeared into the corn. The woods that ran along Cebo Creek were thick with deer. He'd seen wild turkeys come out once near the same place to feed on corn as well, ten, fifteen wild turkeys in a flock.

He climbed into the cab of the combine. It was still chilly inside from the night air. He fired up the engine, listened for a while to its running and got rolling. A quartet of red-winged blackbirds launched itself in front of him from the waterway. He rolled on down to the lower terrace and started in.

On his opening pass across the hillside he nearly got stuck, the big front wheels spinning, but he opened up the throttle and skidded on through. Running the slick spots after that, he watched the picker head and opened up so much that sometimes inside the cab the beeper came on that signaled a loss of twenty

percent or more power to the rotor, the wheels getting the power and wasting some of it spinning. When he started to skid where the slope was steeper he'd steer into the skid as the rear end began sliding downhill and try to avoid knocking down corn in the rows below him. It kept him busy and once Tom slid too far and had to crash on down through four rows and pick up another swath of four. Later, when he could work up from below, he came back to the four he'd slid down from. "She's slicker than a ball bearing in a bucket of grease," he told Sally when she arrived. He worked around, picking up point rows and breaking through.

Sally had found the cab of the GMC full of flies. The window hadn't been completely closed and the flies had crowded in last evening looking for warmth. Before Sally had driven to the field, she'd opened both doors and shooed them out. Molly had barked and leapt into the air to snap at them, Blaze watching with interest from beside the house. Now that it was cooler at night, little Molly slept curled up on Blaze's back, her face buried in the big dog's fur. Blaze didn't mind. It kept her warm too.

Sally had been on the phone with an old friend from her hometown and it reminded her of Sammi's problem the day before. Her friend, Alicia, a woman her own age, had a daughter who treated her like dirt, a sixteen-year-old who was dating a married man who'd been in jail and wasn't any good. She'd totaled her car one day and ordered her mother to come home from work and bring the pickup so she could go to a football game. "Alicia's too good for her," Sally told Tom as she rode around with him in the combine. "Alicia gives her everything she asks for and she treats her mother like dirt. I really worry about our kids with all that's going on these days. I hope they turn out okay."

"They're good kids," Tom said. "Brett needs a little bit of an attitude adjustment about school, but they're fine."

By noon, Tom knew he could finish the field. It'd be nip and tuck with the bin, though. The bin was nearly full. Tom had sent Sally up to the manhole to watch the Stiralator working down inside the bin. Its motor-driven vertical augers, moving from the center to the outside, would slowly level the corn. Then they could shut the Stiralator off and put corn on top, mounding it up under the cone of the roof. The cone would hold about a thousand bushels more.

At high noon, a red-shouldered hawk wheeled above the bins. Tom crossed the empty field, moving on. Even stripped, the field was alive with critters, mice most of all that ran in panic ahead of the combine in the troughs of the rows. Wasps still worked the stobble, spiders, small flies, large mosquitoes. The wind blew the stalk litter and the sunlight bloomed and faded as clouds rushed by. Swifts followed the combine, swooping low. Farming was pirating on the high seas of the sun. You never knew what your haul would be. That was why fall was Tom's favorite season. At least they'd managed to finish one more field.

Dinner was goulash from the crockpot—elbow macaroni, tomatoes, hamburger from one of Clarence's steers—and lettuce in a bowl. They said a blessing, as they always did before they ate. By three that afternoon it was cloudy, heavy cumuli below a thickening overcast. They just had to hope they could get their last forty acres of corn picked before it rained again.

TWO

The next day, Thursday, dawned gray and chilly with a serious threat of rain. Tom was nervous to finish that last cornfield. Wayne pulled up first thing in the morning, home from college early for the weekend, and he and his dad drove over to Landers' in the GMC to collect the combine. The last field was the first field Tom and Sally had owned that they'd sold to Mr. Geizhals and now farmed for him on shares. It was halfway to Plymouth down U.S. 24. Tom led the way in the combine at fifteen miles an hour, slow-moving-vehicle lights blinking under the lowering gray sky. Wayne followed in the pickup with his flashers on to protect the combine from being rear-ended. If a car approached behind him, he'd watch for a signal from his dad. When it came, he'd move onto the shoulder and wave the car past pickup and combine both.

Twenty minutes up the road, Tom and Wayne turned left into a blacktopped lane. The convoy was no sooner off the highway than a light rain began, drizzle streaking the combine's big picture window. Another mile up the lane to the forty acres and the drizzle had thickened to a steady rain. Tom pulled the combine off the road onto the strip of set-aside ground at the near edge of the forty acres and parked it. The combine's holding bin was uncovered to the rain, the tarpaulin that covered it when he parked it outside for any length of time folded carefully and stored on the walkway

180

beside the dump auger. Before Tom covered it again, he thought he'd try to find a place to pull the machine in under a roof. He shut the combine down and took over the GMC. Wayne slid to the passenger side. Jeb Hurder lived a little way up the road, one section south and one section east.

They found Jeb working on his combine in the converted-barn machine shed behind his house. It was the same model Case machine as Tom's. Jeb's face and hands were smeared with grease. He stopped working and cleaned his hands with the waterless cleaning cream Tom called "gojo" and they talked rain and beans and combines for a while until Jeb caught on to what it was Tom had come to ask.

"You want to put that picker into that back shed over at my boy's place?" Jeb asked Tom then. Jeb's boy Joel was a couple of years older than Wayne and married. He'd already started farming with his dad, the same way Tom had gotten into farming twenty-five years ago. "There's just a planter in there now. All we'd have to do is hook her up to the tractor and pull her out."

"I wouldn't want to trouble you none," Tom said. "That planter shouldn't set out in this rain just so my combine can stay dry."

Jeb saw he'd seemed to hint that the planter was a problem. He corrected himself. "Plenty of room for that planter in that new building we just put up."

"I wouldn't want to put you out none," Tom repeated.

"Ain't no trouble. A man sure hates to leave his combine out in the rain."

Tom gave Jeb two more chances to refuse the request he'd never officially made, then accepted the favor with relief. Now he wouldn't have to drive his combine all the way back home and he wouldn't have to leave it out in the rain either. Grinning, Wayne grinning with him, he took off to fetch his machine.

By the time Tom and Wayne arrived, Jeb and his son had already moved the planter. The new building was a prefabricated Butler steel structure some eighty feet long, forty feet wide and twenty feet high, the steel protected from the elements by a baked-on coating of white enamel. The first forty feet of the building had already been in place for a year. Jeb had added a forty-foot extension to the back end.

Tom was admiring. The wide, high building was a step forward from grain bins. Jeb could store his beans in it through the fall. Later, after they were sold, he could sweep it out and use it as a machine shed. It had a high enough ceiling even to take his combine and it'd hold a hell of a pile of beans.

With their sons following, the two men toured the structure. An extended social call was part of Tom's return to Jeb for sheltering his combine. Tom never thought of farming as lonely. From the combine or the tractor he could see deer crossing his fields, coyotes hunting, traffic passing on the highway, the comings and goings of his neighbors. But sometimes a man got hungry for talk. And there was always something to learn. Jeb's wife was working two jobs to help out in the hard times, at the Bendix plant in Kansas City during the week and at Wal-Mart on weekends. Jeb worked harder than almost anyone Tom knew, mostly alone. He'd started out from scratch, like Tom, with nothing but his two hands to help him.

Jeb had nailed up sheets of waste plywood he'd bought at auction to keep the beans he'd be storing in the new building away from the steel outside walls. He'd dug the footings and poured the slab floor himself and then Butler had come in with a crane and put up the building's roof and walls overnight. He and Tom talked it over a good long time, working out its possibilities. The boys just listened. Tom summed up the conversation with a blessing. "I wish I had this building," he told Jeb formally, "and you had a bigger one."

With his new building thoroughly appreciated, Jeb remembered what else they had to show. "Did you know Joel's got a deer fawn?"

The part of him that'd never grown up took over and Tom went boyish. Grinning and excited, he followed Jeb and his son over behind Joel's house to a large pen fenced with chicken wire. The rain had let up a little, back to a drizzle. Inside the pen, a spotted fawn with a delicate black nose, big alert ears, fine black cloven hooves and a flicking tail knelt on a bed of yellow wheat straw. It bounded over to the fence to suck on the finger Tom offered.

"Joel's been raising it on goat's milk," Jeb said.

"Where'd you find that?" Tom asked the boy.

He was shy. "Over t' south of Osage Station," he said quietly. He had a black Labrador pup he was playing with.

"That's a long way to go."

"Joel's good with animals," Jeb said. "Just like Brett."

"Hell," Wayne threw in, "I ain't half bad with them myself." Tom gave his son a look. Sometimes he wondered if Wayne was ever going to grow up.

The fawn dazzled Tom. He talked about its spots, noticed its alert ears, reached over the high fence to pet it. "Boy," he said finally, "wouldn't Sammi like to see this."

"You can bring her over anytime," Jeb told him.

Tom got serious. "I expect you'll be hearing from the game warden."

"Yeah," Jeb said, "we figured we would."

"It's against the law to fence a wild animal," Tom recited the law they all knew. "We got into it once when we dug out a nest of coyote pups. We figured we'd get fined if the game warden caught up with them. We had to thump them. Clarence did the same thing with some he'd turned up. Come to find out we could've kept them if we'd allowed them to roam free. That's what I'd advise."

"We could do that," Jeb said. "Joel's got the little thing all tamed down."

Three deficiency slips had come in the mail from school that week. That was the attitude adjustment Tom had told Sally Brett needed at school. The boy wasn't keeping up in English, economics and typing.

Brett was mortified about the deficiency slips. He didn't want to discuss them. He didn't want his parents to talk to his teachers about them. He'd gone around all week saying he guessed he was just dumb. They'd dragged a little of it out of him. The typing teacher didn't think much of boys taking typing, but he also admitted he wasn't practicing as much as he should. The econ teacher depressed him. All he seemed to talk about was the problems and troubles in the world. He made it sound as if every farm in America was going bankrupt. The English teacher was a former college teacher with a Ph.D. and he put on airs. He'd flat out told them he was only interested in the smart kids. The others could just sink or swim.

Tom wasn't impressed with Brett's excuses, blaming the teachers for his problems. On the other hand, as far as Tom was concerned it was the teachers' job to find a way through to his son and see that he learned what he was supposed to learn. He wanted to hear their side of the story. The English teacher was the same one who'd given Wayne grief about his tests and then come to find out they were mimeographed in purple ink and hard as hell to read. Tom wanted to know if the man was only interested in the smart students. Tom hadn't been a top student when he'd been in high school. They'd had a different English teacher at Plymouth then, a woman, and she'd worked with all of them regardless of whether or not they were smart. That was what they paid taxes for.

Sally called the school during the dinner hour and a little after three she and Tom drove into Plymouth for a conference. The typing teacher couldn't stay after school that day but the econ and English teachers could. They met the Bauers in the counselor's office and led them to a conference room with a round table. The econ teacher was a short man with a paunch. The English teacher was average size. He wore a tweed sport coat and had salt-and-pepper hair. Both men were younger than Tom and Sally.

Econ started explaining about his requirement that the kids read some kind of newspaper every day and bring in a story every week that related to economics. Sally listened until he was finished and then asked him bluntly if he knew he was depressing.

"Brett says you bring up bad news every day of the week. Can't you find some good news once in a while?"

Econ looked surprised. It didn't seem as if he'd heard that particular complaint before. "Economics is about problems and how to solve them," he told Sally. "I never thought of it as depressing."

Tom spoke up. "There's a share of kids in your classes who're farm kids," he said. "It ain't a majority anymore the way it was when I was in school here, but it's still a goodly number. You've got to remember that farming is tough these days and farm kids get a double dose when they hear about farm problems in school. You tell this boy that farmers are going bankrupt right and left and he comes home and wonders when the lightning's going to strike his own house. It ain't all farmers is losing their farms, but maybe he don't know that."

Econ perked up. "I never thought of it that way before," he said. It was a new problem to solve. "I could certainly try to widen my emphasis and look a little harder for positive developments. That's a very good idea."

English had been waiting his turn to take command. "Brett's been improving recently in my class," he told Tom and Sally. "He was slow settling in after the summer. I believe in getting down in the trenches with my kids—"

Tom interrupted him. "Brett says you told them you was only interested in the smart kids, that the others could just sink or swim."

That took the wind out of English's sails. He looked embarrassed. "Why, no, I said nothing of the kind."

Tom didn't think his boy would lie to him, but maybe the truth was in between. He decided to let it go. He was about to say so when English recovered and counterattacked. "Brett always sits in the back," he told Sally, not quite looking at Tom. "He never asks questions, and asking questions is one of the best ways to show class participation, which I grade them on every day. He can make up for a lot on tests and so on if he participates in class. But if I direct anything his way he gives me that *look* of his." Sally nodded. English smiled. "You know what look I mean."

Econ came in. "I remember that same look. It's kind of contemptuous. I had to talk to him after class about it. He stopped doing it after that."

"I've been ready to talk to him on several occasions," English said. He sounded as if he'd been afraid to. "Maybe I should go ahead and do it."

"You ought to," Tom agreed.

"Well, then," English said, "I will."

They talked on about study requirements and grades, focusing mostly on Brett's English class. Eventually Tom sat forward, put his arms on the table, spread out his big hands and laid down the law. "We want our boy's grades to get better," he told the two teachers bluntly, "and we intend to do whatever's necessary to see that they do. We'll be here every Monday to talk to you if necessary."

"Every *day* if we have to," Sally added.

"I know Brett's got an attitude problem," Tom went on. "He's got to take responsibility for his work. I'll see to that." Tom sat up straighter and seemed to get bigger. "But the way I look at it, you're just like my feed man or my propane man. You're paid to do a job, and that job happens to be teaching these kids. If one of them's not learning, then you're responsible for finding a way to make him learn. We'll make sure Brett does his homework and straightens out his attitude. But you have to take it from there." Tom looked sternly from one teacher to the other. "Fair enough?"

Both men looked nervous. Like father, like son. Brett was big and physical too.

Econ recovered first. "Fair enough," he said.

"Fair enough," English added. His voice sounded a little strangled.

Tom and Sally talked over the problem on the drive home. Sally worried about Brett because he was their middle child and Wayne and Sammi were both good in school, Wayne even with his handicap. Brett had taken Sammi's Iowa Basic scores hard. Sally was proud of her little girl's IQ scores but concerned about her middle son.

"Brett's not dumb," Tom told her.

"I didn't say he was," Sally defended herself.

"I knowed you didn't," Tom soothed. "He's like me is what he is. He has to be pushed. I had to be pushed at his age. You can see it in his farm work. Wayne just about won't quit. Brett's ready to quit after a while. He gets restless. Bored. I remember my dad pushing me the same way. I didn't have any idea what I wanted to do until Dad came down to Fort Sill to talk to me about farming. Before that I'd just been having fun."

"Chasing women," Sally said drily.

Tom dodged that one. "Well, I'll speak to the boy tonight."

He did. Sally and Sammi went to an open house at school and Tom sat Brett down and just told him he had to graduate from high school whether he liked it or not. "You can't do anything in life anymore without at least a high school diploma," Tom told his son.

"I could farm."

"You couldn't keep up with all the changes, son. My dad didn't keep up when the big change came in fertilizer and chemicals. It was all just too much for him. He didn't want to start over and learn a bunch of new ideas. I'll come up against that wall one of these days. You'll have to learn a lot more than I did, chemicals, computers, what all." Then Tom realized what he'd heard and stopped to look at his son. "You mean you want to farm?"

"I don't know," Brett shrugged. He didn't want to be pinned down. "Maybe."

Tom couldn't figure if Brett's talk about farming was serious or just designed to throw him off the scent. He decided not to let his enthusiasm show. "Whatever you decide to do," he said sternly, "you've got to get your diploma. That's your job this year and next just like my job's farming. You may not like it, but that's what you've got to do. Is that understood?"

Brett gave his dad one of his looks. "Yes, sir, understood."

"We're with you and we'll be keeping track of you."

"I knowed you will," Brett said glumly.

Friday they went to work on the last of the corn, bringing the combine out from the Hurder place, cutting ruts in the wet field with the big front tires and finding water standing even at the top of the slope. Since they were five miles away from home, Wayne started worrying about Sammi coming from school to an empty house. He volunteered to fetch his sister on his way back from Comstock's, delivering grain, but she got off the school bus on her own out on 24 at the lane that led to the forty acres and turned up walking across the muddy field in her new white Reeboks with her book pack on her back and her arms full of corn ears the combine had missed that she'd picked up as she came. Tom and Sally watched her crossing the field from the cab of the combine. "Ain't that a sight?" Tom asked his wife. Dark-haired Sammi and her sweet smile. "I'll clean my Reeboks," she greeted her mom cheerfully, getting the jump on Sally's complaint.

Waiting in line at Comstock's, early that evening, Tom got to talking on the CB with a friend of his waiting behind him in a semi. The CB was a backup in that particular truck to the portable business-band radio. Tom hadn't been able to afford to install built-in business-band radios in all his farm equipment yet. The friend asked him how it was going. He said he could finish picking his corn if the elevator would just stay open until ten thirty, but he'd have to haul the last load in a grain wagon with a tractor. The semi man offered to haul the last eight hundred bushels in his truck if Tom could load it out on the road so he wouldn't risk getting stuck. It started to rain while they were finishing up, but with the semi to dump on, they delivered the last of the grain before ten thirty, at ten cents a bushel for the hauling. That was the end of it: the entire corn crop was in.

That weekend Wayne announced that he wanted to farm and his parents might just have to find some more land for him.

"You too?" Sally asked him.

Wayne was surprised. "Who else?" he asked his mother.

"Brett," Sally said. Tom had told her about his conversation with their younger son.

Wayne went off to digest that news. Tom and Sally were skeptical about Wayne farming, given his eyes. It was still something to dream on. Tom thought the two boys were opposites. "They'd make a hell of a team," he told Sally the next morning. "But then you'd have to worry about the wives and whether they'd get along."

"Girls these days don't know how to work," Sally said.

Tom rolled his eyes at her. "That's what my sisters said about you. You turned out okay."

"It takes a special kind of woman to live on a farm and not want fancy things and help her husband," Sally insisted.

"You're right about that," Tom agreed.

Saturday, Tom drove the combine to the converted barn on the upland of the Ward place, eased the picker head inside, smeared used motor oil on the surfaces the corn had worn to bare metal and put the attachment away for the season. He hadn't squared it up as precisely with the barn wall as a barracks inspector would have liked but there was plenty of room in the barn. "A blind man won't see it," Tom told himself, "and a smart man won't say nothing."

He drove off to collect the combine's grain header, parked in the barn on the Dixon place. He was ready to combine soybeans.

THREE

Migrating blackbirds crossed the wide sky these days in giant flocks, a stream like a dark river sweeping back and forth through a blue plain. Tom wouldn't even try to guess their number. Tens of thousands at least. Down on the ground, sulphurs, the little pale-yellow butterflies, met in pairs and played in the space just above the grass. Sometimes a doe appeared in a pasture, jumped the fence into a cornfield and fed on the corn left from picking. Mornings there'd be a hard frost, white frost over the rich green grass of this wet fall. Siegelstecher's orchard, across the road from the Elms, still had apples for sale, glowing red in their bushel baskets of pale new wood, but the draw now was pumpkins, a pile of pumpkins, and cider in the cooler case. Neighbors set pumpkins and shocks of corn out along the roadside, and over at the Galens', Clarence's wife, Jessie, had stuffed a scarecrow and given it a pumpkin head and leaned it against the corner post next to their entrance gate. Jessie Galen was a small, trim woman with a big smile, as cherished in the neighborhood as Clarence was. She put together a new scarecrow every year. Tom always looked twice when he saw it, because she always dressed it in Clarence's old clothes, and just like Clarence, it was thin and loose-jointed-looking, but with a happy-face orange head.

Tom had to change over the combine before he could begin

189

combining beans. The big twenty-foot header was parked on the grass south of the workshop now where the picker head had been before. Molly stalked around it, hunting in the lush grass. The header's black-paddled reel made it look light and bulky at the same time, like the box wings on an old biplane. The reel served to bat the soybean stalks into the auger that turned behind it that fed the beans to the combine throat. The lower leading edge of the header, under the reel, bristled with a row of pointed teeth. These were brackets bolted onto the header pan through which flat, triangular, serrated sickle sections like large sawteeth riveted to a bar sliced back and forth when the machine was running to cut the beanstalks close. The entire header, which stuck out three feet on each side of the combine and nearly matched it in scale, floated on flexible skid plates attached to hydraulics that automatically kept it positioned in operation an inch or two off the ground.

The first thing Tom did was to replace broken sickle sections, chiseling the heads off the rivets that held them to the cutter bar with an air hammer hooked up to his shop compressed-air supply and fastening on new sections with lock washers and small bolts. Some of the sections he replaced weren't broken but only dented, but a dent would grab a soybean stalk rather than cutting it cleanly through, shaking the beans out on the ground.

In Osage Station, at Case International, Tom picked up a wooden bearing he needed to replace one that wear and tear had wallowed out. The parts man kidded him about getting rich in this bumper-crop year. Tom kidded back. "If I had all your-all's money," he told the parts man, "I'd be rolling in tall clover." "Yeah," the parts man complained, "we get paid so much." Tom had ordered an upgrade kit for the combine's clean-grain auger and the kit had come in the day before from Kansas City. The bicycle-like chain that ran the auger had slipped its sprockets twice when Tom was combining corn. The upgrade kit contained the parts with which to build an idler into the chain, a spring-loaded weight that would keep it taut. The cost of the kit had gone down since Tom had last priced it, which made him suspicious that the parts man hadn't ordered all the parts it called for. The parts man explained that the design had changed. Tom was doubtful—when did prices ever go down except the prices farmers got paid for their crops?—but he took the man's word.

Tom had followed Wayne into Osage Station to make sure his son got the best deal on a new muffler for his car and left him at the muffler shop. Wayne waited for the installation and then drove home to help his dad change the combine over for beans. It was a cool, dry, sunny day, the humidity down to thirty-five percent, good for drying out the beans and a nice day to work. Tom wore lumberjack shirts and his red windbreaker these days against the cooler air. Boy and man hauled the heavy steel contours, scoured shiny as new-minted silver now by all the corncobs they'd cracked, out from under the combine rotary. They wanted to reinstall the rods they'd taken out for corn to make the contour grid smaller again for beans. Tom clamped onto a rod with locking pliers and hammered on the pliers to force the rod into the contours through the holes in the steel bars of the grid. Wayne used a screwdriver to guide the end of the rod into the holes for him. Forcing the steel rods, thick as a man's little finger, through a curved grid of steel holes made for banshee harmonics, each rod a heavy-metal harp string sliding up the scale.

The combine's spreaders—rotating cones of sheet metal fitted with fan blades—had been removed for the corn harvest. While Tom disappeared inside the combine body to install the new idler, Wayne remounted the spreaders above the rear discharge outlet. The empty soybean pods and broken stalks would blow from the discharge outlet into the path of the spreaders. Spinning, they'd disperse the litter uniformly into the swath behind the combine, returning nutrients to the soil and mulching it. Without binocular vision, Wayne had to feel for the bolt holes with his fingers. He had trouble finding a nut he'd left on the ground. He'd devised ways to see, but sometimes it took a little longer.

The next afternoon, the middle of October, Tom opened up the first bean field, a hilly Landers field back behind the Elms. He'd turned cattle into the harvested cornfield next to the beans and confined them to the field with an electric fence. To get into the soybean field he dropped the electric fence and ran the combine across it. He cut across a header width of outside rows of beans as

well before turning parallel to the fence and beginning a first round clockwise. On his second pass he'd return counterclockwise and pick up the fencerows, making an outside cleared area forty feet wide where he could turn the combine around when he harvested the rest of the field.

He ran up the rows on his first pass only long enough to put some beans into the combine's holding bin. Then he stopped, raised the big header and climbed down from the cab to take a look. Kneeling in the swath behind the combine, he smoothed the litter aside and counted beans lost to the ground. He found five or six per square foot. "Too many beans," he told himself. "Now I've got to figure out what's causing it."

He was a scout now, studying the ground for sign. A bean or two on top of the litter meant the last shaker screen before the discharge might need adjusting. The shaker screens were levered like venetian blinds to control the size of the material they let through. Tom cranked the last screen down a notch. Beans under the combine probably meant the header reel was threshing out pods before they made it into the combine throat. He decided on two remedies for that problem. He wanted to speed up the threshing so that the beans had less time to fall ahead of the combine. That would mean more material coming in at the combine throat, and to process it more vigorously he adjusted the contour screens closer to the rotary by tightening a turnbuckle rod with a wrench.

The second remedy could wait until he was back in the cab. First he wanted to see the crop. He climbed to the holding bin, leaned over and scooped up a double handful of the cream-colored beans. They were the size of small pearls, black streaks marking their hila, the scars where they'd attached to their pods. He let them stream off his hands back into the bin and suddenly he was elated. They didn't look half bad, not nearly as bad as the beans he'd studied with Donald Landers a few weeks before. Drying out had improved them. "We'll have to see what that old elevator's going to say about the damage," he cautioned himself.

Back in the cab and preparing to run again, Tom punched up the rotary speed from 350 RPM to 410. With the contours tighter, that adjustment would also thresh more beans faster. But adjustments were always trade-offs. Now he'd have to watch for cracking. If he worked the beans too hard, some of them would split, damage that the elevator would dock him for.

"A man could make a million if he figured out how to get the beans the combine leaves behind," Tom would tell Clarence when they talked over harvesting. The header could knock beans out of their pods before the reel could sweep them in. Wind and rain could shatter them—put them down where the header couldn't reach them. Or they could shatter when the cutter bar cut them, beans flying up to pop against the combine windshield like BBs. Adjusting the header reel was crucial. Run it too fast and it hit the beanstalks like a hammer. Run it too slowly and it pushed beans down ahead. "You want it to just fall over onto the stalks and sweep them in," Tom had coached Sally and then Brett.

With beans there was none of the clunking noise in the combine that corn ears made. The sound of soybeans being harvested was smoother, like hay dragged across a barn floor, and the reel turned to a higher, lighter rhythm. Beans put up a cloud of trash into the air, though, mold and dust and the fine, choking hairs that grew on the plants that tickled the legs of deer and made them shy from walking through bean fields. Tom hadn't forgotten the years of open-air farming. He thanked his stars for enclosed cabs and their efficient filtering systems. The more ground you covered, the more exposure you had, and the big machines farmers operated today covered two or three times more ground than the machines his dad had used.

Tom worked on through the afternoon, starting up rabbits and mice, setting ground martins running in the rows of beans ahead of the combine. It took longer to fill a truck with beans than it had with corn. He unloaded the first truckload into the Landers bin. The second he decided to drive to Riverton, to Comstock's, to see what the dock was going to be.

On the way to Riverton, Tom noticed two dogs scavenging a four-point buck deer dead in the ditch at the side of the highway. It must have been hit by a truck. At the crest of the bluff leading down to Comstock's, a line of trucks waiting to dump at the other elevator there nearly blocked his way. He threaded through, inched down the steep bluff road with his engine racing as its compression braked the descent, crossed the railroad tracks and swung around to enter the unloading area from the east. There was a semi in front of him but no line. The unloader had tilted the whole truck up into the air. After it had emptied, the unloader lowered it back to the ground and a small, pretty woman came out of the scale room, climbed up into the cab like a cat into a barn loft and drove it away. Probably some farm wife helping her husband, Tom figured. He pulled his truck through the shed onto the scale.

A local boy he knew, a part-time farmer, was running the scale. "Y'all see that old dead buck by the side of the road back there by Swanson's orchard?" Tom asked him.

"Yeah," the scale man nodded.

"There's two old hound dogs chewing on him."

"You see any quail in the fields?" the scale man asked in turn.

"Not as many as other years," Tom told him.

"You hunt quail?"

"Never shot a quail. Shot a lot of coyotes." Bird hunters and animal hunters were a different breed.

After a pause, the scale man said, "You hear they changed the grain quality standards?"

"No, did they?"

"Yeah, went back to the old ones."

That was good news. "Wonder why they did that."

"Don't know."

Tom pursed his lips. "Usually when they got a man by the seeds they hang on."

The scale man gave Tom a wink and went to work. He didn't even bother checking Tom's beans for damage. He wrote in one percent foreign matter, which was standard. The beans tested at fifteen percent moisture. The elevator wanted thirteen percent, so that was a twenty-cent dock per bushel, not bad for a harvest plagued by rain. The load weighed in at 20,420 pounds, 340.33 bushels at 60 pounds to the bushel.

When Tom was growing up in the 1950s, before chemical fertilizers came into general use, Missouri farmers still grew soybeans to no better purposes than fodder for cattle and so-called "green manure," applications customary in the United States since the mid-1920s. The plant cooperated symbiotically with nitrogen-fixing bacteria that lived in nodules on its roots to enrich the soil.

Farmers cut it green for hay in those days or disked it green into their fields to add nitrogen to boost their yields of wheat and corn.

The soybean was a grain legume, a plant of small round beans that grew in pods that was domesticated at least thirteen thousand years ago in northeastern China. The Chinese counted the soybean one of their five sacred grains. Its beans contained as much as forty-five percent protein and twenty percent oil, making them a potentially highly nutritious source of human food. Amino-acid inhibitors in the raw beans interfered with human digestion, but the Chinese learned to counter their effect by fermentation and other processing. The cultivation of *Glycine max* spread to Korea and then to Japan before the birth of Christ.

A German botanist, Engelbert Kaempfer, who lived for two years in Japan, brought the soybean to Europe at the beginning of the eighteenth century. The Jardin des Plantes in Paris received seed soybeans from missionaries in 1739. Benjamin Franklin probably brought soybeans to the United States among the many seeds he collected, but the first recorded growing of the bean in the United States was in Philadelphia in 1804.

Only in the twentieth century did the soybean begin to catch on among American farmers. Between the 1950s and the 1980s American markets developed for its oil and, secondarily, for its protein. From about two million acres in 1924, the area of its planting increased to sixty-one million acres in 1986. Total production increased during the same period from 134,000 tons to 60 million

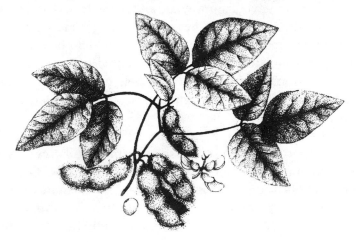

tons. In 1973 the soybean overtook wheat and corn to become the most important cash crop in the United States, the value of its production reaching a height of more than $14 billion in 1979, dropping to $9.3 billion in 1986 when prices were significantly lower. It accounted for about three-fourths of the U.S. production of vegetable oil, some 11.6 million pounds, two-thirds of which went into edible products such as salad oils, margarines and shortenings. The protein cake that remained after the oil was extracted, which farmers called soybean meal, became the principal source of protein for hogs and chickens. Tom wouldn't have a chicken on the place, but his hogs grew and thrived on corn enriched with soybean meal. Americans only slowly increased their intake of soybean products during the same period, preferring meat protein to vegetable. The Japanese enjoyed their miso and tofu, the Chinese their soy sauce and bean curd.

The market for soybeans seemed to be bottomless, and it was the one crop that Tom grew that he could plant unrestricted by government controls. He would have planted more, but keeping up his wheat and corn bases so that he could continue to participate in government programs took first priority since the return was guaranteed. Government programs skewed the marketplace, to the advantage of grain companies more than farmers. There was a glut of corn in the world. In an uncontrolled marketplace, farmers might have been better off planting more soybeans.

Sally had spelled Tom at the combine when he drove to Comstock's. Back at Landers', he took over combining again, hoping to deliver another truckload before the elevator closed at seven. By 6:30 he saw he wouldn't make it. He and Sally went ahead and moved the trucks and the grain wagon they were using to the next field farther south from the highway. They parked them in the lane, where Tom could dump on them over the fence. He was going to keep working through the evening. "Less than a month to have a hundred acres of wheat sown and all these beans combined," he told Sally before she left to fix supper. "If Mother Nature would just cooperate we could do it, but I don't think she's going to."

There was a harvest moon that night, rising at dusk big and

orange as a pumpkin. Tom finished up the first Landers field south of the Elms, dumped on the diesel truck and took off down a waterway for the next field. The header was too big for the gate. Tom had to pull up a fence post with his bare hands and fold back a section of wire fence to make room. He knew the field layout from planning and planting it and drove along the edge of its waterway midway to one side where rows came out at a diagonal. He opened up the field from there, glad for the little daylight still left in the west. He hated to open up a field in the dark. Once it was open he didn't mind night combining.

With the setting of the sun the beans began to toughen, dew infusing their stalks and making them less brittle, harder to cut and to crush. As they toughened, the beeper that warned Tom that the rotary had lost twenty percent of its RPMs would begin to screech at him, cautioning him to slow down or risk packing the combine throat tight. He settled in to keeping ahead of it.

After dark, the moon high, Tom noticed the Big Dipper marked out on the northern sky as clearly as on a star map. Night combining was slower, but it was also more peaceful, closed in by darkness in the quiet of the cab. He found himself reminiscing.

A high school classmate he hadn't seen in years had turned up one day a few months back. They'd gotten reacquainted. He seemed to be a good old boy. Tom and his brothers Dale and Warner had spent some time with him. He'd said his wife worked at Cook's Paint in Kansas City, and one day he'd offered to get them all the Cook's Paint seconds they could use for three dollars a gallon. The Bauer boys were always looking for a bargain. They'd talked it over for a while and decided that three dollars a gallon for paint was a good deal. Seconds would mean the color was off, but that didn't trouble them. It'd still be good enough to use around the farm.

The classmate said he had to have the money up front, so they each wrote him a check for seventy-five dollars. He also asked them not to write the reason for the check onto the little memo line in the lower left-hand corner. He took their checks and went off.

Tom thought over that memo-line request for about an hour. Then he saw the light. "Boys," he told his brothers, "we've been had."

They called the bank in Plymouth to stop the checks. The classmate had already cashed them. They jumped into Tom's pickup
and rolled into Plymouth, looked up the sheriff and told him
what'd happened. There wasn't much he could do, he said, but
he'd do what he could. Probably the guy had already hit the bars
and was drinking up their money.

That was a Friday. The sheriff put out an APB, but his deputies
didn't find the con artist until Saturday morning. By then he had
twenty-five dollars left in his wallet.

The sheriff threw him in jail and went to work on him. "When
you messed with the Bauers you done messed with the wrong
bunch of boys," he told him. "They're likely just to kill you if
they find you. I put you in jail for protective custody, to save your
ass."

"What can I do?" the con artist asked the sheriff, scared.

"If I was you I'd scrape up the money somewhere to pay them
boys back," the sheriff told him. "Pronto."

So the bastard got hold of an aunt who owned a restaurant and
talked her into loaning him the money. By then it was Sunday. He
sent the money through the sheriff to pay Tom and his brothers
back. After that the sheriff let him go. When he cleared the jail he
just lit out. They'd never seen him since. The sheriff said he was a
known con artist. He'd even conned a police officer in Sally's
hometown into paying him thirty dollars for a .38 special he
claimed he had.

The wrong bunch of boys. That was a good one. Hell, they
hadn't known. The joke was, they couldn't have done anything to
him if they had.

Tom chuckled at the memory. He reached down the two-way
and called home.

"Sally, do you copy?"

After a moment Sally answered. "Go ahead, Tom."

"You remember that Cook's paint I nearly bought you?"

"I remember," Sally said drily. "You still need to paint that
barn."

"You got my supper ready?"

"It's in the oven. I'm keeping it warm. How much longer you
think you'll be?"

"Beans are starting to get tough," Tom radioed. "I want to keep on a-going as long as I can. What time is it?"

"Eight o'clock."

"Maybe a couple more hours."

"Okay then. I'll see you when you come in."

"Not if I see you first, darlin'."

Sally decided not to dignify that response with an answer.

Well into another round, Tom heard a change in the rhythm of the header. "Sounds like a machine gun," he told himself. He opened the door and listened while he drove. From the location of the sound it was likely the Pittman system, the box of gears that drove the cutter bar. The Pittman took a lot of punishment.

Farther down the row, the cutter bar abruptly stopped cutting. Tom had to move fast to stop the combine before it tore up a bunch of beans.

He was running with lights now, six of them in front like the compound eye of a giant spider. He raised the header through the headlights and climbed down from the cab to see what was wrong. The cab had been warm. He hadn't realized the night air was so chilly.

The heavy, blackened steel bolt that attached the cutter bar to the Pittman arm had fallen out of its hole. He found it lying under the left end of the header. He found the washer next. He had to climb to the cab and back up the combine to find the nut. It was a special locknut. A jam nut that screwed down on top of it was supposed to hold it in place but the jam nut was gone. Without the jam nut, the locknut had worked loose in the terrible vibration of the cutter bar, the loosening allowing the noise to begin that had alerted Tom to the problem.

He tightened on the locknut and went back to combining. Rather than lose the locknut, he stopped at the end of each pass through the field to tighten it. That got old after a while. He tried locking it by gashing the bolt threads with a chisel and hammer. Another pass and he found the nut loose again. This time he drove over to Babe, which was parked outside the fence to give him transportation home, found a new jam nut and solved the problem.

But he'd no sooner fixed the cutter bar when the rotary started acting up. It refused to come up to full speed and gradually began slowing down. Tom had to slow his forward speed accordingly or risk packing the combine throat. He found himself combining more and more slowly until he was down to one mile per hour. The beans had toughened too much to combine anyway. He'd fix whatever the problem was in the morning. He raised the header, wheeled the big machine around under the star-filled sky, followed the waterway out to the fence and parked his ailing cornucopia for the night.

FOUR

First thing next morning, Tom hauled a truckload of the beans he'd combined the night before to Riverton and waited in line an hour to dump. Back at Landers', he decided to hold off hauling the second truckload until the line at Comstock's had time to thin. He went ahead and serviced the combine, greasing it up, refueling it with high-grade diesel from the tank behind Babe's cab, checking the cutter-bar bolt he'd had to repair. When he was through servicing, he started up the engine to see if the rotor was working again.

It wasn't. The toggle switch that speeded it up and slowed it down wouldn't move it more than 10 RPMs either way, from 140 to 130 and back. The toggle switch drove an electric motor that turned a chain that moved a gear in and out to control tension on the big pulley belts that delivered power to the rotor from the engine. Something was seriously wrong.

Tom climbed down from the cab and up to the engine platform and opened the engine well to access the electric motor. He slipped the chain free, returned to the cab and tried to run the motor again unloaded. He could tell it was working fine because it made a high-pitched whir on the auxiliary CB radio in the cab. He'd be better off if it wasn't—now he didn't know what was wrong.

He remounted the chain, shut down the combine, hiked to the loaded truck and drove off to deliver the rest of last night's beans, his mind chewing over all the problems he could think of that might be causing the rotor to drag. It made him restless. "Boy, these beans are a slow boat to China," he complained to a farmer waiting in line ahead of him at Comstock's. The morning was cool, dry and sunny again. Tom wasn't fooled. The six o'clock weather report had said showers at the beginning of next week. Serious rain could start again any day now and screw up the program. He needed to get his soybeans out to get his wheat in. He usually took his problems in stride, but he didn't like this one at all.

He cut short dinner. He and Wayne drove the GMC and one of the unloaded trucks over to Landers' before one o'clock to start combining beans. Tom had barely gotten rolling when the rotor completely stopped turning. Back on the engine platform with Wayne beside him, he opened the engine well and checked everything over. When he got to the two main drive pulleys, flanged steel castings big as manhole covers that the combine's diesel engine turned through industrial rubber drive belts, Tom found the bolts that held the lower of the two pulleys jammed against a slide plate. The pulley had slipped out of position upward on its shaft.

"Well, will you look at that," Tom said unhappily.

"Pretty disgusting," Wayne agreed.

Tom climbed down into the engine well and studied the pulley bolts. "Look here," he directed his son. "They're worn along one side. They've been creeping up on that shaft for a long time."

Wayne nodded. "Looks like it."

If the pulley was only loose, then moving it back into position and tightening its bolts tighter should solve the problem. Wayne fetched a long wrench from the combine toolbox and Tom loosened the nuts on the slide plate, hoping to slide it out of the way. It wouldn't budge. Tom retrieved the big railroad-scale wrench, the one he'd used to move the rotor when Sally had jammed it with dirt, and tried to turn the rotor shaft as a way of turning the pulley. That didn't work either. He tried loosening the big nut that held the rotor itself onto its shaft. Even that didn't free up the jam.

Tom decided he needed a crowbar to pry the pulley away from the slide plate. He wished he'd driven out in Babe with Babe's full assortment of tools. He and Wayne jumped into the GMC and headed for the house. From there Tom called Case and talked to a mechanic, who told him about four more bolts he'd have to loosen to move the pulley. He left the GMC and returned to the field in Babe.

But loosening the four bolts didn't do it, and removing them entirely in the hope of finding a big nut underneath that held the pulley on the shaft didn't do it either. What it did do was release the entire pulley assembly to slide on the shaft, slide plate and all, with the pulley bolts still jammed uselessly against the slide plate. "Well," Tom told Wayne, "I guess we go into Osage Station." If he'd had a parts book, with all its exploded views of combine subassemblies, he probably could have figured out the problem without the trip, but only dealers had parts books.

Back in the big concrete bay at Case, Tom and the mechanic climbed up onto a combine the man was fixing and Tom showed him the problem. It was worse than Tom had thought. The mechanic guessed that the splines on the shaft that held the pulley in place might have sheared, locking up the assembly. That would be a major repair, hours just to get the pulleys and belts and shafts out of the engine well, more hours in the shop at Case.

"Damn it to hell," Tom swore driving back to Landers', "I'm going to be down for days." What worried him most was that it was Friday. Mechanics didn't work on Sunday and rarely on Saturday. He'd like to be back in the field by Sunday at the latest. He'd have to move fast to get in under the wire.

"It's the pits, Dad," Wayne sympathized. He was nervous enough about the breakdown to do a Donald Duck imitation. "Oh, boy," he quacked. His dad gave him a glare and he cut it out.

Taking the back road from Osage Station that would bring them out on 24 near Landers, they passed the missile silo. Tom was staring ahead and didn't notice. He was thinking about whether he should move the combine to the workshop or work on it in the field. Assuming it didn't rain, the test was whether he needed electricity or not. He decided he didn't. He wouldn't be cutting or drilling or welding, just trying to disassemble something that didn't seem to want to come apart.

He caught himself pulling a long face and remembered one of his dad's sayings. He passed it on to Wayne. "Your granddad used to say that machines don't break down when they're sitting in the shed. I guess we'll just have to go to work and get things fixed. I sure wish we'd had this when we was sitting around waiting for the rain to quit, though."

"Huh," Wayne agreed. "So do I."

They worked through the afternoon to extract the pulley assembly from the combine. It was attached in a dozen places, some of them around behind and under shafts and chains black with thick grease and hard to get at. They had nuts to unscrew that needed loosening first with penetrating oil and pulley belts that had to be released and then disconnected. They skinned knuckles, pinched fingers and smeared their blue jeans thick with grease, but finally the assembly was free.

It weighed close to two hundred pounds. Wayne didn't see how they were going to lift it out of the engine well. "We about need that portable shop hoist, don't we, Dad?"

"We could of," Tom told him, "but I think we can manage it between us. Jump down and fetch my lariat, son."

Wayne retrieved the lariat from one of Babe's compartments. Tom used it once in a blue moon to rope a cow or a calf. He slipped one end of the lariat around the pulley shaft, threaded it through its iron-sleeved eye and pulled it tight. He slipped the other end around the shaft on the other side, drew the rope down to a loop big enough to serve as a double handle and tied it into place. Then he braced himself on the engine platform and took up the loop. Down in the engine well, his feet set on narrow ledges, Wayne gripped the shaft.

"Ready?" Tom asked.

"Ready."

"*Lift*," Tom started them off. He strained his back and arms. Metal ground and the assembly shifted and began to move. Wayne lifted from below until the two of them had the assembly up to his chest level and then turned his hands so that he was pushing instead of pulling. Tom was holding most of the weight. The strain showed. His legs shook. His face was getting red and the knuckles were white on his hands. As the assembly came up out of the engine well, he had to move back to make room to set it down, and he staggered a little. Wayne felt the extra weight and pushed. The

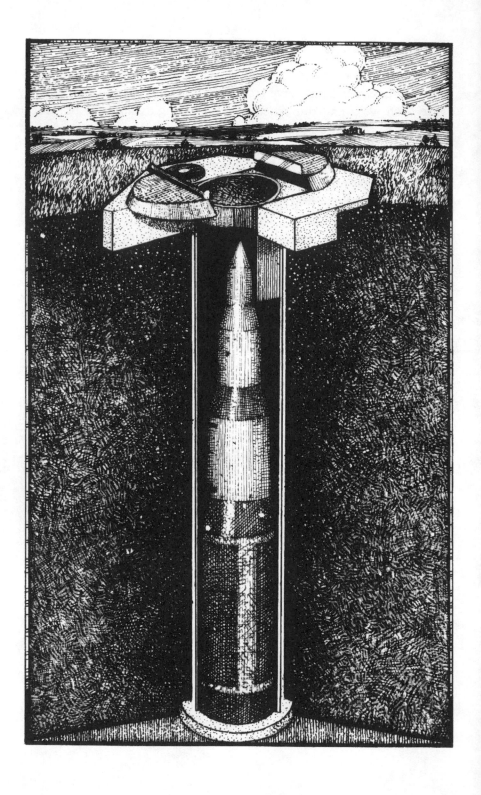

heavy assembly cleared the edge of the well. Tom lowered it down hard on the platform. Then father and son grinned, panting from the strain. "All *right*," Wayne cheered.

When they'd caught their breath they duck-walked the assembly over to the edge of the platform. It looked like two railroad wheels on a short shaft dangling with chains and plates. Tom winced to see it stripping curls of red enamel off his beautiful combine as they turned it, exposing the bare sheet metal underneath. A little spray paint would touch the scratches up, though. Wayne climbed down and backed Babe directly under. Tom redid his lariat. With Wayne up on the platform again they lowered the assembly onto the truck bed with the rope.

From the house Tom called Case in Osage Station and learned that they couldn't work on his problem until the combine they already had in the shop was fixed. That decided him to take his problem all the way to Franklin to the other Case dealer there.

He worked with a young Case mechanic in Franklin until seven o'clock that night trying to figure out what was wrong. They finally tracked the problem to a missing spacing collar. It was supposed to space the two pulleys apart on the pulley shaft. The original part was missing. It'd never been installed at the factory when the combine was manufactured, way back in 1979. None of the Franklin mechanics had ever even worked on that particular subassembly because when the thing was put together right at the factory it was trouble-free. Without a spacing collar, the back pulley had wobbled on the shaft until it was galled up. That's why it'd jammed. They'd have to replace both pulleys and the shaft as well. It looked as if the whole repair job would cost more than two thousand dollars.

The kid brought the assembly back out on Saturday. He was embarrassed to admit he didn't know how to install it. Tom guided him through. They didn't use the lariat this time. Tom kept a tractor mounted with a manure loader at the Elms to use cleaning out the cattle sheds. He drove the tractor over and lifted the pulley assembly up to the engine platform with the manure scoop. They lowered it in by hand.

Tom picked beans late that night, until they toughened up along about nine thirty. He came out again on Sunday only to find the combine's alternator shot. That was another damned delay, another hundred dollars in repairs, but he got it fixed too and went back to combining.

Donald Landers stopped by on Sunday afternoon to see how things were going. He didn't know about the repair problems. Usually Tom was courteous, but today he was blunt. "Donald," he told his landlord, "I haven't combined any beans for two days and I ain't got no time to talk." Landers backed off. Tom worked late again Sunday night and got a grain wagon loaded besides the two trucks. He was combining again, but what a lot of damned trouble it'd been. And with another owner before him on the combine and the warranty long since expired, he sure as hell wasn't going to see any money back from Case.

Monday morning, no sign of those showers, leaves blowing and the sky blue with scattered clouds, Tom unloaded the grain wagon into one of the Landers bins, serviced the combine and drove down to a bottomland field in Babe to see how wet it was. Too wet, he decided, and decided he'd have to combine on the hills that week. Crowds of deer tracks in the cornfield he passed on the way down and back made him smile.

He picked up Sally at the house then, switched to the GMC and drove over to the Ward farm upland, where the big Oliver tractor and disk were parked in the shed. The tractor needed readying to disk the fields where he planned to sow wheat. Sally followed him home in the GMC with her emergency lights flashing.

He worked through the morning servicing the tractor and the disk and came in for dinner at noon. Sally had cooked ham and beans for him even though she was allergic to beans herself and couldn't eat them. They made her face and hands puff up and her throat swell shut. She was playing with a diet anyway and had a salad instead. They bowed their heads and said a blessing. There was iced tea and bread and Tom as usual got out the jelly.

"You know we only averaged $5.02 for those Chernobyl beans," Sally told him when they'd started to eat.

Tom was surprised. "The hell you say." By now he'd delivered the three thousand bushels he'd contracted for in full to Comstock's.

"Was you gigged for any damage?" Sally asked him.

Tom shook his head warily. "I didn't see any dock on the ticket." Suspicion of the grain boys was in his blood and he was always ready to believe the elevator had cheated him.

So was Sally. "Well, let's go over it." She got out the computer sheets she'd been given when she'd picked up the checks and they compared them side by side with the scale receipts. They'd been docked for excess moisture. There were taxes paid. The extra deduction seemed to be a soybean checkoff, a few pennies per bushel Tom had agreed to donate to the American Soybean Association to promote soybean sales. "Did you remember that?" Sally asked him. "I didn't know about it."

"I forgot to tell you, hon," Tom apologized. "I plumb forgot about it myself, as far as that goes." They'd received a little more than fifteen thousand dollars for their three thousand bushels of beans, still a deal better than the current market.

After dinner, Tom got moving. He drove Sally to one of Landers' bean fields, opened up the field and left her combining. Back at the house he called the MFA co-op in Osage Station and asked the manager for a price on fertilizer. It was down, the manager told him, from twenty-three dollars to eighteen.

"That's the first damn thing that's been down this year," Tom said with pleasure, the memory of two thousand dollars' worth of pulleys still fresh in his mind. He asked the manager to spread a load of liquid fertilizer that afternoon. The man said they couldn't do liquid but they could do dry. Dry was okay, Tom agreed. He told them to spread enough for thirty-three acres on the field south of the red house at the Landers place. The red house was the house that Landerses rented to the old couple from town. "We're going to disk in behind you," he cautioned, "so if you don't get the whole field, be sure to let me know where you stop so we don't overdisk."

The odd number, thirty-three acres, came from a visit Tom had made a few weeks previously to the ASCS office in Osage Station to find out what his wheat base would be, the amount of wheat the government would let him grow and still qualify for the various grain programs. Since his wheat base was determined by the acreages he'd planted to grain in the previous three years, it changed every year. This year the numbers were complicated worse than usual because the year before had been a bad year when a lot of farmers, Tom included, hadn't even gotten their wheat planted. The base calculation took that disaster into account. There were new rules as well. The result was a slightly smaller base, about a hundred acres in all. Tom had filled out all the necessary forms with the help of one of the women in the office, a cheery redhead whose husband was a farmer. The forty-acre field he was about to plant had a seven-acre set-aside, land he was required to leave fallow. The government took aerial photographs across the county on a regular schedule to check. You had to fallow land in the same field with the land you planted, too. Otherwise everyone would have fallowed the worst patches of ground and planted the better land. As it was, he planned to fallow the steepest seven acres in the field, down at the far end from the red house. No law against that.

Next Tom called MFA in Osage Station for his Hybrix wheat. The twenty bags of the new hybrid seed he'd ordered were in. He needed another twenty and he ordered Calwell Certified to fill out his supply.

He still had work on the tractor and disk. For added traction pulling the heavy disk, the tractor needed a second set of tires attached to its big main tires that extended out from under the cab. Tom had to run the tractor up on blocks to install the big duals. Each one was eighteen inches wide and five feet high and weighed, with its rim, about four hundred pounds. He rolled them out of the shed one at a time, careful to keep them upright, and strained to brace them in position next to the inner tires while he hooked clamp brackets over their rims to hold them.

During the morning he'd noticed that the frame on his disk was cracked in two places. He set up his arc welder and welded the fatigue cracks solid again. In better times he'd have replaced the old disk by now. Now he was making do.

By midafternoon he was disking, cutting the soybean waste and the pellets of fertilizer the MFA truck had spread into the rich brown soil of the Landers field that started across the gravel work area from the grain bins and ran south to the big Landers pasture where the cows and calves and two bulls grazed. The disk was hydraulically mounted behind the tractor and controlled by levers inside the cab. It was twice as wide as the tractor. For road travel it ran on two rubber-tired wheels with its wing sections folded up and in like the wings of the old carrier-based Navy fighter planes in the Second World War. In the field, Tom pulled the steel pins that held the wings safely upright, lowered the wings hydraulically and dropped the seventy-two disks to the ground by raising the wheels. He'd make a pass across a field following the contour, dust drifting up behind, and then with a single lever at the end of each pass he'd raise the disks a foot off the ground and spin through a quick turn, braking one set of tractor wheels to keep the turn tight, then drop the machine again into cutting position as he came back into line. He disked from terrace to terrace, cutting the crop waste into two-inch pieces that would rot during the winter and release their store of nutrients, turning the fertilizer three or four inches under where it would wait for the wheat roots to arrive, leaving behind at each pass a wide swath of well-worked earth.

On toward dusk, Sally brought out a supper of ham-and-cheese sandwiches and Pepsis. She arranged the meal on the tailgate of the GMC. She'd brought along a can of Cutter insect repellent. They needed it. The mosquitoes were still around, a cloud of them, large and hungry. Tom went back to disking and Sally to combining under a sunset of gold and red, blue darkening westward into purple, the wide sky over their cultivated prairie pretty as a stained-glass window.

When Wayne arrived home from college at eight o'clock Tuesday morning to help, Tom had already driven in to Osage Station and picked up his wheat seed. Father and son hauled the grain drill out from the shed where it was stored on the Landers place, across from the grain bins, and worked together to clean it up. It was two-wheeled, an eighteen-hole planter with a long tongue that attached to the tractor drawbar. It had wooden boxes across its width that fed seeds into elaborately geared counters that spaced them down tubes that spit them out into eighteen parallel furrows opened by a row of small steel disks. A set of wheels lined up behind the tubes closed the furrows over the seeds and lightly tamped them. The gears clicked like clockworks whenever the grain drill was moved. Compared to the big disks and chisel plows

Tom usually hauled, it was a precision instrument, planting each seed carefully spaced at exactly the right depth.

They'd driven out a smaller tractor with an open seat to pull it. Wayne would do the planting and he needed all the visibility he could get, but Tom preferred the open seat himself for planting even with his keen eyes. The trick with wheat was to make sure you didn't leave any rabbit paths. That's what his dad had called them, little bare strips where the outside planter rows hadn't been matched up right from one pass to the next. Come spring and they'd grow up in weeds. You could see them a mile away. Weed seed in wheat was always a bad dock at the elevator. A rabbit path usually showed where someone forgot to overlap the planter's wheel tracks. His dad had a saying to remind you of that. "That wheel don't sow," he'd warn Tom every time they planted. His other saying about planting almost didn't fit this wet fall. "Sow wheat in the dust," it went, "oats in the mud." The ground on the upland field Tom had been disking was just about right. Oats were for horses, so they didn't grow oats anymore.

When the drill was ready, Tom backed the GMC up next to it, dropped the tailgate, found the strings at one end of the top stitching of the nearest brown paper bag of Hybrix and ripped them away. The Hybrix bag had a fancy bronze wheat head printed across the front along with the guaranteed analysis information, but when Tom hoisted it and began pouring the seed into the planter box he was horrified at what he saw. The seed was dyed

pink as he'd expected, for fungus control, but it was also withered and shriveled-looking and he thought he saw a lot of rye and weed seed mixed in.

He stopped pouring and set the bag upright on the ground. "By God," he swore to Wayne, "will you just look at that. What the hell kind of goddamned seed we got here?" Wayne took a handful and studied it up close and shook his head.

They talked it over. Tom had been wary of this new seed all along. Now he saw he had reason. He'd wanted to get an early start that morning. It made him damned mad. "They figure they can pawn that crap off on some old sleeping farmer out here," he told Wayne angrily.

He closed the tailgate on the GMC and raced home to call about the seed. He called from the workshop, standing in the open shed next to the phone on the wall. The manager wasn't in and he got put on hold long enough that he finally hung up in disgust. Pete, his feed salesman, arrived and heard the story. He started to commiserate, but Tom didn't have time to shoot the bull. He flung "a thousand pounds of cubes" over his shoulder at Pete and raced on. As he turned off 24 into the lane that led back to the Landers bins, Wayne raised him on the radio to ask him if he wanted the fertilizer man to start. MFA hadn't finished fertilizing the field the afternoon before and was out this morning with a second load.

"I'm up here at the road," Tom answered. "Tell him to wait." Maybe the driver had seen hybrid wheat seed and knew something about it.

Johnny, the driver, was a stocky redhead. He stood on the planter's wooden running board, dug out a handful of the hybrid seed and looked it over. "Tom," he said then, "I think it's supposed to look that way."

"It's sure sorry-looking," Tom snapped. "I think that's that blight hit all that Missouri wheat last year."

"I'd swear this isn't last year's seed, Tom," Johnny defended his outfit. "Nobody planted any last year. I'm pretty sure they retested and recertified it. I think it's supposed to look like that."

Sally came onto the GMC radio and got into the act. She suggested calling the MFA manager from the phone in the rental house. Tom remembered instead that the fertilizer truck had a radio. He marched Johnny over to the cab of the big white truck and had him get the manager on the radio. After Tom read the man the riot act, the manager's voice came crackling back swearing that the new seed was okay, it was supposed to look the way it looked, it was presprouted and that was why it looked withered, the weed count was accurate and low, he'd seen hybrid seed before and Tom should trust him that it was okay.

Tom was suspicious, but he'd planted a hybrid corn once that looked bad that made a good crop. Hybrix came from a German company with a good reputation. He decided he'd take a chance and go ahead and sow the strange stuff. It came with a guarantee. If it didn't germinate, MFA could eat it. He made sure Johnny had loaded some extra fertilizer to compensate for a four-acre shortfall yesterday. Then he strode over to the wheat drill, threw back the lids and dumped bag after bag of withered pink seed wheat into the bins, seed that was supposed to yield him a hundred bushels to the acre if the weather was right.

The rest of the day was a three-ring circus. The MFA truck spread a forty-foot swath of red and white pelletized fertilizer. Tom came along behind, disking a twenty-foot swath. Wayne followed farther behind with the planter, working a ten-foot swath crosswise, sowing wheat and straining to see. Tom had opened up the field for his son first, planting the edges where it was hard to navigate. Sally was combining, and he went off at one point to open up a new field for her. Other times he unloaded beans into the big auger and up into the northernmost Landers bin.

In the afternoon, after Sammi's school, needing another hand, he picked up his daughter and had her drive the GMC as part of a general move of vehicles up from the wheat field to where Sally was combining beans, Sammi peeking out from under the steering wheel and inching along in low gear. Brett arrived from football practice and saw his little sister driving the pickup and imitated a terrified crowd, clowning. Then he jumped in and rode alongside her to back her up. When the pickup approached the gate into the bean field, Sally called on the two-way for Sammi to drive on through and Brett threw his hands over his head and surrendered. Brett was feeling good. He'd heard that day that he'd been chosen to be a People to People student ambassador on a trip next summer to New Zealand and Australia. He'd never thought he'd be picked. Wayne had gone to Europe two years before. "I'll never get it," Brett had told his dad. "I'm too dumb." And here the invitation was in the day's mail.

Wayne had a long day, but he finished the wheat field well before sunset. He made damned sure there weren't any rabbit paths.

FIVE

Sally went off that weekend to the ceramics show she'd been working so long to get ready for. Sammi got to go too. Sally's brother, Cary, had rented a delivery truck and she'd packed its shelves with the bisque they'd molded and fired in the past months. At the store they sold only greenware. Greenware was too fragile to transport to Kansas City, so they took fired pieces to the show. Sally had wrapped each piece carefully in newspaper.

They drove in to the convention center at a hotel in northeastern Kansas City, near Worlds of Fun, and parked behind the center in the sale lot with trucks loaded with molded ceramics from all over the United States. This was the big annual show, with classes and seminars and hobby competitions as well as exhibits. It was strictly wholesale. There were ninety-four exhibitors that year from as far away as Texas, Ohio, California, Louisiana and Florida. "By producing a ceramic show," the show catalogue said, "we hope to introduce the art to more people—young and old, men and women—to show how satisfying it is to make many beautiful things in ceramics and to learn a gratifying hobby."

A lot of people who got into the ceramics business were former hobbyists who thought they'd make a killing. Sally had seen that kind come and go. Cary had been a hobbyist when he'd started out, but he was in the business to stay. It was a sideline for him.

He was a barber by trade. He went to the show for connections with other businesses and to see what the trends were in molds. The money was in the molding.

They had a double booth on the east side of the hall. A lot of exhibitors who were selling bisque just displayed the plain bisque in their booths. Cary displayed glazed, finished pieces. That whetted the buyers' appetites. The year before, when he'd exhibited for the first time, he'd had the only bisque booth in the show. Now there were more. Normally, Cary favored animal pieces, but since the holiday season was coming up, he and Sally had put together an exhibit mostly of Halloween and Christmas items. They had ghosts and scarecrows and pumpkins, Santas and angels and Christmas trees. Some of the pieces were lighted. The trees had flashing lights and little electronic units in their bases that played carols and some of them were even scented with pine or cinnamon. Cary used a special clay that turned pure white when it was fired. It cost a little more, but it made his stuff popular. He sold slip made with California talc. He had a black business card with white lettering. It listed his store hours as "open when we're here, closed when we're gone."

You could see everything at a ceramics show. There were Indian booths and porcelain-doll booths, booths with figurines and families and clocks and steins. Skulls with spiders on top catered to the teenage market. Goose and duck items were popular. Cows were supposed to take over from geese this year, but they hadn't. Geese turned up on tablecloths and afghans, window appliqués, pencil erasers, ashtrays and all kinds of dishes, appliance covers and aprons as well as ceramics. Sally swore if she saw one more goose stuck around anywhere she was going to throw up.

Sally and Sammi ran Cary's exhibit. People studied the finished pieces set up around the booth. If they bought the bisque versions, Sally or Sammi ran the ticket out to the truck to Cary. Business was so brisk he was stuck in the truck most of the weekend. If the buyer only wanted a piece or two, they'd bring it back in to the exhibit. More usually, they'd send the buyer around in his car or truck to pick up his order from Cary. Cary never knew where anything was. He'd send in to Sally to ask where she'd put such-and-such a piece. Sammi got tired of running back and forth and

had her mother do a diagram. Before long she was advising Cary on what was where.

Sally enjoyed ceramics, but she wasn't crazy about them. She liked to keep busy and it was something to do. She'd started helping out her brother after she'd come home from the job with the gas company in Plymouth. She loved porcelain dolls, though. Maybe it was because she'd never played with dolls when she was a girl. She'd made a doll to represent each of her children, Wayne, Brett and Sammi. They were eighteen inches tall, carefully painted, and she'd sewn the suits and party dress that clothed them. Porcelain dolls were expensive. It cost about sixty dollars to make one, but they sold for three hundred.

The ceramics show was fun. You got to meet people.

Molly was pregnant. Nobody could figure out how she'd gotten that way. She'd been a skinny little thing and now she'd started rounding out in the belly. She wasn't more than nine or ten months old. She shouldn't even have come into heat yet but there wasn't any doubt she had. There'd been a couple of stray males around the neighborhood. One of them must have done the deed. Sammi was excited about the prospect of puppies but Tom didn't like it. He hadn't even decided if he wanted to keep the little female. He was waiting to see if she was going to grow any more. She'd been the runt of the litter and she was still a runt. She was a sweet little dog but he didn't think much of runts in general. He'd wait and see about the puppies. He doubted if they'd keep them. He didn't plan to pay out good money to feed a bunch of Heinz 57 dogs and there wasn't any place to dump them. The country was the end of the line. City people dumped puppies and kittens out on the road all the time. Why they thought farmers could afford to feed them, Tom and Sally never understood. Tom would probably have to thump Molly's puppies and he didn't much like that either.

Brett was starting to pull up his socks in school. Vocabulary was one subject where studying harder could make a difference and Sally checked to make sure Brett brought home his word lists and studied them every night. She made him look up each word in the dictionary even though the English teacher had given them a list of synonyms. Sometimes the synonyms looked off base to her and sometimes she thought they were at least as hard for Brett as the word itself. She didn't think defining "exuberance" as "exhilaration" helped much. "Conjure" didn't seem much like "charm" to her and "atrocious" didn't seem much like "devilish" or "outrageous." Using the dictionary gave Brett that much more exposure to the word, whatever it was, which never hurt.

The test was on a Friday and Brett felt he aced it. That same Friday a friend of his who got tired of hearing him say he was dumb told him he wasn't dumb, he was twenty-fourth in a class of ninety-six. Brett didn't believe him. The friend took Brett into the counselor's office and showed him the ranking list. Then, Friday night, the football coach put in the B team in the last quarter of a game Plymouth was winning and the plays came Brett's way and he made three tackles. When he got home that night he took his time getting to the shower so his dad would notice how muddy he was. Tom could see that Brett was feeling good about himself.

Monday Brett found out he'd gotten an A on his vocabulary test. It was a good lesson. It proved to him that he could do as well as his brother and sister if he'd just work at it.

Brett had posters up on the walls of his basement bedroom of Hulk Hogan, the big bleached-blond professional wrestler with the pirate mustache. When Brett had to write an essay for school about someone he considered a hero, he chose Hulk Hogan. His dad thought that was pretty funny and pinned him down for a reason. Brett squinted to show he'd thought it over and to put a little spin on his answer. "He's different," he told his dad. "He's got a style of his own. It sets him off from the crowd. It takes guts to go your own way. That's why I like him."

Sally wasn't surprised Brett admired Hulk Hogan. It seemed to her that her son had always gone his own way himself. When he was six, she took him with her one time to visit her brother's kids. Brett watched his teenage cousins swing on a rope out over a forty-foot ravine. He swung once on his own, the same way they did. The second time, he deliberately let go and fell all the way to the bottom of the ravine. Sally was pregnant with Sammi but she climbed down to fetch him. He had a cut above one eye where a branch had scraped him. But the worst part was, he didn't say a word. Sally was nearly panicked. She was afraid he'd had a concussion. She carried him out, talking to him all the while and getting no response, and rushed him to the hospital. Eventually Tom showed up. Brett was on a table in the emergency room, silent as a stone. Tom leaned over him to check him out. Right away he opened his eyes and looked up at his dad. "Dad, I ain't no Tarzan," he told him. Sally just about died. Six years old. To this day she was convinced Brett had been calmly watching her panic. Then and now he seemed to stand back cool and amused and study adults making fools of themselves.

Tom drove into Osage Station one evening to attend a meeting of the Crevecoeur County ASCS committee. The conference room was in the back of the ASCS office, through the open pool area where all the new computer terminals stood silent. When Tom arrived it was crowded with farmers with weathered red cheeks and white foreheads. A lot of them, Tom included, looked older with their seed caps off because their baldness showed. The younger men had dressed up a little in trim new jeans and Western shirts with pearl snap buttons. Tom didn't especially favor Western shirts. He'd put on a new button-down cotton tattersall and dress jeans, his arms as always a little long for the shirtsleeves even in the big-man sizes Sally tracked down for him at specialty stores in Kansas City.

FARM   221

Rowland Howell, the ASCS director, started out explaining the new rotating election system for ASCS committee members. It was designed to make sure there was continuity on the committee from year to year by only electing committee members each year from two of the eight townships in Crevecoeur County. That meant some members would be facing election right away and some others would stay in office the full three-year term. Each township elected three members and two alternates, so there were twenty-four people in all on the Crevecoeur County ASCS committee and another sixteen backing them up.

Not many Americans knew the names of their townships any more. Farmers did. The township system was old. Townships were geographical divisions of counties, marked out in the original land surveys authorized by the Congress of the Confederation Ordinance of 1785 and usually made up of thirty-six sections of land, which was thirty-six square miles. Crevecoeur County was divided into Revolution, Plymouth, Seward, Devon, Smith, Vin-a-ton, Murray and Jefferson townships. The Plymouth and Devon names showed where the first towns in the county had been. The original surveyors who laid out the county chose the other names, based on local preference or just fancy. Townships weren't exactly political divisions, but when the constituency was farmers it made sense to use townships as political units, because farmers were pretty well spread out across the land. Anyway, land was what they had to do with.

Rowland had a new federal program to explain, Sodbuster. It was about as complicated as the rest of them. The ASCS director, who was lanky and loose-jointed, liked to talk and had a good sense of humor. Those were real talents when it came to explaining a government program. "Not in a row crop or wheat between 1981 and last year as of the twenty-third of December, that's the definition of sod," he told them. "If a farmer has plowed out sod, anything plowed out after that December date is plowing sod according to this new act.

"You come in and tell me you did that," Rowland went on, "and I'll say, '*Stop.*' I can't do anything for you in this office until I've looked over that field you plowed and made an erodibility decision." "Erodibility" meant the land's potential for soil erosion.

The federal Soil Conservation Service, the SCS, next door north of Rowland's operation, was responsible for erosion control. "If SCS decides that's erodible land you plowed out, then you're going to have to seed it back or put it in terraces and waterways before any farm you own or have an interest in can have anything done for you at all in this office."

Rowland looked over the crowd. Everyone was listening. He was telling them that plowing up former pasture to plant grain without government authorization would result in expulsion from all the government loan and price-support programs on which they depended to make a living. "Now, the really spooky thing here," he went on, "is that by this definition, alfalfa is sod." Alfalfa was a legume crop, planted with a drill like wheat, that dairy farmers grew for hay. "My advice to you is, don't bust any sod. You can see that sign-up for our programs here is going to be like a snail. We can do a hundred farms a day here, but Johnny over in the SCS office can't make a hundred erodibility decisions in a day."

"A lot of us have already busted sod, Rowland," someone complained.

The ASCS director nodded. "I know that. If it's terraced I think you have a good chance of getting passed. I see a real conflict developing between wheat bases and Sodbuster. The godfathers on the Potomac haven't looked that far ahead, but I do. Johnny tells me that most slopes of four degrees or greater are going to fall into this program."

"Hell," someone said, "that's just about all the land in Creve-coeur County except the Lundbeck Bottoms."

"Yep. You got to jump through Sodbuster hoops in order to get your payments."

"What about those checks they said we was to get paid by the middle of November?" someone else asked.

"Horse's stuff," Rowland scoffed. "That's just because there's a congressional election going on. No way on earth we can get those checks out by then." He turned back to explaining Sodbuster. "The erosion on Sodbuster fields has to be under control by 1990."

"It's about ten years too late," an older farmer said.

"I know it. Old Earl Butz, old Tricky Dicky's secretary of agribusine-culture, told you all to plow from fencerow to fencerow and now here they come telling you you can't bust sod without putting in a hell of a lot of conservation improvements. I will say this, though, Crevecoeur County is way ahead on this because of past conservation efforts. We led the whole country in terracing until a couple of years ago."

Tom spoke up. He had his chair leaned back against the door frame. "You're not anticipating any trouble with all this, are you, Rowland? It's just the paperwork, isn't it?"

The ASCS director nodded. He'd wanted to make that point. "That's right, Tom. We're not going to fight you over it. Our policy is to bring you into compliance—to help you into compliance."

He went on to talk about hidden corn and hidden beans, deficiency payments and set-asides, preventive planning and paid diversions. Most of the farmers followed him. Washington, he told them, sent him ninety thick three-ring notebooks a year full of interpretations of farm program rules. One rule alone had 1,004 changes in one year. He studied them day and night, trying to distill out what Crevecoeur County farmers needed to know.

"You take the wheat program," he said. "There's a hook here. It's called cross-compliance. You can't plant over your base on any grain—*any* grain at all—or you're out of the program. So you think, sure, I'm in compliance on corn, I'm in compliance on wheat. But you plant three acres of oats to bale some straw for old Dobbin. Not to sell. Just to bed down that old swayback you keep for the grandkids to ride when they come out from the city to visit. Well, you just lost it. Plant three acres of oats without an oats base and you lose *all* your bases—your hundred acres of wheat, your two hundred acres of corn.

"But here's something weirder. If you've got a wheat base and you don't plant it in wheat, then by the new rules you're allowed to plant your wheat base in corn. That's wheat corn and it's perfectly legal."

"They shouldn't allow that," Tom spoke up, farmers around him nodding agreement. "They're supposed to be trying to reduce the surplus. That just increases it."

"I know it, Tom," Rowland said. "I'd like to take those guys on the Potomac and shake them."

"And baling oats," someone else said. During the bad drought in the South the previous summer, the government had relaxed its restriction on putting up hay from set-aside land that some farmers had planted to oats. "How come they allowed that? Cattlemen complain?"

"I think so," Rowland said. "Southern farmers saw a good thing."

"They *want* us to grow too much," a wiry younger man said, rehearsing an old grievance among farmers. "The city people want to know there's plenty around."

Rowland Howell was an outspoken Democrat who'd never have kept his job in a Republican era if Washington made county-level ASCS appointments. He and Tom had sat in his office more than once chewing over the farm problem and the future. Rowland had told Tom it looked to him as if the Reagan administration and Congress wanted to reduce the number of farmers. What with bank foreclosures and natural attrition, he expected to have twenty-five percent fewer farmers to deal with a few years down the road. He thought fifty-fifty share arrangements with landlords would probably change, too, to get farmers a larger share with machinery and input costs going up. They already had in areas like northern Missouri where the soil wasn't as good and the farmers had been harder hit. More farmers would go part-time, he thought. Federal loan guarantees were scheduled to decline, which meant bankers who counted on those guarantees to justify making operating loans to farmers were going to tighten down the screws. That was going to drive men out of business who had to borrow money to operate. Consolidation was coming, he predicted.

"I don't see how I can farm any more land than I do," Tom had told him. "Hell, I have to run day and night just to keep up with what I've got."

"The big are going to have to get bigger, Tom," Rowland had said. "The small guy just isn't going to be able to make it anymore. But I think the final answer has to be production quotas. I think we're going to have to forget about feeding the world. Let farmers grow as much as they want but only allow them to sell so much. It's not politically palatable, but it's the only answer. If the farm program keeps on being based on acreage controls, all you farmers will just keep on improving efficiency, keep on boosting yields."

One way or another, the government had always been involved in farming. Back in the earliest years of the republic, national leaders bent on raising revenue had debated whether to sell the public lands in large tracts for cash or in small parcels on credit. The speculators had beaten out the settlers. The Ordinance of 1785 had authorized minimum lots for sale of 640 acres, one square mile, at a minimum price of one dollar per acre, cash money. Gradually and grudgingly, Congress had lowered the minimums across a hundred years and some six major land acts. By 1862, the Homestead Act had offered homesteads of up to 160 acres free to American citizens willing to settle and improve them. For that and other reasons, land in farms more than doubled between 1870 and 1900.

With improving technology, total farm output increased by 135 percent during the same period. But the American population grew less than half that fast, and exports expanded too slowly to carry away the surplus. The difference between supply and demand marked the beginning of the "farm problem," which then as now was the same problem, overproduction in relation to available markets. Farm prices declined, farm income declined and farmers had trouble paying off loans for land and machinery, trouble their great-grandsons would face again in the Reagan years.

Prosperity came along in the decade before the First World War. Prices were particularly high and stable during the golden years 1910 to 1914. In the second half of the decade, American grain fed a Europe at war, American mules hauled French and British artillery and prices climbed even higher. By 1920 they had more than doubled their 1916 level. Farmers moved during the war years to buy land to cash in on the boom, bidding land prices up by sixty percent. After the war ended, in the 1920s, farm prices dropped again by almost one-half. Thousands of farmers who couldn't meet their mortgages went bankrupt in the 1920s while the rest of the country seemed to be enjoying unbridled prosperity.

They turned to the government for relief. At a national conference called by the secretary of agriculture, two businessmen connected with the Moline Plow Company of Moline, Indiana, came up with a plan they called Equality for Agriculture. It was based on the notion of parity, which they defined as "a fair exchange value for all farm products with that of all other commodities." The idea was that farmers should earn an income equivalent to what factory workers earned, an early twentieth-century version of comparable worth. In practice, parity came to mean a package of benefits that would help a farmer earn purchasing power equivalent to the purchasing power he'd enjoyed in the golden years 1910 to 1914.

Farmers liked the idea of parity, but Equality for Agriculture didn't fly. Congress considered and sometimes passed six different versions of the plan during the later 1920s. Calvin Coolidge and then Herbert Hoover, both champions of laissez faire, promptly vetoed every parity bill that reached their desks.

Between 1929 and 1933, the Great Depression added its burden to the problems of agriculture. Durable goods production in the United States declined by eighty percent and unemployment in the cities rose above twenty-five percent. During the same period, net farm income declined by more than fifty percent and another rash of farm bankruptcies and foreclosures followed. At the bottom of the Depression, in the whirlwind first one hundred days of the new administration of Franklin Roosevelt, Congress passed the first farm bill, the Agricultural Adjustment Act of 1933. Many of the AAA's historic approaches would survive through the next five decades of farm programs, including payments to farmers, commodity programs designed to reduce production, price supports based on crop loans and commodity storage. The AAA proposed to raise prices by controlling production, limiting the number of acres a farmer could plant to particular crops. Since farmers were free to plant their leftover acres to other crops, the limits didn't work very well. Severe droughts in 1934 and 1936 probably controlled production better than the AAA.

The Second World War pulled American farming out of the Depression. High prices for farm commodities persisted until the early 1950s, when they declined enough to trigger acreage control programs again that had been lying dormant. Through the 1950s Congress debated whether to support farm prices with production controls and supply management or let them fall to their unsupported market levels. The debate culminated in 1965 in the Food and Agriculture Act, a compromise that made price supports and income payments contingent upon voluntary acreage controls.

With that linkage the modern farm program was essentially in place. From it followed many of the consequences that city people concerned about the quality of their food and people who find virtue in smaller-scale farming deplore. A farmer who agrees to limit the number of acres he plants in exchange for a supported price on the crops he grows has been encouraged thereby to maximize his yield per acre. The predictable outcome in Missouri, for example, was corn yields increasing from an average of 73 bushels per acre in 1970 to an average of 109 bushels per acre in 1985. Wheat yields increased during the same period from 31 bushels per acre to 39, soybean yields from 27 to 30. Successful farmers did much better. Tom routinely saw corn yields around 160 bushels to the acre and soybean yields between 50 and 60.

Farmers boosted yields to offset acreage restrictions by farming more intensely. They mechanized their operations, fertilized more heavily and used pesticides to control weeds and insects. Any farmer who didn't keep up with his neighbors in the technology race was almost certain to be forced out of farming, acreage restrictions or not. But federal price supports coupled with acreage controls increased the pressure to farm more acres, to mechanize and to apply chemicals to boost yields. By 1987, U.S. agriculture used more than half a million tons of pesticides, mostly herbicides, per year. Nearly half that tonnage was applied in fields planted to corn and soybeans.

The obvious benefactors of this skewing were the agribusinesses that manufactured farm equipment and refined fuels and chemicals. A cruel saying came into vogue in the 1970s: a farmer is someone who launders government money for a chemical company. Agribusiness was a powerful lobby in Washington. So were the various commodity organizations, the grain companies in particular, that benefited from manipulating the vast surplus that farmers produced in their struggle to grow enough to prosper.

Surpluses, which acreage controls coupled with price supports all but guaranteed, meant cheaper food. A cheap food supply looked good to urban legislators, but lower prices always force farmers to increase production, just as a cut in wages would force a worker to work more hours to take home the same pay. Over the last twenty-five years, agricultural productivity had seen gains greater than any other sector of the economy of comparable size, making farm goods highly competitive in foreign markets and American agriculture, in the words of one expert, "one of the nation's last indisputable world-class industries."

The boom-and-bust cycle nevertheless continued. Poor world grain harvests in 1972 and 1974 pushed up farm prices and income. The Soviet Union decided to improve the nutritional level of its population by buying grain abroad. Because of inflation, the value of the dollar was falling in relation to other currencies, making U.S. exports a bargain. They increased during the 1970s by more than eight percent per year. Secretary of Agriculture Earl Butz talked confidently about feeding the world. Between 1970 and 1981, acres planted in the United States to corn, wheat and soybeans increased by fifty-four percent. Land values increased during the same period because land looked like a good hedge against inflation. Low and even negative real interest rates (the difference between the nominal interest rate and the rate of inflation) encouraged borrowing. Farm debt to finance the export boom, secured by the increase in land value, rose by more than ten percent per year. By 1980 it had tripled.

The boom began to go bust late in 1979 when the Federal Reserve Board decided to counter inflation by limiting the supply of credit, pushing up interest rates. The dollar began a sharp rise in value on world money markets and exports plummeted. At the worst possible time, Jimmy Carter imposed a grain embargo on the Soviet Union in response to its invasion of Afghanistan, a warning to the Soviets and other nations not to count on U.S. grain exports. Deliberate budget deficits during the Reagan years further boosted the cost of the dollar. Other nations, notably Canada, Australia, Argentina and Brazil, saw gains in agricultural productivity and made more of their harvests available for export. The European Economic Community, faced with agricultural overproduction comparable to that of the United States, maintained farm policies that subsidized export just as vigorously as American farm policies did. Dirty U.S. grain shipments encouraged buyers to look elsewhere. Farm income declined. Farmland values shrank by an average of twenty-nine percent nationwide—by fifty percent or more in the Midwest—and farmers who had invested heavily in land and machinery once again couldn't come up with more collateral to secure their loans.

The farm crisis of the 1980s was the direct result of government fiscal policies. It would have been less severe if a shakeout hadn't been overdue, delayed by the 1970s boom. Agriculture had been shifting in the direction of fewer and fewer farmers farming more and more land—becoming more industrial and less agrarian— since the turn of the century. The number of farms had been declining steadily, from 5.7 million farms in 1900 averaging 147 acres to 2.2 million in 1982 averaging 440 acres. Thirty million Americans, 42 percent of the U.S. population, lived on farms in 1900, but only 5.4 million, 2.2 percent of the population, did so in 1982. In 1987 the number dropped below 5 million. Nearly half of those 5 million lived in the Middle West. The farm crisis of the Reagan years accelerated the decline. In one year in the middle of the decade, 240,000 Americans left the farm. Fifteen thousand Missouri farmers went out of business between 1984 and 1987 and more than half of those remaining turned to part- or full-time jobs off the farm. "It ain't the way it used to be," Tom told Clarence once when he heard about all the farmers with jobs. "Used to be, if you couldn't find a job in town you could always go out and farm, feed your family. Now it's the other way around."

Bankruptcies and foreclosures made the evening news. Declining sales of farm machinery were another measure of the severity of the crisis. Sales of farm tractors fell from 166,153 in 1980 to just 95,280 in 1986. Combine sales collapsed, from 25,760 in 1980 to fewer than 7,000 in 1986. Total farm machinery sales declined during the same period by eighty-eight percent.

It wasn't that corporate farms were taking over. The 1980 U.S. census discovered only 7,140 nonfamily corporate farms in the entire United States, specializing in cattle feeding, poultry raising and the growing of fresh vegetables and fruits. Even counting farm operations run under contract with large corporations, corporate farming accounted for not much more than ten percent of total farm output. Large-scale farming continued to be more agrarian than industrial, and government policies that limited maximum benefits encouraged individual or family ownership. Up to a point, technological change favored larger farms and the substitution of machinery and chemicals for labor. Since 1950, labor had fallen as a percentage of total farm input from thirty-eight percent to thirteen percent. Purchased inputs—fuel, fertilizer, chemicals and machines—had increased during the same period from forty-five to sixty-two percent. American farmers steadily increased efficiency and productivity. The winnowing process that accompanied that steady change drove less efficient, less productive or just unlucky farmers off the land. By the later 1980s, farming had a better debt-to-asset ratio than most industries, a sign of its general health. At the same time, about one-fourth of American farmers were in serious and probably fatal trouble. Those were the farmers reporters wrote stories about and Hollywood made movies about. But the more numerous three-fourths were in good shape, even if, like Clarence, they foresaw potential disaster down the road.

Farming in the second half of the 1980s continued to be a tough and risky business. The new farm act that Rowland Howell was explaining to the ASCS committee members, the Food Security Act, alleviated some of that risk. In its first year of operation, it would pay out more than twenty-five billion dollars to agriculture. Though not nearly all that huge input reached farmers' pockets directly, its average of about five thousand dollars for every man, woman and child still left living on a farm would begin to turn farm economic indicators up from the deep depression they'd reached by the mid-1980s. Farm program costs dropped by almost half after that first year, but it remained to be seen how long urban America would continue to pay such generous subsidies. When there was talk of budget cutting, early in the new administration of George Bush, the first program to which legislators looked was the farm program.

Tom didn't much like pesticides. He would have been happy to farm without them. He just didn't see how he could. When he and Clarence debated the question of price supports, they always came to the same conclusion. "I'll take a free market for agriculture,"

Tom would say, "if the price of my supplies will go up and down too. But the farmer's the only man who can't get his own price. These big chemical companies do. Oil companies, farm machinery. I don't see how it's going to end. We're already a net importer of agricultural products. What are you going to do, give the land back to the Indians?"

The truth was, suppliers were few and there were millions of farmers. Machinery and diesel fuel and fertilizer and everything else went up while grain prices went down. The only strategy Tom and Clarence could see was boosting yield. They still had a lot further they could go if they had to. There were farmers growing for yield contests under ideal conditions who did better than 250 bushels per acre on corn and close to 100 per acre on soybeans. It might be that Rowland Howell was right about production controls, except there were still plenty of people going hungry in the world. It was a shame to idle land or restrict production when some folks didn't have enough to eat. That was the real problem. Someone in the government ought to come up with an answer to that one. American agriculture was the hope of the world, and a lot of it was just going to waste.

SIX

The opening of the deer season was just a week away. School was out for the day because of a teachers' conference, so Brett could drive around with his dad to look for deer sign and check the blinds.

Over the years, Tom and the boys had built blinds in all the best places. Most of the blinds were strung out in the wide stretch of timber that ran north and south along Cebo Creek on the western edge of the Landers place. Tom and Brett drove there first, parking Babe along the fence of the stobble field. They took an ax and a hatchet and walked in.

It was a gray morning. A wet wind out of the south blew across the land. Tom got onto tracking right away. He spotted buck rubs everywhere and it wound him up. A buck would choose a sapling about an inch in diameter to use as a tool to rub the velvet off its new antlers. Rubbing would shred the bark and expose the white sapwood underneath. Tom spotted the white patches against the background of browns and grays in the winter woods. Once he'd found one, it just jumped out at you. The bark hung in shreds like the tassels on party favors.

Another deer sign was a buck scrape. Pretty soon Tom found one of those along a trail. A buck would scrape away leaves and trash on the ground and then urinate on the space it'd made. The scent attracted passing does, which urinated on the scrape in turn.

The buck made regular rounds inspecting its scrapes. It could tell by the odor whether a doe was in heat.

Tom could read tracks as well as he could spot buck rubs and scrapes. The find of the day turned up at a place upstream from where a feeder creek ran into Cebo from the east, a crossing stamped and wallowed with hoof marks. "Looks like forty head of cattle went across here," Tom told Brett happily. Fresh deer tracks had sharp edges that softened with age, so an experienced tracker could date them. There were fresh, sharp tracks no more than a few hours old on both banks of the crossing. You could see where the does had jumped the narrow creek. There was a buck scrape halfway up the bank on the other side. Bucks usually crossed separately from does. Brett went upstream looking for the buck crossing and found it higher along. In the meantime Tom moved down the feeder creek toward Cebo and located another set of crossings.

There were trails running back from the crossings through the timber. The men stayed off them to avoid spooking the deer before the hunt. Tom had blinds up in the trees in the neighborhood of the feeder creek. Some were made of oak pallets braced in the crook of a tree. A few were made of steel water tanks cut out with firing slots that looked like oversized knights' helmets turned upside down. At each blind, Tom and Brett walked out the lines of sight and cleared any brush that had overgrown since the deer season last year.

They hiked back to Babe when they were finished and followed the fence south to a gate near the end of the field. Brett hauled open the gate, nothing fancy, a homemade business of barbed wire strung to a wooden post, and Tom pulled Babe into the timber. Wayne had a special blind back near the creek, a steel tank up in a tree above a place where a deer trail crossed a glade. Tom wanted to check it.

The glade was overgrown with brush. Tom shouted to Brett to put Babe into four-wheel drive and gun the truck through to knock the brush down.

"You sure, Dad?" Brett called back, happy for the chance to hot-rod.

"Yeah, I'm sure!" Tom called. "Just don't get her stuck!"

Brett climbed out of the truck and locked in the front wheels. Back inside the cab he gunned the old engine, slipped the clutch and crashed through the crackling brush heading straight toward his dad waiting under Wayne's tree. Tom coolly stood his ground and saw his son grin when he skidded through a muddy patch. "Kids," Tom said to himself, shaking his head. Brett stopped the truck short directly in front of him, dust from the dead brush billowing up behind, and jumped down from the cab.

"Think I'm ready for the monster truck competition, Dad?" he asked.

"Maybe the Hot Rod Hall of Fame." Tom was looking behind the truck, waiting for the dust to settle.

"I done good, huh?"

The pruning looked okay. "That'll give Wayne a clear shot," Tom said. "I'd love for him to get a deer. He ain't had much luck."

"Maybe he will this year."

"I sure hope so."

Across a fence to the south there was a fallow field grown up in reeds. Tom pushed through the understory toward the fence to see if he could find where the deer crossed to escape into the reeds. This time Brett was the first to spot a buck rub. They shifted eastward to line up with the rub and Tom found a trail nearby that led directly to the fence.

The reeds in the fallow field showed a change of color about halfway up, where flood spreading from Cebo Creek from all the fall rain had left its high-water mark. "You'd never find an old buck in there," Brett announced. He pointed to a twig broken off at shin height.

"That's a fawn," Tom interpreted the broken twig. "Look at the top barbed wire. Is it muddy?"

"Yeah."

"That's where they jumped over. The does hide out in that old field. We'll put one of Cowboy's boys in this farthest blind. That way, he'll have a chance to pick up any does that work their way down here to dodge all the shooting."

"You can put me in here."

"I've got a better place in mind for you, son. You and your cousin Dennis."

"He's so crazy. How come I get stuck with him?"

"You two get along real good."

"Yeah," Brett said warmly, "I knowed we do."

Driving back toward the Elms, they passed the first wheat field Wayne had planted. The wheat was green, the new blades up a couple of inches and tillering beginning, shoots coming off the main stems. The slight growth spread over the dark brown soil like a green haze. The grass on the waterways still showed green, but otherwise the wheat was the only green left on the fields now that it was late fall. By winter the wheat would glow like emerald wherever it wasn't covered with snow. It was soft red winter wheat and it needed low winter temperatures to prepare it, come spring, to switch from putting out leaves to pushing up a stem and a head of grain.

Tom looked for rabbit paths to see how well Wayne had planted. He didn't find any at all. "Old Wayne really did a good job," he told Brett. "There's not a rabbit path anywhere in the field." Brett grunted. He was watching a Cooper's hawk, its tail striped like a raccoon's, swooping from terrace to terrace chasing a mouse.

Before heading home, Tom drove down through the big Landers south pasture to a stretch of dense woods along Little Cebo Creek. The creek meandered westward to join up with Cebo near the fallow field. "Let's keep it down around here," Tom cautioned Brett. "This here's that neighbor's woods I told you about."

"You mean the one that stole them cows you bought?"

"We never proved he stole them, son. He don't hunt, and there's no use letting a fine woods like this one go to waste."

Stealthily, they climbed the fence that led into the woods and worked their way back to the creek. It had cut its meandering channel down a good ten feet below the level of the land. Tom kept an eye out and soon found a deer crossing. He looked around for a site for a blind. There was a creek bend downstream from the crossing. They hiked around to it up on the land and found a deer trail passing the point of the bend. A hunter hidden at the point would have a good shot of the trail and, over his shoulder, of the crossing as well. The deer trail was tracked to where it looked more like a deer superhighway. They went to work making a blind.

The ground they fixed for Brett and his cousin was off on the Dixon farm, a couple of miles east from everyone else on the other side of the home farm. It was another stretch of woods along Little Cebo, south of the bottomland field that Tom had reclaimed with tiling. It wasn't as heavily trafficked as the woods they'd inspected farther west, but there was plenty of sign around, tracks and buck scrapes. They located the main trail and built two blinds positioned to cross-fire it.

After a dinner of sausage and rice casserole that Sally had left for them in the crockpot, Tom unlocked the gun case in the living room and handed Brett a .25-caliber deer rifle. Brett grinned to have his dad's personal hunting weapon and then frowned. "What're you going to use?" he asked his dad.

"I've got my elk-hunting rifle," Tom told him, taking the bigger weapon out of the case. Both rifles were mounted with telescopic sights. Tom had bought the elk-hunting rifle a few years ago, when he'd gone hunting in Wyoming. It was a seven-millimeter that fired magnum shells and it kicked hard, but Brett had missed getting a deer last year and Tom wanted to give his son every possible advantage this time around. The .25-caliber was a beauty. It was accurate and it handled well.

They took boxes of brass shells in the two calibers and went out west of the workshop to sight in the rifles. Tom paced off fifty yards from the fuel pumps and set up two empty oilcans and a used white oil filter. He paced another fifty yards, which reached the edge of the soybean field, and set up a row of used oil filters and an empty grease bucket, a larger target. He and Brett hauled a couple of sacks of feed out of a shed and laid them on top of the diesel tank at the fuel pump to make a gun rest and then for the next hour they took turns firing, walking out to check their patterns and adjusting their sights. Over the soybean field as they began firing, a red-tailed hawk beat from thermal to thermal to gain altitude and then soared, observing the proceedings. It only took three rounds before Tom had a sore shoulder from the seven-millimeter mag but he wouldn't fire more than a few rounds hunting deer. With deer if you missed the first shot you waited a few hours for the next one.

Tom had been thinking about shipping a load or two of hogs. The batch on the finishing floor was about the right weight. He wanted to sell as many of them as possible before the Thanksgiving season began. Holidays were turkey and poultry days, not red meat days, and hog prices usually went down.

He and Sally started paying closer attention to the morning hog prices on the six o'clock farm report. Tuesday, prices started to sound good. When he'd had a cup of coffee and Sammi and Brett were stumbling around half asleep, getting ready for school, Tom called the Wilson buying operation in Plymouth and got a quote of $52.75 a hundredweight. He reserved judgment and called Swift & Company in Grants. The buyer there offered $52.50. "I done got you outbid," Tom told him, quoting the Wilson offer. The Swift buyer came back with $53. "Fair's fair," Tom told him. "The other guy outbid you first. I might bring you a second load, though." He called Wilson's again and told the buyer to expect a load later that morning.

Winter had finally blown in, the first serious cold weather of the season. It was fourteen degrees Fahrenheit outside with a cold wind, overcast and gray. In the mud room, after he had his work coat on, Tom pulled on an old pair of blue denim coveralls and set his feet in heavy rubber boots that came up over his calves. He took a dirty, foam-lined cap from the row of seed caps hanging in the mud room and turned down its fleece flaps to cover his ears. He dug out an old pair of orange fleece work gloves. Loading hogs was smelly, messy work. You waded through hog manure and got splashed. Tom wanted to protect his regular work clothes so that he wouldn't have to undress all the way to his skivvies to eat dinner.

Taking along his stockman's whip, made like a long buggy whip with a switch at the end, he hiked out to the workshop to retrieve his Hot Shot cattle prod. Blaze and Molly larked along behind. Their breath made clouds in the cold air. Tom hadn't used the battery-powered prod since he last shipped hogs. It looked like a policeman's nightstick except that it was bright red and had two prongs sticking out of one end like the prongs on an electric plug. To test the prod, Tom pushed the thumb button that was recessed into the handle, but no spark jumped across the prongs. It didn't work any better when he shook it. It used special high-capacity batteries. He took the GMC then and ran into Osage Station to MFA. The store clerk installed new batteries and the damned prod still didn't work. The clerk was ready to sell Tom a new capacitor, the device that stored the battery charge and built it up to a powerful but harmless shock, but Tom tried scraping the contacts clean on the old one first with his pocketknife and when they reassembled it with the new batteries the prod worked just fine, a jagged blue-white spark jumping across the prongs.

At home again, standing on the truck bed working his powerful back, Tom unbolted and wrenched up the grain gate on the International truck and set a livestock gate into its place. The plain wooden side racks were fine for hogs. Tom backed the truck up to the sand pile west of the old silo and scooped a few shovelfuls of sand onto the bed to give the hogs footing. The wooden bed was slick with oil crushed out of the soybeans the truck had hauled.

Sally had stayed home that day to help him with the loading. He picked her up at the house and drove down to the finishing floor. Around behind it, where the ground sloped down to the sewage lagoon, he backed the truck up to a loading gate, set the brake, hauled up both gates and tied off their ropes. That opened the aisle along the hog pens to the truck. Blaze and Molly had trotted down behind the truck. Big-bellied Molly stood alert and watchful but Blaze had already lost interest in the hogs and was happily chewing away on a frozen clump of hog manure. She was a farm dog through and through. You didn't want to encourage her to lick your face.

The hogs stirred and grunted. They were curious about what was going on, surging in and out of the shed sections of their pens. Tom stuck the cattle prod into his back pocket, tucked the whip under his arm and took up his crowding board, a piece of battered plywood like the lower half of a Dutch door with slots cut in the top for handles. "You run the gate, hon," he told Sally absent-mindedly, already studying the first pen of hogs. As if she hadn't helped a million times before.

With Sally holding the headboard-like gate of the first pen, Tom slipped in and began cutting out hogs, judging them with a practiced eye for fullness of ham and breadth of back, signs of adequate finish in the long, lean, modern animals he grew. He liked to ship them at between 225 and 250 pounds. Below 225, he wasn't getting full dollar for his work of raising them. Above 250 and the packing company docked the price for overweight. No one wanted lardy hogs anymore. These were almost all pink animals with white hair and long white lashes that made them look sunbleached.

When he spotted an animal he liked, Tom used the crowding board to block it from slipping around behind him and keep it moving toward the gate. Sally's job was to close off the gate to the other hogs and then quickly swing it wide enough to let the hog through that Tom was crowding. The work called for nice timing. They'd had twenty years of practice. The less the business of loading and shipping stressed the hogs, the better. Shrinkage, usually from stress-induced diarrhea, could take their weight down five or ten pounds each before they weighed in at the buying facility. Since they grew up in confinement, these weren't well-exercised animals. They could easily overexert themselves even in the winter cold.

With Tom pushing, blocking and snapping the whip and Sally timing the gate, the Bauers cut fifteen hogs into the aisle from the first pen before they closed the pen gate behind them. The only exit for the hogs now was onto the truck. Tom slipped around behind them to begin crowding them up the aisle in that direction. Sally climbed over the fence and took up station out of the hogs' line of sight, holding the rope to the truck gate. She needed to drop the gate shut once the animals were aboard before they came pushing back off.

Whenever he loaded hogs, Tom had sore thighs and a sore butt

for a week afterward from the effort of moving several tons of live
hog up the aisle by pushing his legs against the crowding board.
The hogs moved willingly up the aisle until the first one came to
the truck bed. It stopped and sniffed and began to back up. It
bumped the next hog and wiggled in beside it, wedging the narrow
aisle. The chain reaction of backing hogs reached Tom. He braced
the crowding board with his legs and applied the whip, reaching
over to sting the forward hogs on the rump to convince them to
move ahead again. They started squealing then and he started en-
couraging. "Yo!" he called. "Yo!"—and to Sally at the gate rope,
"Get ready, hon." With the whip he packed the herd solidly between the crowding board and the open gate at the end of the aisle.
The first hog was still braced against crossing over into the truck.
The animal had never known any surface but concrete. The truck
bed was wooden and foreign and it didn't trust it.

That meant Tom had to use the cattle prod. If he didn't get the
herd moving while it was at its maximum compression, one animal
and then another would begin to back up. With fifteen hogs pushing backward there was no way he'd be able to hold them. He was
sweating just from the effort of moving them forward. He leaned
over the solid mass of animals and zapped the first hog with the
prod. It squealed in fright and bolted across the gap into the truck.
The next one in line followed, but to keep up the momentum Tom
zapped a hog a couple of animals back and it tried to climb over
the one in front in its frenzy to get away from the shock. Then all
atumble the animals were crowding into the truck and when the
last one had just cleared the gate Sally dropped it shut.

One load aboard, Tom and Sally cut another ten hogs from the
next pen. One smaller hog with a spotted back, too curious for its
own good, kept pestering Sally to let it out of the pen into the aisle.
Tom finally used the whip to move it out of the way. It wasn't big
enough to send to market.

Twenty-five hogs was a good load. Tom dropped Sally at the
driveway to the house and drove on to Plymouth, the sky breaking
and the sun coming out along the way. Near town, he noticed
cows grazing in someone's soybean field. He frowned his disap-
proval. Grazing soybean fields was bad management. The cattle
would eat the beans and get the scours.

The Wilson operation in Plymouth was housed in a former sale barn. Pens and ramps and runways of weathered oak sheltered under a common roof, twelve-by-twelve beams supporting the low roof and two-by-eights slatting the pens. The wooden unloading chute extended up high enough to accommodate the second deck of double-decker cattle semi's. Tom found the ramp stuck in its second-level position. Urine from unloaded cattle had frozen it to the sides. He jumped up and down on it to break it loose, but it wouldn't budge. He went looking for the Wilson buyer, a handsome, dark-haired younger man in dark coveralls. The buyer had fought the ramp before. He fetched a six-foot pry rod and pried it loose.

With the ramp in place, Tom began quietly working his hogs out of the truck. The buyer went ahead inside, opening and closing gates to make a way for the hogs to walk to the scales. Once the last hog was down the ramp, Tom followed, herding the lot along. It was gloomy inside the holding pens and it took his eyes a minute to adjust. When he could see again, he noticed a hog that still had one of its seeds. He or the boys must have missed it when they were castrating. He alerted the buyer and the man shunted it off into a stall by itself for separate weighing. It would go onto the bill of sale as a boar. Since boar meat was gamy, Tom wouldn't get as good a price for it.

Shooing the hogs along, watching out for the ones that wanted to turn around and slip by him going the other way, Tom worked the lot into a twelve-by-twelve-foot pen. The buyer swung shut the heavy oak gate and slid a bar through a slot in the corner post to secure it. Under the oak floor of the pen was a scale. The men cut through a door next to the pen into the old auction room. Sunlight streaming in its one high window made cobwebs glow above three tiers of steep bleachers. The abandoned auctioneer's stand and the scale gauges took up the fourth side of the room. The buyer weighed Tom's hogs and stamped the weight onto a heavy cardboard sale ticket. He figured on the back of the ticket with a pencil. He was a lefty and held the pencil cocked under his left wrist. "They average two hundred thirty-four pounds, Tom," he concluded.

Back in the aisle, the buyer set up a tattoo station next to a corner where the aisle made a right turn. He had a box of cast-metal blocks like headline type but with two-inch spikes protruding that were arranged so that their points formed numbers. He assembled the numbers he'd assigned to Tom's lot of hogs in a holder with a handle like a hammer. Dipping the tips of the spikes into a pot of indelible purple dye, he signaled to Tom to let out the hogs. Tom opened the scale gate just wide enough to release one animal at a time. Once the first one had braved the gamut, they followed each other out. The buyer hit them solidly in the shoulder with the tattoo hammer as they passed, twenty-four surprised grunts, permanently marking them with a lot number. The tattoo would mark the carcass. If one of the animals turned up diseased, the rest of the lot could be traced and checked and, if necessary, disposed of.

The buyer had a one-room metal shack outside the old sale barn where he worked. He and Tom dropped in long enough to get warm and to tote up the value of the hogs. It'd be just as easy to bring the second load to Wilson's, Tom decided. He'd collect one check for both loads.

It was a fine, cold, sunny day now and Tom got the second load to Plymouth by eleven o'clock in the morning. This time he included two large older hogs left over from a previous litter and a sow with a bad leg. The sow had been stubborn and hard to move. With Sally's help again at the gates, Tom had crowded thirty-nine animals onto the truck. They came off slowly. He needed the cattle prod to move them. The buyer weighed the market hogs first, the two heavies next and then the crippled sow. He accepted the sow on contingency and herded her into a stall with the words QUARANTINE PEN painted in white on its gate. Tom figured the sow had an abscess in its right shoulder. They'd discard the right shoulder at the slaughterhouse and credit him for the rest.

In the warm office shack, the buyer filled out a full bill of sale and wrote Tom a check for more than seven thousand dollars.

Tom drove off to the bank to deposit the check. Hogs really helped pay for a farm, especially these days when the ratio between corn prices and hog prices was so wide, as wide historically as it'd ever been. Those banks that put a lot of old boys out of business ought to have been kicking themselves about now. If they'd kept their farmers in business and let them raise hogs the boys would've been able to pay back their loans.

He'd made good money selling the hogs, but he had plenty of obligations. The annual payment was nearly due on the Dixon place mortgage and on the home place as well. Plus, he was down more than a few thousand dollars in unexpected expenses, mostly for combine and tractor repair. But he was happy with the hog sale and seven thousand-some dollars richer than when he woke up in the morning. He still had to hose out the back of the truck. That was a stinking job. Then he could get out of his coveralls and eat some dinner. They were predicting below-zero temperatures tonight. He'd need to haul some bales of straw out to the gilts in the east pasture, to give them some nesting material in their houses along the creek out there. Also to check the heating system that ran warm water through the concrete finishing floor. He didn't want to lose any animals to the cold. You shipped them out for slaughter. That's what it was all about. But in the meantime you tried to take the best care of them you could.

SEVEN

Deer season always put a twinkle in Tom's eye. He liked venison and he liked to hunt deer. He knew there were city people who thought hunting was cruel. It seemed to him the only people who had a right to speak to the matter were vegetarians. Otherwise it was just a question of whether you did your own killing or someone else did it for you.

The season would open first thing Saturday morning. Everyone had arrived at Camp Kookamunga by five o'clock Friday afternoon. By then it was already getting on toward dark. Tom's brothers Dale and Cowboy came, Dale up from south of Kansas City where he had a farm near the air base, Cowboy up from the Lake of the Ozarks where he carpentered. Cowboy had stopped at the house to let off Grace, his better half, and then followed Dale back through the soybean field and across the structure dam into the camp grove. His two sons came along soon after, crazy Dennis first and then Duke, his older boy. It looked as if everyone had a new pickup except Tom. They pulled them up side by side under the trees on the bank above the structure, facing away from the old baby-blue trailer. Wayne and Brett rode out from the house with their cousins. Counting Tom and a city man Tom had invited to join them this year, they were eight in all. By five thirty Cowboy had the hamburgers on.

The trailer's small, white-enameled propane stove worked well enough. The rest of its fittings were defunct. There wasn't any electricity. Tom had rigged two Coleman lanterns overhead in the long living area for lights. There was a hand-lettered sign over the entrance door that said REST ROOMS, meaning if you had to go you could go out in the woods. They hauled water from the house for coffee. Anyone who didn't want coffee could drink soda pop. Next to the stove there was a Formica table with one end attached to the wall and a pegboard behind it that was hung with skillets and pans. Food was potluck. Everyone brought something and stashed the sacks and boxes wherever there was room. There was a wildlife poster on the wall opposite the door that showed all kinds of large-eyed animals, a bear, a deer, a raccoon, an eagle and the like, surrounding a bulldozer. It was captioned SAVE SOME FOR US. Beside it Tom had stapled up deer tags—hunting licenses—unused from previous years' hunts. "Contributions to the Conservation Commission," Dennis called them. A bunch of them were his. He hadn't shot a deer in seven years, since he was fourteen. A deer tag cost $7.50. This year for the first time the Commission had sold a few doe tags as well as the usual tags for bucks. The deer population in Missouri was pushing the limits of the available habitat and the Conservation Commission was letting hunters prune it back. Deer no longer had any natural predators in the state except man. The panthers and the bears were long gone. If the deer weren't hunted they'd keep multiplying until stress and disease limited their numbers.

At the far end of the room Tom had set up four olive-drab canvas army cots. There were rough four-by-four wooden braces propping up the sagging roof at that end and a scruffy-looking buck head mounted above the windows, its eyes and nose missing, a seed cap jaunty on its antlers. A cracked mirror for shaving hung on one side of the door. Pinned to the wall on the other side of the door was an aerial photograph of his farms that Tom used to point out where to find the deer blinds. The Bauer brothers and the city man would sleep on the cots, the boys in the bedroom beyond the kitchen area on platforms that Tom had built for bunks.

There was plenty of laughing and cutting up before supper, the brothers getting into it almost as much as the boys. They'd been hunting together all their lives and the boys had grown up with it. But the Bauer brothers, these three at least, were none of them solemn. Cowboy was the middle in age of the three, gray-haired and almost skinny compared to Dale and Tom. He had a higher-pitched voice, too, that made him sound more like a TV version of an old farmer. With his long arms and legs he was spry and gawky at the same time. He used the gawkiness to clown with, flailing around and scratching his head. Even in the Bauer clan he was special. He'd do just about anything for you. He had a warm heart.

After supper, the boys went off together to raise some hell. The brothers sat around the table sipping a little peach schnapps and reminiscing. None of them drank enough from one year to the next to notice, but deer season was a celebration.

Mostly they remembered their dad, what a man he was. They agreed that he'd been tough but fair. "I always used to come up with new ways to do things," Dale claimed. "You recollect what Dad said about that? He'd say, 'You young smart aleck, you think you know better than me.'"

"You *was* a smart aleck, too," Cowboy kidded him. "He was right about that."

"Still are," Tom drawled.

Dale grinned. "Well, I did come up with some good ideas."

"Yeah," Tom said, "and some lulus too."

"Hah," Dale told Tom, "the trouble was I didn't know how to get around Dad. That was *your* specialty." He puckered his lips and imitated a sucking calf. Cowboy laughed. "You'd pull a long face," Dale finished, "and Dad'd give in."

"Lewis was the real troublemaker," Cowboy said.

"And Warner always did exactly what Dad told him to do," Tom added.

"Didn't Lewis love to hot-rod that tractor, though?" Cowboy went on. "He couldn't wait until he could get that thing in high gear."

"Dad'd box his ears," Dale said.

"Covering up the corn he was cultivating," Tom finished the story. He went on to another one. "You remember how Dad hated them runt pigs? He'd see a runt on an old sow and he'd just grab it up by a hind leg and toss it over the fence."

"Yeah," Dale said, "and I'd salvage it and raise it."

"I remember one time when Dad gave Warner a dollar," Cowboy embroidered, "and you only fifty cents and Mother asked him why he wasn't treating you fairly. He told her, 'You don't have to worry about Dale. He's got money.' "

"Them runts did all right," Dale agreed. "I couldn't see wasting them."

"There sure wasn't much spare change around in those days," Tom said. "I recollect getting my first pair of new jeans. It'd been old overalls and hand-me-downs up to then. I was just about growed. Fifteen years old. I went to shop class and some clown ran an electric drill up my butt. I didn't care about my butt but he tore up my new jeans and I beat the crap out of him." Dale and Cowboy were chuckling. "He went crying to the teacher and by God if the teacher didn't say, 'Looks to me like you deserve it.' That surprised me."

"Was that Mr. Fletcher?" Cowboy asked.

"No, it was that kind of cockeyed shop teacher came after Fletcher left."

"Don't look at me," Dale said. "I didn't know the feller. I was long gone by then."

"What was his name?" Tom persisted.

"Was it that Mondello?" Cowboy tried again.

"No, he was the Italian. Had the accident with the lathe. I know," Tom remembered. "It was Mr. Smith."

Cowboy looked disgusted. "How the hell could you forget a name like Smith?"

"Live long enough and you'll forget everything you ever knew, brother," Tom defended himself. "But I remember being surprised because Smith'd seemed like such a hard-ass. I didn't expect him to take my side."

The boys came crashing back in, goosing each other and stumbling over the door frame. They'd been out road-testing Dennis's new pickup. They settled in around the men. Dennis had a book of dirty jokes and he set up to read them. He rattled off five or six jokes one after the other. They were pretty raunchy. Everybody laughed at first but then the laughing started sounding forced. It was a little awkward between fathers and sons to be hearing raunchy jokes about women and sex. Finally Cowboy told Dennis they were just about laughed out. Dennis didn't take the hint and read another joke. Cowboy said, "That's enough now, son," after that and the boy stopped.

The men got to playing blackjack for pennies. The boys went on back to the back room to shoot the bull. Ten thirty was lights out. Everyone zipped up in his sleeping bag. It was warm in the trailer. The bitter cold had moved on. There was a full moon outside and a clear sky, the night laying down a good hard frost.

Tom woke early, at 3:30. He'd had trouble sleeping. The trailer sloped down on that one corner. He'd forgotten to bring a pillow, so his head had been down. Cowboy heard him stirring and opened his eyes and they talked quietly. Dale woke up next. The boys slept on until the alarm clock rattled at four. Wayne was up first then as he'd predicted he would be. He jumped down and banged off the alarm clock.

Used to be they'd cooked full breakfasts before they went off hunting. That finally got old. Cowboy made coffee and Tom broke out the cereals, Grape-Nuts and Cap'n Crunch. Breakfast cereal reminded them of Euell Gibbons, the natural-foods spokesman who'd done cereal advertising. "Why did Euell Gibbons wear purple undershorts?" someone asked, and answered his own question: "To match his grape nuts." They'd heard stories that Gibbons had died of malnutrition. They talked over the possibility. They thought he was a weirdo. He was something of an enemy because their livelihood depended in part on raising beef and pork.

There was milk in a cooler to go with the cereal. Tom and the other smokers lit up morning cigarettes. A procession of people filed out to take a leak. One and then another began suiting up. They'd be sitting out in the cold for the next three or four hours and they dressed accordingly. Long johns went on first, two or three layers of socks, layers of shirts and sweaters. They all had heavy, padded coveralls of olive drab or brown canvas but they saved those until they were outside. If they put them on inside they'd sweat them out. They had their rifles and shells, winter hats with earflaps, fluorescent orange hunter's safety vests to put on over their coveralls, heavy gloves, flashlights, knives to gut their kill, little bottles of buck scent to smear on the bottoms of their

boots to cover their tracks when they walked in. The scent smelled gamy and medicinal at the same time, strong in the bottle but almost like perfume diluted on their boots.

Tom pointed out on the map where everyone would be stationed. They trooped out into the night, the full moon well over into the western sky by now, their breath blowing vapor. Pickups fired and revved, clouds billowing from their exhausts. A three-wheeler crackled. One by one they pulled out. Headlight beams swept across the dam and up the waterway through the bean field. Brett and Dennis took the three-wheeler and Dennis's four-wheeler over to the blinds on the Dixon place. Everyone else drove through Devon and around on 24 to Landers' to string out along the bottom woods on Cebo Creek.

Tom and Wayne dropped off the city man first at the fence to the neighbor's woods on Little Cebo. Tom was going to hang out with Wayne to give him some help. They waited until the city man had suited up and then took off.

The city man had never hunted before. He'd qualified as a marksman with a carbine in the Air Force, but that'd been twenty years ago. He was hunting to see what hunting was like. Inside all the layers of clothes and the bulky coveralls he felt like an astronaut suited up for space. He could barely move.

He smeared scent on the soles of his boots, wrestled himself over the barbed-wire fence and stumbled into the woods, flashlight in hand. He knew the markers back to the blind, a brush pile and then a leaning tree. He located the brush pile by tripping over it and falling down. He no sooner found his feet when there was a terrible scream and then two more from somewhere over to his left. They froze him in his tracks. They had to be human. Once his blood uncurdled he tried to figure them out. Since they came out of total silence he decided they must be someone trying to let him know he was holed up in a blind over there so that no one would shoot in that direction.

Later on he'd ask Tom about it and Tom would say it was probably just a screech owl. So that was what a screech owl sounded like.

The city man found the blind on the land above the sharp bend in the creek and settled down to wait. Tom had said to try not to

move even a little toe. The city man settled into a comfortable
position on the log around which Tom had built the blind. His
breathing slowed as he cooled out and his eyes adjusted to the
dark. The light wouldn't come up until about six, so he had an
hour and a half to wait. He began to see what all the heavy
clothing was about. It'd been right at freezing when they'd left the
trailer. The cold seeped into his gloves and boots first of all. He
moved fingers and toes to warm them and to have something to
do. He didn't see how the deer would know. He drifted down to
sleep and woke himself up and drifted down again. It got darker
instead of lighter. The stars crowded the sky. He realized the moon
had gone down. He'd been able to see the tree trunks in silhouette
before but now he was sitting slowly getting numb in nearly pitch
darkness.

He nodded again. When he came up he could see the trees in
silhouette again. Minute by minute, the trees emerged from the
background, branches next and then leaves, so slowly he couldn't
quite catch the change. He had his rifle across his lap. He slipped
off his right glove, took hold of the cold breech, released the safety
and found the trigger.

Leaves rustled, small sounds. The city man didn't know what to
listen for. He felt stupid. He hadn't even thought to ask.

Then over to his left, from the west, came a sound like a small
man walking through the leaves, cautiously starting and stopping
and starting again. Then several more in concert. The city man's
heart began to pound. It had to be deer, a nest of them waking up
now that it was beginning to be morning. They were coming his
way. But they could just as easily have been hunters. The walking
sounded exactly the same. He'd have to be sure of what he was
shooting at before he shot. The last thing on earth he wanted to do
was to shoot someone.

He had his rifle ready, a .30-caliber Winchester with open sights.
A doe came across from the west, wary, not twenty feet in front of
him. He didn't think about does and bucks. There were doe tags
in the group if anyone needed them. He brought up the rifle. The
doe saw the motion and swung away and bolted. He fired, a huge
noise after the hours of silence. The rifle kicked his shoulder and
the barrel came up and he already knew he'd fired over the doe's

back. Its flag flashed ahead of him and disappeared into the darkness. He'd fired the first shot of the season. He only hoped he hadn't spooked the deer for everyone else. He checked his watch. It was 6:13.

He settled back to waiting. After a while he heard other hunters shooting to the east and the west, usually one or two rounds at a time but once five. The light released more and more detail from the woods. The city man found his attention wandering from watching for deer to noticing the complex patterns the trees made as they competed for light in the forest canopy.

A sound behind him alerted him. He turned his head as quickly as he dared and saw deer crossing the creek upstream twenty or thirty yards. He had another straight shot if he could only turn around. He found the trigger on his rifle, set his hands in position on the breech, swung himself around ready to fire. But he'd made too much noise. The deer were gone. He'd seen at least two does and he thought he'd seen a buck.

Men and boys began reassembling around nine o'clock on the waterway above the Cebo woods at Landers'. Cowboy got a doe. Tom and Wayne had seen a big, handsome buck with two does skylighted on the upland in the pasture east of Cebo but they'd been too far away for a shot. The animals had drifted into the woods where the city man had his blind. Tom thought they were probably the deer the city man had seen crossing the creek behind him.

Dennis came in grinning from ear to ear. He'd gotten a fine buck after seven dry years. Brett was happy for his cousin but wry about it. "I seen him," he told them with a wink. "I let old Dennis have him."

Dale was the last in. He'd shot a small buck with a big rack. He hadn't dragged the carcass out of the woods yet. Tom went off with him to haul it out. They gutted the buck at the edge of the woods, a small pile of steaming entrails. The coyotes would have a good feed.

Back at the trailer they cooked that big breakfast, Dale and Cowboy frying bacon and eggs. Tom wanted something more like dinner and chowed down on a ham-and-cheese sandwich and some potato chips. He'd decided he needed to combine. The moisture in

the soybeans was down to fourteen-and-a-half percent. Cowboy
volunteered to help. He'd bagged his limit on deer and handling
the trucks would free up Brett and Wayne to sunset-hunt. Before
they went back out, though, Tom told them, they'd need to grind
some feed and feed the hogs.

Cowboy, Dale and Dennis drove to Plymouth later that morning
to have their kill checked. They parked across from the sheriff's
office at the side of the courthouse. There were lots of hunters
around, city men mostly in new hunting clothes. They came over
to see the racks on the two bucks and looked envious. Inside the
sheriff's office, under wanted posters at a dusty desk, a sheriff's
deputy filled in forms for them. There was a fingerprinting stand
on the corner of the desk. The deputy brought tin inspection bands
out to the pickup, verified the tag numbers and handed up the
bands to Dennis to be snapped into place around an Achilles
tendon on each animal.

Back at the workshop, Cowboy rigged baling wire from the
center rafter and strung the three carcasses up to cool them out.
Sally and Grace came along to see. The men were taking turns
being photographed with their kill and inspecting the carcasses.
Tom rolled in from combining the hillside field at Ward's. The
ground had thawed and turned slick. The deer were light-brown
and lean. Their small black cloven hooves almost looked polished.
Cowboy had gotten his doe head-on, the bullet entering one eye
and exiting the side of the jaw, a burst of meat against the soft
brown hair. Dale had exploded his buck's heart. It fell out when
Cowboy hauled the carcass up below the rafter. Molly was sniffing
around the blood on the workshop floor. When the heart came
tumbling down she snatched it up, oversized and ghastly in her
mouth, and trotted it off somewhere. She came back later with
Blaze to lick up the fresh blood dripping from the deer.

Dale had three hundred acres of beans still standing. Since he'd
shot his limit, he left that evening to get back to combining. Sally
had cooked up a big pot of stew that the men heated on the stove
in the trailer and served out in soup bowls with crackers. After
supper they went into the house and got cleaned up to go to
Saturday-night Mass. Cowboy used the cracked mirror and shaved
in cold water out at the trailer so as not to crowd the house.

Tom, Sally, Cowboy, Grace, Sammi and all the boys went to Mass. It felt like old times.

Sunday was cleanup. Anyone who didn't have a deer yet went out again before dawn. Late morning they gathered at Landers' for a drive. One group stayed on the upland. Another hiked down into the draw of a creek that fed into Cebo and began working downstream. By now the deer were dispersed from their usual nests and trails. Driving the draw should flush some of them out. Then either the men in the draw would have a shot at them or the men up on the land.

Tom led the men through the draw. It was grassy because the creek flooded it too often for brush to gain much purchase but it was wild in places with twisted, flood-washed trees. They'd hiked about a quarter of a mile when all of a sudden a buck and a couple of does flushed from cover down the way. The men fired at them, calling out to the party up on the land. The deer didn't try to hide out. They swerved and kept running swift as the wind, dodging from one side of the twisting draw to the other and then right up the side. As they went over the top, the firing began from the men up above and the buck took a round in midair. It was obviously a mortal wound but the animal kept on running another hundred yards before it collapsed. The does didn't stop and the men kept firing until they were out of sight back down in the draw around the bend.

Someone went for the three-wheeler to haul the buck out. Tom kept his party moving through the draw. It opened up at Cebo Creek, which had a floodplain a good hundred yards wide, a steep bank on the other side and a flat lowland on the near side dense with brush. They followed along on the lowland side, still after the does but thinking there might be more deer. It was harder going through the black, tangled brush but everyone was excited. Sitting silent as a stone in a blind was one thing, stalking down a creek draw in broad daylight was something else entirely.

They flushed a flock of wild turkeys. The birds had big, almond-shaped bodies with striped feathers, the stripes almost zebralike. Tom had never seen so many wild turkeys so close up before, right out in the open. He counted thirteen birds. They kept a set distance between themselves and the hunters but didn't even seem frightened. They acted as if they knew it wasn't turkey season. Finally, a long walk upstream, they all took off flying over to the west across the creek.

A doe and a yearling buck flushed just then, out from under a brush pile near the creek. The men were on them and firing. The animals headed for the creek and jumped in. Only their heads showed so they made a smaller target as they swam and no one had any luck hitting them. When they climbed out on the other bank they went straight up the steep side and over the top. So that morning the men only added one deer to their total. Duke claimed the fatal shot and everyone agreed the buck was his.

Sunday afternoon was leave-taking. The air had warmed and sunlight streamed through the trees. Tom was sitting with Cowboy in Cowboy's silver pickup at the entrance to Camp Kookamunga, waiting for the boys to finishing loading and follow them out. The city man was standing in the middle of the camp at the picnic table getting ready to unload his rifle. He'd be riding out with Duke, bringing up the rear.

The Winchester was designed so that you shucked rounds through the chamber to unload them. It was awkward and unfamiliar but the city man thought he had control. Instead of pointing the rifle barrel up into the air as he ought to have done, he held it parallel to the ground. He shucked a round from the magazine into the chamber. The hammer slipped under his thumb. The rifle fired. The terrible explosion blew through the woods.

Everything stopped. The city man looked in horror where the barrel was pointing. It seemed to be pointing between Cowboy's pickup and Duke's. The city man felt a surge of relief. Then Cowboy jumped from his cab, flailing his arms. He snatched off his seed cap, bobbed up and down, rubbed the top of his head.

I've killed him, the city man thought. I've shot him in the head and killed him. He just doesn't know it yet.

Cowboy didn't fall. The city man laid down the rifle and went to him. Tom came out of the pickup to his brother's side. "You were white as a ghost," Tom told the city man later. The city man began to hope he hadn't taken a life, brought grief to a dozen families, ruined his own life as well.

Cowboy was starting to realize he'd been shot at. He'd turned white too. He'd had a heart attack once and he didn't need fancy embroidery on his excitement. "What the hell happened?" he asked. His voice sounded a little strangled.

"I slipped," the city man said. "I'm sorry. I was trying to unload a round. I'm sorry."

Tom was watching, checking it out. His eyes flicked to the rifle abandoned on the picnic table, the city man, Cowboy's head, Cowboy's hat. "Let's see your head," he ordered Cowboy. Cowboy bent down. Tom inspected. He let out his breath. "Not a scratch," he pronounced.

Cowboy turned his cap over in his hands. "Will you lookee here," he said with amazement. He poked his little finger through a hole in the crown, pulled it out and pointed to another hole just above the sweatband. A tuft of gray hair, Cowboy's hair, stuck out from the hole in the crown. "Jesus Christ," he said, "where'd that round go?"

In their excitement, the two brothers ignored the city man. The boys were coming over, looking at him strangely. The thought crossed his mind that it wouldn't have been safe for him in that stretch of woods if he'd killed their father and uncle. He still felt horror but growing past the horror was a powerful feeling of shame. He'd been out of his depth and his carelessness had nearly killed a man. He knew one thing: he'd put away guns forever.

Tom and Cowboy were climbing on the truck. "My God," Tom said, "will you look at that." They'd found the entry point for the soft-nosed slug. It'd drilled into the pickup cab just above the rear window. The two brothers jumped down from the back at the same time and climbed into the cab.

"Lookee here," Cowboy called out. Everybody was listening. "It channeled along under the roof."

"Windshield's cracked," Tom added. "There's where it exited. How'd you get that hole in your cap?"

"Damned if I know," Cowboy said, relief filling his voice. He turned down the sun visor. "Here. Here's a hole. Bullet fragment must of gone through."

"I'm sorry," the city man said from outside. "It was stupid. Just stupid."

Cowboy hadn't felt enough relief yet to be gracious. His pulse wasn't back to normal. "It was an accident," he was able to say. The boys came close and studied the evidence. They didn't know what to say. Once they saw Cowboy was really all right, when he'd demonstrated two or three times the holes in his cap, they dispersed to their trucks and drove off. They'd say their goodbyes up at the house. The city man rode to the house in the pickup he'd ventilated, between the brother he'd nearly killed and the brother who was his friend, and he didn't know what to say either.

The brothers knew what to say. They asked the city man not to tell Grace about what had happened. "She lost a brother in a hunting accident a few years back," Cowboy explained. "I'll tell her later when things calm down."

A little afterward, when people were leaving, Cowboy chewed a stick of gum and used the wad to plug the hole in the back of his cab so it wouldn't whistle in the wind. The city man asked him to send him the bill for a new windshield and the bodywork and told him once more that he was sorry. Cowboy's pulse was back to normal and he could be gracious again. "If you'd meant to do it that'd of been one thing," he said. "But you didn't mean to. It was a accident pure and simple."

"We all know about gun discipline," Tom consoled his city friend, "but we all get a little careless after a while. I'm partly to blame. I should have gone over it with you and made sure you knew. We grew up with guns. You didn't."

"It was stupid," the city man said. "*I* was stupid. I wasn't thinking about what I was doing. I thought I had control."

"It was careless," Tom told him, generously finding the good in it. "But we'll remember it for years to come and it'll remind us all to be careful."

Cowboy wrote the city man later, after the man had paid for the pickup repair. "I look up to the *Man* above a lot more now and give thanks," he wrote. "And for you, *Practice Practice Practice* (just kidding). I hold no bad feelings against you and I'm glad that we met."

They'd add it to their stories, the city man thought. They'd add it to their stories and go on hunting. It would fade to a story told in the trailer over stew. He was damned lucky it wasn't any more than that.

EIGHT

In December's cold, the sky overhead was dark blue, pale blue and greener nearer the horizon. Long highways of white clouds crossed it. The colors of the ground in morning light had changed. The soybean fields that had been dark green in summer had reversed to white now with hoarfrost. Curving lines of buff stobble contoured cornfields marked with strange salmon-colored patches, the frozen remains of the pale green volunteer corn that had sprouted and leafed in the wet fall. Wider bands of dark umber loam showed where farmers had plowed eroded terraces to build them back up or where bulldozers had shaped new ones. Big yellow flatbed dozer carriers waited parked at field gates. Brown and black cattle grazed in the pastures and the cornfields, dark points moving across the lighter ground.

Combining had been like sleigh-riding lately. The top one or two inches of soil would thaw by late morning, but the ground underneath would still be frozen and the beans would still be tough. Even at the top of a terrace the combine would slide greasily in the mud. "I ain't going to have this next year," Tom had told Sally. "Next year I'm going to drill. I'm sliding because she wants to get off these ridges the planter made. We've been using a planter so's we could cultivate for the weeds but with this new chemical this year them weeds ain't been so much of a problem. I stayed

ahead of the harvest last year. We hit it hard enough early enough that we missed that spell of bad weather."

"I remember we did," Sally had agreed.

"But this year I'm not doing any better than the rest of them. I'm going to buy me a new header, sixteen foot instead of this big awkward twenty, and a drill for the beans."

Sally hadn't argued. They'd look at what it'd cost.

Waiting on the weather, Tom arranged for MFA to soil-test the Ward and Landers farms. He did that every couple of years to see what minerals and fertilizer he needed to apply and whether he'd need to lime. He was particularly interested in the Ward farm since he'd only taken it over this year. He thought he might give it an extra five or ten pounds to the acre of fertilizer to build it up.

The soil testing was free since it encouraged fertilizer sales. MFA sent a man out and Tom spent a morning showing him which fields he wanted tested. The man took samples from different parts of each field, mixed them to make field composites and sent them off to Nebraska to a soil-testing laboratory. In a month or so MFA would get back a computer printout that showed soil levels of nitrogen, potassium and potash, the three basic plant nutrients, plus soil acidity and the important minerals. If the soil was too acid, Tom would have the field limed. On shared fields, the land-lord paid for lime, since it lasted three or four years and was in that sense semipermanent, and they split the cost of the fertilizer.

The gilts had started farrowing. Three of the sixteen young sows had litters the first week. Tom set up a board with a hypodermic, a pair of small wire cutters, a bottle of iron dextran and a pan of iodine. When a litter was a day old he took a red plastic milk-carton basket, lifted the new pigs out of the crate one by one with a finger across their throats to keep them from squealing and alarming their dangerous mother, settled them in the milk basket and went to work on them. He picked up one pig at a time from the basket and held it by its head with a finger through its mouth. Disinfecting the pliers in the iodine, he snipped the pig's four needle-sharp eyeteeth one by one. That protected the sow's teats from damage and cut down on the number of injuries when the pigs fought for dominance. After doing the teeth he snipped off the pig's tail, then gave it a shot of iron in the long muscle of its neck.

If he encountered a runt he'd leave the teeth to give it a little advantage.

Mid-December the new mower came in at Fleckmeier's. Tom was excited. He enjoyed new tools the same way kids enjoyed new toys. He hooked up his old crimper mower to the GMC and hauled it in to Osage Station first thing the next morning to trade it. It was a clear, sunny day, warming up into the forties, great weather but not great enough to dry beans. Tom had heard that someone had delivered a load to Comstock's at twenty-two percent and taken a $2.40 dock on it.

The new mower was a Dutch design made by Fiatagri, a simple, sturdy system. Larry Fleckmeier walked him through the warm shop and out onto the sunny back lot to see it. Larry was about Tom's age, wiry and intense, a good friend. He didn't just sit in the front office. He was the best mechanic in the place. He knew his machines.

He and Tom hadn't always gotten along. When they first started doing business, a few years back, Larry seemed kind of a tough nut to Tom. You never knew what his mood would be. Some days he was friendly and some days he was sarcastic and short.

It came to a head when the crankshaft broke on Tom's big tractor. Caterpillar had made the engine and the drive train. It had a reputation for quality products. Tom asked Larry if Caterpillar might allow something on the engine since it only had fourteen hundred hours on it. Tom had bought the tractor from Fleckmeier's, but he'd bought it secondhand. "I wouldn't dare ask them," Larry snapped. "They'd laugh me out of the office."

That didn't seem right to Tom. He called Caterpillar in Kansas City a couple of times and finally got through to the right man. "We build our engines better than that," the man told Tom, and he promised to allow something on the crankshaft.

The bill came in from Fleckmeier's, twenty-seven hundred dollars, and Tom and Sally sent the damaged parts to Caterpillar for evaluation. It wasn't more than ten days later when they got a dunning letter from Larry that said things like, "My employees have to eat too." Then he called and started chewing Sally out. She told him to talk to Tom. Larry went on with Tom for forty-five minutes. Tom just waited him out. Then he fired back. "If you're through," he told him, "it's my turn. The problem ain't the engine, Larry, it's your goddamned personality." Tom ran through the list. There was the disk he'd bought from Ford, down the road from Fleckmeier's, because when Larry had quoted him a price and he'd asked, "Can't you do any better than that?" Larry had sneered, "How much better do you think I should do?" There was the crankshaft business. There was rudeness reported by other farmers. Tom wrapped it up by telling Larry, "I don't think a man should mistreat the people who come in to buy from him."

Larry's answer dropped Tom's jaw. Instead of arguing, he agreed with Tom and thanked him for being honest. He said he knew he wasn't much fun to be around and he'd try his damnedest to improve. And that was how it worked out. Larry got it together and became someone you liked to do business with. With the way people had been starting to take their trade elsewhere, Tom's little talk might have saved Larry's business. Farm implement dealers were going bankrupt right and left these days, so it couldn't have hurt. Tom learned later that Larry's wife had been ill through that period and maybe that accounted for his foul moods.

The new mower was a long, low rectangle of steel painted bright orange. It didn't run on wheels. It mounted on the back of a tractor, sticking out one side, suspended hydraulically and operating through a power takeoff. It had two fanlike sets of blades that rotated at nearly 3,000 RPM. It would lay grass and weeds right down and there wouldn't be any worrying about sickle bars and broken mower blades.

Tom was surprised to see it set up sitting on the ground. He'd figured from the catalogue that it stored standing up. The blades connected to the PTO through oil joints, though, and he supposed that if it were stood upright, the oil would leak out. There was a kickstand support for the far end of the mower threaded with a bright orange braided nylon rope that seemed to pull the wrong way. Larry showed him that the kickstand was spring-loaded and pulling the rope from up on the tractor would release a latch.

A heavy vinyl cover snapped on over the whole unit to hold down the dust and flying debris. "I bet that don't cost too much to replace," Tom said drily. Larry lifted an eyebrow but didn't commit himself. Larry had already had the machine greased. They went around it together and checked out its operation. "It's my first foreign machine," Tom told him. "I hate to take the work away from my own kind."

"It isn't made over here yet," Larry reminded him.

"I know. I wouldn't have bought it otherwise." Larry had given him a good deal. He'd proposed to trade in the crimper. The mower cost $4,580 new. He'd gone to one dealer who offered him a $2,200 difference. Case had offered $1,200. Larry had offered to buy the crimper for $4,080 in trade, a difference of $500. He knew Tom's machines and knew how well Tom cared for them. He didn't even drive out to look the crimper over. "Hell," Tom had told Sally, "five hundred dollars ain't nothing."

He'd wanted the mower primarily for Wayne, who did most of the mowing in the spring and summer and couldn't see mice nests. The crimper got caught up in that kind of tangle and left unmowed clumps behind, which embarrassed Wayne when he saw them afterward. He'd go back and try to clean them up. Mice nests wouldn't stop this new machine. Tom wasn't sure it wouldn't take down small trees. For five hundred bucks he had a slick new mower, the first of its kind in the neighborhood.

Tom had other errands to run before he loaded the Fiatagri. At the GMC dealer in Osage Station he checked on parts for his car, but they weren't in yet. At the Keller Machine Works he checked on his grain auger, which he'd brought in for repair. It wasn't done yet. At the junkyard he checked on body parts for Brett's car to replace a fender Brett had bent last weekend in an accident. They cost too much. It looked as if it just wasn't his day where repairs were concerned.

One of Larry's men chained the Fiatagri to a high-loader and loaded it onto the GMC. Coming round the bend toward his farms, Tom decided to store the mower in the old barn on the Dixon place. He lifted it off the pickup with the loader on one of his tractors and parked it on a two-by-four to keep it off the ground. "There, she's dry," he assured himself, and drove on home. Clarence had finished his beans and brought his old Gleaner over to Tom's. It was parked in the Dixon barn, ready to help Tom combine if the ground ever cooperated.

At the end of the day Tom loaded a feed cart with hog feed and wheeled it down the aisle of the farrowing house. He had a bag of Rootin' Iron for the baby pigs and sprinkled the dark, medicinal mixture onto their heating pads as he moved from crate to crate. The sows knew it was feeding time and kicked at the metal front gates of their pens. There were pigs everywhere, pigs standing on their mothers' backs, pig heads lined up along a row of teats, pigs squealing and scratching, and more to come, into a dimly lit world where the air was mellow night and day with country-Western songs.

Tom started the next day feeding the sows again. When the chores were done, he hooked one of the grain wagons to Babe and drove it over to the Elms to store in a shed there. It was full of beans from one of his fields that he'd decided to save for seed. He'd planted the field west of the house for seed, but it was still too wet to combine and the quality of the beans there was deteriorating.

For a week he'd been enticing the cows and calves at the Elms into the feedlot by leaving the gate open and putting out corn and hay. He wanted to get them used to coming into the lot because he was preparing to wean the calves. After he'd unhooked the grain wagon, he parked Babe in the backyard behind the antebellum house where Landerses had lived for more than a century, a two-story brick house with chimneys at each end and a long front porch. Walking past the sheds behind the house, he picked up two five-gallon buckets and let himself into the feedlot. He stored corn in a miniature grain bin not much taller than he was at the east end of the lot. The bin had a door cut into one side that came up to his waist. Once he'd loaded his buckets with ground corn, he moved fast to dump them into the feed troughs, calling the cattle at the same time with a long, warbling, drawn-out bellow. The cows always came running when they heard him. He hurried to dump the feed because they didn't mind at all knocking him down and trampling him. One big palomino cow didn't like corn and stood aside from the feast looking sour. The smell of the cattle lot was different from the smell of the farrowing house, the hogs musky, acrid and complex, the cattle sweeter, vegetable, fermented.

The calves followed their mothers into the lot. The younger

calves began playing, butting each other and kicking up their heels, little puffs of vapor jetting from their nostrils. The older calves took the bounty seriously and tried to work past the cows to the troughs. Tom left them to feed. At the tractor gate, he carefully unhooked the electric fence wire that ran along the top, tested it by zapping sparks between its ends and left it disconnected. He hiked over to a shed west of the house and wheeled out yet another of his tractors. This one was a red International with a bale lifter installed on its drawbar, two steel prongs about four feet long and as big around as a man's arm that stuck straight out in back. Tom used the bale lifter to haul four round bales of hay, one at a time, into the cattle lot. He wheeled the tractor fast through the gates, practiced at its operation, clearing the fence posts by inches. The sky was sharp and blue, clear and cold and feathered with cirrus. It'd frosted hard. Isolated hummocks of grass in the cattle lot looked like silver-white sea anemones, something you'd see on *Jacques Cousteau*.

Tom returned the tractor to its shed, strolled back to the lot and quietly skirted its periphery, closing the gates to close in the cattle so that he could sort them. Two calves still hung behind in the pasture. Tom left one gate open and circled wide around them. Seeing him stalking them, they broke suddenly for the safety of the herd. His stalk looked like a hunter's stalk. The truth was, raising animals was a long, drawn-out version of hunting, a permanent surround.

After dinner, Tom drove back to the Elms and found Clarence there in his old red pickup already waiting to help. Donald Landers turned up a few minutes later. He was fresh from a trip to Hawaii. He didn't seem to have acquired a tan but he'd carried home a can of macadamia nuts for Tom. Tom had never eaten one before and he accepted the can with curiosity.

First off, they hauled the orange plastic feed troughs around to make a funnel leading from the large main lot into a holding lot at one side. Next they drove the cows and calves through the funnel into the smaller lot and closed the gate. Donald stood aside to watch them and Tom and Clarence went to work. Tom had brought along his drover's whip. Slowly and quietly, with soft calls and an occasional flick of the whip, the two men sorted cows from calves much as Tom and Sally had sorted hogs before, working the cows to the gate and opening it at the right time to pass each cow into the main lot and bar the calf's way. They culled some cows and kept them with the calves—the cow that didn't like corn, several cows with cancer eye and one undersized animal that always dropped runts. Tom planned to ship them for slaughter.

As soon as the healthy cows realized they'd been separated from their calves, they began bawling. Donald shouted over the din that you could hear them all the way to Plymouth. The calves made less ruckus. They hadn't figured it out yet. They'd be bawling their heads off soon enough. Once the men had finished sorting, they drove the cows from the main lot out into the pasture. Then they hauled the feed troughs back into line and let the calves and the cull cows out into the lot again. Tom dumped four buckets of feed into the troughs to start the calves feeding and to distract them from their separation. The cull cows headed straight for the feed, but the men had to drive the calves over to the troughs from the fences where they crowded to look for their mothers. The youngest calves were the hardest to move. The older ones showed about equal interest in their mothers and the feed.

The men got to talking later about rabbits. Clarence remembered killing hundreds of rabbits a day when he was a kid. Those were the Depression years. They sold them to an itinerant butcher. "One time I got on top of an old brush pile," Clarence said, "and shot me twenty-seven rabbits, just one after another, bam bam bam. Just thump my foot on the pile and another one would come out. We'd get them and the man would salt them, throw them into a barrel and off they'd go."

"You remember how we cleaned them?" Tom asked him.

"Hell, I ought to. I did it often enough." Clarence demonstrated, imitating cutting, pulling off the skin, popping the guts out top to bottom like finishing off a tube of toothpaste, flinging the guts away. "There was a lot more then than now. We didn't have coyotes then and there was a lot more clover."

"Lots of groundhogs, too," Tom remembered. "One time my dad and my uncle killed four hundred ten groundhogs in one year on one farm. You had to clean them off the land. They was dangerous. Groundhog holes killed many a farmer."

"Yeah," Clarence added. "Old tractor drop into a groundhog hole and turn right over."

The moon was full that week, orange and huge on the horizon, cool and clear at the heights. Rusty Mars and spotlight Jupiter had come into rare conjunction. Christmas stars, Sammi called them, walking out with her dad to see them after supper one night. Tom had lighted up the welded iron star on his FM antenna over the house. He'd taken some kidding about that star. It was two triangles he'd welded together with their points overlapping. Someone had told him it was a Star of David. That was okay with him. He left it up all year round and turned it on at Christmas. It might be a Star of David, but it was a Christmas star too. "You know Jesus was born a Jew," Clarence had deadpanned the afternoon they sorted the calves, working his bushy eyebrows under his old green seed cap like Groucho Marx. "Yeah, he was born a Jew, but he grew up and became a Catholic."

NINE

Sally decided to decorate the Christmas tree with white lights and red bows this year. Sammi helped her decorate. They put a blond ceramic angel at the top with wings and a halo. Pretty soon you couldn't see the base of the tree for all the presents.

Five days before Christmas, on a Saturday, Tom and Wayne took the cull cows in to the Kansas City stockyards. Tom hated to ship cows. They got scared and let go all over the truck. He remembered once seeing a cow butted up against the stock rack of a truck directly above an open white convertible at a stoplight, some guy and his gal, and thinking, oh-oh, there's trouble, and sure enough a great yellow stream came pouring out and down into the convertible onto the gal and the guy took off right through the red light.

Tom had hoped to get some combining done later that Saturday, but about the time he was ready to start, the clouds and fog rolled in and the beans toughened up. "I sure ain't taking no two-dollar dock," he told Sally. He knew he was balancing the penalty against the possibility of a total loss to mold and snowstorms, though. He was already finding more stalks down on his field inspections, rotted at ground level and then just fallen over. A heavy snowstorm would be a disaster at this point. He was glad the weatherman wasn't predicting a white Christmas.

Saturday night, Tom and Sally had driven back into Kansas City to the annual Bauer family Christmas get-together. Relatives came in from all over, almost as many as during the summer family reunions. The crowd had supper at the Gold Buffet in North Kansas City and then moved out to the Independence VFW Hall for dancing.

Then, Monday, Tom and Wayne had shipped hogs. The hogs went to Grants this time instead of Plymouth because Swift & Company was paying twenty cents more a hundredweight that day. One hog was down on the first truckload. Hogs raised on concrete didn't have much stamina. This one had probably been knocked down by the other hogs. A downed hog will exhaust itself struggling to get back up, which was probably what was wrong with this one. They had to drag it out. They got it into the chute but it was too overheated to move. From the looks of it, it had a dislocated or fractured hind leg. Hogs had hips about as bad as quarterbacks' knees. They left the hog panting and miserable in the chute while they drove the rest of the load through to the scales. It was still down when they got back and the buyer told them he'd deal with it. Tom was insured in any case. If the hog died, he'd collect for it based on the average price of the rest of the load.

They hauled in a second load, including a sow that didn't breed, and then they had the messy work of cleaning up the truck with its splatter of hog and cow manure, urine, corn and sand. They backed the truck up to the outdoor faucet beside the farrowing house. The wash from the hose drained down into the pasture and a contingent of nine sows and two boars soon arrived to inspect it, finding the corn that had passed through the cows to their liking. "It's a crappy job," Wayne laughed about the cleanup, "but someone's got to do it." The boars' scrotums that had been swollen like balloons in the heat of summer were drawn up against the cold now. Wrinkled and tight, they looked like brains the boars carried between their legs. For boars at least, it was true what women said.

So by Christmas Tom was a little frustrated. He'd have combined on Christmas Day if he could have, but the weather wasn't going to let him do that. He figured he might as well quit worrying for one day at least and take it easy. He'd get the beans in somehow.

It was a good Christmas. Everyone got piles of clothes, the way they always did. The big presents were the most fun. Sally got a Magic Chef microwave. They'd had one that was built into the oven of the electric range, so that you were supposed to be able to roast and microwave at the same time, but it was an early model and didn't have much power. This one had a digital keypad and power to spare.

Sammi got a two-speaker boom box, one of the little slim ones, just her size. Tom and Sally had discussed getting Brett a shotgun for his bird hunting. He'd taken to the idea of duck hunting from a blind on the big pond over at the Elms. But he'd been talking about overhauling his car, so they got him a set of socket wrenches instead and Wayne gave him a toolbox to put them in. Everybody chipped in on Wayne's present, five more belt buckles for his Hesston belt-buckle collection. He'd accumulated more than two hundred Western-style belt buckles in his collection, nearly all that Hesston had released over the years. He'd had the collection professionally appraised the year before, when he was thinking about selling it. He'd put it together buying up buckles at sales and flea markets. The appraiser had said it was worth seven thousand dollars.

Tom got a drill press. He needed it for the workshop. It was a honey and it really rounded out his shop tool setup.

Sally was cooking ham and turkey both for Christmas dinner—the ham for Tom, who didn't like poultry. There'd be dressing, noodles, mashed potatoes, salads, broccoli and cauliflower, and for dessert Sally's special chocolate cream-filled cupcakes and pecan pie. Christmas Eve, when Sally's kin traditionally came to visit, she'd served an old family favorite that her mother used to make, barbecued raccoon.

Tom drifted over to the piano while Sally was finishing up cooking Christmas dinner. Sammi wanted him to sing her favorite song, "Billy Bayou." It sounded like an old folk song but it was a Roger Miller song that Jim Reeves recorded. Tom had sung it to Sammi for years, ever since she was a little baby. She was getting too big to sit on his knee. He let her sit there one more time and reached around her to play the bass chords and she sang along with him against his rich bass in her sweet voice:

Back about eighteen hundred and some,
A Louisiana couple had a redheaded son;
No name fitted him, Jim, Jack or Joe;
They just called him Billy Bayou.

> *Billy, Billy Bayou,*
> *Watch where you go,*
> *You're walking on quicksand,*
> *Walk slow.*
> *Billy, Billy Bayou,*
> *Watch what I say,*
> *A pretty girl'll get you*
> *One of these days.*

Billy was a boy kind of big for his size,
Red hair and freckles and big blue eyes.
Thirteen years from the day he was born,
Billy fought the battle of Little Big Horn.

> *Billy, Billy Bayou,*
> *Watch where you go,*
> *You're walking on quicksand,*
> *Walk slow.*
> *Billy, Billy Bayou,*
> *Watch what I say,*
> *A pretty girl'll get you*
> *One of these days.*

One sad day Billy cried, "Ho, ho,
"I can whip the feathers off Geronimo."
He smarted off and the chief got mad,
That like to have ended our Louisiana lad.

> *Billy, Billy Bayou,*
> *Watch where you go,*
> *You're walking on quicksand,*
> *Walk slow.*
> *Billy, Billy Bayou,*
> *Watch what I say,*
> *A pretty girl'll get you*
> *One of these days.*

Sammi liked the pretty girl part. Her daddy always flirted with her when they sang those lines.

One day in eighteen seventy-eight,
A pretty girl walked through Billy's front gate.
He didn't know whether to cry out or run,
And now he's married 'cause he did neither one.

> *Billy, Billy Bayou,*
> *Watch where you go,*
> *You're walking on quicksand,*
> *Walk slow.*
> *Billy, Billy Bayou,*
> *Watch what I say,*
> *A pretty girl'll get you*
> *One of these days.*

Four guys put together the band Tom had led after high school. They called themselves the Castaways. They had electric piano, drums, lead guitar, bass guitar. Tom played electric and acoustic guitar both, by ear, just like the piano. They performed for three or four years, part time, mostly on weekends. They played every Saturday night at the public dance the Lions Club sponsored in Hamilton, sixty miles up the road.

"I was the money box," Sally told the kids over Christmas dinner, reminiscing. "Mom'd throw a sandwich out the back door and I'd get my cigar box and we'd go. We'd get home at three or four in the morning because I couldn't stay out overnight."

"Why not?" Sammi asked coyly, as if she didn't know.

Sally shot her a look. "They were so handsome up there on stage. They had matching royal-blue coats with 'The Castaways' embroidered on the pockets, black pants, let's see, black patent leather shoes, white shirts, black ties."

"We was El Swifto's," Tom said. Brett grinned. "We got a gig all the way to Des Moines once. Had to leave your mother behind for that one."

"What'd you play?" Brett asked.

"Lots of Jerry Lee Lewis. Elvis and Beach Boys songs, Everly Brothers. 'California Sun,' 'What'd I Say?,' 'Love Me Tender.' "

"Real antique stuff, huh Dad?" Wayne kidded.

"I don't like that hillbilly music," Tom said seriously, "old Ernest Tubb and all. Don't like that fiddle. Don't like bluegrass. I like country today with a big band."

"We know," Brett said. "You don't have to tell us. We're your *kids*."

"The guys felt sorry for me because I couldn't dance at the dances," Sally said.

"Why couldn't you dance?" Sammi asked.

"Because I was going with your father."

"*That's* no reason," Sammi started, hoping for a debate.

"What d'*you* know about it?" Brett chimed in.

Tom cut them off. "We went into this little nightclub. This guy had never hired a band before. He didn't want to guarantee us nothing. We said, 'You stick a man at the door and we'll take the money and you'll get the booze money.' We started packing them in."

"Your dad was a clown onstage," Sally told them.

"I just kept them happy. Anyway, we went that way for three weeks. Weekends. We was working during the week. This guy all of a sudden wants to split the door money. He was making a mint on the booze but he got greedy. We said that wasn't the deal. He wanted us out of there after that. We knew it was a setup job. This henchman at the door supposedly turned around and the money box disappeared. We saw the guy going out with something. We had a gold mine developing there. Then the guy took the money box and that was that."

Sally always counted her blessings at Christmas. Most of all she counted the improvement over the years in Wayne's eyes. She blamed herself for his handicap. Tom said she shouldn't, but she did. It was sent for a purpose, though. She knew that much. She used to think it was God punishing her for becoming a Catholic when she married Tom. She did. Her family was against it.

Wayne had been her first pregnancy and she'd just been ignorant. No one had told her. She hadn't known anything about babies. She didn't know how to eat right. She didn't know what a baby should feel like. She'd carried Wayne to term, but she'd had a partially detached placenta that kept him from getting nourishment. The doctor kept saying, "He isn't growing, Sally," "He isn't growing, Sally," but he never said why or told her what to do about it. Wayne had only weighed four pounds, four and a half ounces at birth. They'd put him in an incubator for a week after he was born. The incubator caused the damage—too much oxygen. They were supposed to cover all their senses in an incubator, eyes and ears and noses, to protect them from the oxygen. They hadn't done that with Wayne. Sally didn't blame the doctor. It was an accident. They didn't sue for malpractice because they didn't believe in that. That was all they heard from some people, sue this and sue that. That wasn't their way.

The doctor who'd delivered Wayne claimed there wasn't anything wrong, but Wayne's eyes even as a baby didn't follow your finger. Sally went from doctor to doctor trying to find someone willing to treat his eye problems. One doctor told her, "He just doesn't want to look at you." Luckily for them, Wayne had a problem with his hip, a bone problem that ran in Tom's family. When he was two and a half they took him to a bone specialist to have it looked at. The bone specialist told them he could fix the hip. But when he saw Wayne's eyes he said, "Mother, let's get these eyes taken care of." He ordered braces and correction shoes. When they arrived, Tom put them on Wayne and said, "Look, that straightens that hip right up." Wayne took off walking then and walked straight into the wall. Tom turned him around and he walked straight into another wall. At least he was walking. Before that he'd just hung onto Sally's legs.

The bone specialist directed them to an ophthalmologist in Kansas City. Wayne got glasses. A few years went by. Wayne's corrected vision in his right eye at that point was 20/100 and in his left eye 20/300. That was *corrected*. When Wayne was six years old, the doctor recommended surgery to improve his head position, his tendency to turn his head to the right to look at objects straight ahead. The surgery involved moving some of the eyes' muscle attachments farther back and releasing some others entirely. After all that was over there wasn't much improvement. Even the doctor said so.

Sally met Dr. Matthewson's wife at an estate sale in Excelsior Springs, an old resort town north of Kansas City. Her daddy was auctioneer. Mrs. Matthewson had flown up from Houston antiquing. She'd mentioned to Sally's daddy that she was a doctor's wife. He'd said, "I've got a grandson I wish he'd look at." He didn't even know what kind of doctor Dr. Matthewson was. He just knew Houston was a medical center and wanted to get Wayne in there any which way. Dr. Matthewson was a heart surgeon, as it turned out. He'd worked with Denton Cooley and Michael De-Bakey. But along the way he'd gotten interested in acupuncture, and he was using it to treat eye problems. He'd gotten interested because he'd noticed his own vision declining.

Tom and Sally's daddy took them down to Houston the first time. When Dr. Matthewson saw Wayne, he wanted to start right away. He got mad when he read the surgical report. "How can anyone cut on some little baby when he knows it won't help?" he asked Sally.

So Tom and her daddy flew home and Sally had to stay with Wayne. It was the first time she'd ever flown on a plane and the first time she'd ever been away from home that long. She was just beside herself. Wayne bucked and kicked so bad when Dr. Matthewson put in the needles. They went in at three points around the eyes, in the bridge of the nose, in the hands and in the elbows. They had to stay in thirty minutes. She had to hold Wayne down. She'd call Tom at night and just boo-hoo on the phone.

Wayne was mad at Dr. Matthewson the first week because Dr. Matthewson had promised him it wouldn't hurt. It did hurt. Wayne told her later the acupuncture needles felt like hypodermic needles going in. He hung on her legs at first. It was a big day when he finally went into Dr. Matthewson's office alone. The doctor made it up to Wayne about the hurt. He took Wayne up in his little plane and flew him over Houston.

When Tom went back to Missouri, he left Sally the money they'd brought. They'd talked to Dr. Matthewson about fees. Tom had said he'd go to the bank for a loan if need be and Dr. Matthewson had said, "Don't you go to a banker, I'll be your banker. You just pay me when you can." That just went straight to their hearts. Who would imagine?

They went to Texas for seven years. It was every other week at first, then every two weeks, then one week a month and so on until at the end they were going once every six months. Wayne had a total of 167 treatments. Sometimes they flew from Missouri to Houston but usually Sally drove straight through to save the cost of an overnight stop, eighteen or twenty hours of driving. She usually drove the Indian Nation Turnpike through Oklahoma because it didn't have any speed limit and she could make some time. Sometimes they'd stop overnight in Paris, Texas. Wayne remembered those stops. They'd pig out on creole food. Then on to Texas the next day and two treatment sessions, one in the morning and one in the afternoon, this little kid running around the doctor's office with needles sticking out of his head, peeking out into the waiting room. Dr. Matthewson would say, "Wayne, are you scaring off my patients again?"

The first regular trip, one of Sally's cousins drove to Texas with her. Her daddy went with her one week and stayed. Tom flew down one Friday to drive back with them. Sammi was born during that time. They went down to Galveston and Wayne carried Sammi out to the ocean when she was two weeks old. Sally had a car wreck in Houston. Her CB radio was stolen in Houston. She lost Wayne once at a big shopping center in Houston. Oh, she got an education in Houston.

Wayne was Dr. Matthewson's youngest patient. A lot of Sally's friends who drove to Texas with her went to see him with problems like arthritis and stomach ulcer. He was using acupuncture for those too. He cured a bleeding ulcer. He told Sally's friend, "Go on home, you're leaving that ulcer behind in Texas." The doctors in Plymouth were amazed. The ulcer was just gone, healed.

Dr. Matthewson lived on a ranch northeast of Houston and flew his own plane to work. He asked Sally to stop over there sometimes when they drove in. He'd put them up in a little house in the backyard. That was when he observed Wayne. Wayne would come out in the morning to play with the dogs and Dr. Matthewson would watch him.

The first time she stayed at the ranch was with her daddy. Dr. Matthewson wanted to take them to eat steak. Her daddy said he'd pay. They drove out to this old store. The groceries were so old on the shelves they looked like antiques. The tables were all wriggledy, the chairs didn't match, there wasn't one plate that didn't have a chip in it. They weren't sure it was all right but they figured Dr. Matthewson knew what he was doing. He said steak all around. They had steak and potatoes and salad. The steak was cooked on an old wood stove and it was the best steak Sally had ever eaten in her life. There was too much. It just hung over their plates. You couldn't eat it all. And you know what Dr. Matthewson and his wife did? They asked for doggie bags and took it home. Sally figured they were going to feed it to their dogs but they told her they had it for breakfast the next morning. They were so common, just down to earth.

The acupuncture corrected the up-and-down motion. It wasn't officially supposed to work on nystagmus, but it did. Wayne said it did and Wayne knew his eyes better than anyone else. Dr. Matthewson told Sally he hadn't found the nerve yet that would control the side-to-side motion. He was still trying when he was killed. They called Sally when his plane crashed. He'd just gotten a brand-new plane and it had a mechanical defect. He and his wife had four kids.

The one time Sally got furious about it all was when the IRS was running an audit on them down to every last detail. The auditor told them he was going to disallow their travel expenses for Wayne's acupuncture in Houston because there were plenty of acupuncturists in Missouri. The IRS was trying to humiliate them, Tom and Sally decided. They ended up humiliating the IRS instead. Tom saw it as a challenge. It just made Sally mad. The government didn't have the right to tell her where to go for medical care. The IRS didn't have to do that. She'd driven straight through all the way to Texas with her little boy to save the motel cost. The IRS didn't have to do that. They took the whole audit to tax court and won.

Wayne had surgery once more when he was eighteen. That time it helped. It slowed the eye motion even more and improved his vision to 20/60 on the right and 20/70 on the left. He could read by holding the reading material up close. Not that his eyes ever stopped him. He was carrying a double major in college in agriculture and agricultural economics and doing just fine. That was the best Christmas present anyone could ask for.

Tom finished combining beans on the third of January. He lost as much as a quarter of his crop in the bottomland fields, where it was wetter. The last days of combining, he'd noticed the white inner lining of the bean pods shining in his headlights at night, which signaled that the pods had split open, lost their beans and curled inside out. He still averaged fifty-four bushels to the acre overall, which meant his yield would have been up around sixty bushels if the rain hadn't damaged the beans. When he was done he told Sally, "I think I'll get me a fifth of whiskey and just sit around here for a couple of days." He didn't, though. He had calves to castrate. Sally reminded him that he had a pile of honey-do's. He groaned about those and threatened to reconsider that fifth of whiskey. But it all got done in good time.

III

PLANTING

ONE

Winter was a time for mending fences and catching up. Hogs and cattle demanded about as much work as ever, but the fields got a rest for a while. The sixty acres of wheat Tom had sown, as much as he'd been able to get planted in the wet fall, vegetated green and sturdy under the patchy winter snows. The other fields lay fallow.

Jack Ward had come out to see the work Tom had done on his fields. He'd been impressed. Tom had already made more money for him by boosting grain yields than his previous tenant had done. Jack authorized Tom to go ahead and have the field terraced where the new tiles had been laid last fall. Tom was a little nervous about spending so much of Ward's money even though he knew the improvements would earn it back and then some. "If he's got money to spend, though," he told Sally, "I sure know where to spend it."

Tom could see years of needed improvements on the Ward farm. He had a bulldozer come in during the winter and build terraces along the hillside that the tiles had reclaimed. While he was at it he had the old Ward homestead bulldozed that was fallen down on the upland. Jack had asked Tom to save two of the big oak trees that marked the site, just for the memory. Trees in the middle of a field make trouble. Tom managed to save one at least. With the house and all the brush they scraped together they had one hell of a bonfire.

The upland and the bottomland were now all one wide, beautiful stretch of land. Come spring, Tom planned to cut the dam on the old pond in the wet area toward the west end of the field. That would drain the pond. Then he'd run a lateral line of tile through the pond area. In another year the field would sweep clean and sweet from the west fence to the creek, up the slope and all the way back to the south boundary.

Molly had her pups, four in all. Tom took them as soon as they were born, so that Molly wouldn't get attached to them, and thumped them. He hated to do it. There just wasn't any place on the farm for four more Heinz 57 dogs running around. It made Sammi sad, but she had her hands full with her rabbits. The doe would drop a litter and then kill them and eat them. It took Tom a while to figure out what was wrong. The buck was caged directly above the doe. Tom figured that was too close. The doe probably felt threatened. He helped Sammi set up two separate cages. That solved the problem and pretty soon they had some baby rabbits.

Molly was back to normal soon enough, lean and hungry and happy, running around. She gave up being matronly and reverted almost to puppyhood. She could be a real clown. That happened one day when Tom was trying to refinance the mortgage on the Dixon place. His regular bank didn't write farm mortgages, which he resented since he'd banked there for thirty years. One day two bankers from another Plymouth bank came out to look over the place to consider a mortgage. One of them was the president of the bank. They drove around in the bank president's white Chevy with burgundy velour interior and Tom showed them all the improvements he'd made—terraces, tiles, bulldozing the old Dixon homestead and the well, cleaning up the fields. They came back to the home place and stood in the gravel lane outside the workshop talking business. Molly came trotting up then with some kind of gray lump of stuff in her mouth, probably a dead mouse. In the lane Tom had burned a pile of straw that had fallen off a truck. It'd left a little pile of ash behind. In full view of Tom and the bankers, Molly proceeded to dig a hiding place in the ash pile for the mouse corpse, just as if the humans weren't there. She dropped in the mouse, covered up the hole, looked around to see if any *important* animal had noticed what she was doing, raised her head proudly and trotted off. Even the bank president laughed.

Tom bought a used tractor that winter to replace the old 1953 Farmall. It wasn't much newer or more powerful, but the difference in price was only seven hundred dollars and it had more usable features—a three-point hitch, power steering, a high-low gear and an independent power takeoff. The old machine had a PTO connected directly to the engine, which meant it kept turning even when the clutch was disengaged. On a mower that could be dangerous. You wanted to be able to shut a mower down before you got off to clean it or whatever.

They bought a backup generator for the farrowing house. Tom had been looking for one for two years but hadn't found one he thought he could afford. This one was almost new. It belonged to a dairy farmer who was going out of business. No one at the farm sale, up near Chillicothe, seemed to know what it was for. Tom told Sally, "Don't look at it. We'll just see if we can get it." Sally told him to go ahead and spend a little more if necessary if it was what he wanted. They didn't need to. They got it cheap. Tom hauled it to Plymouth for servicing the same day and the man there said he'd give them triple their price for it. Now, if the electricity went out, summer or winter, the sows and their litters wouldn't be at risk from heat or cold.

Clarence bought a new pickup, a Dodge, painted metallic silver. "That's my Silver Bullet," he told Tom. It had a V-6 engine, air-conditioning, stereo. He was proud of it. Tom was looking to replace Babe. She still ran, but the body was just about rusted out. He had an eye for one of the used service trucks the electric utility put up for sale every year. They had the same kind of toolboxes mounted on the sides that Babe did.

The board of the Elms Corporation, Donald Landers and his sister and their spouses, had Tom and Sally to supper one evening in Plymouth early in the new year. It was a fancy candlelight dinner with wine and all. It looked to Tom as if they were worried about the harvest having taken so long and maybe worried about keeping him. He'd done their crops first and then his own had been delayed by the weather, with some loss. They asked him if he was

happy with the fifty-fifty split and he told them he was. Sally
thought they might have sensed that Tom had doubts about con-
tinuing to farm their place. He'd been thinking about finding a
piece of land that laid better that wouldn't be so hard on his
machinery. He told them honestly that their farm was good land
but labor-intensive compared to the other farms he worked. The
soil was good. It was just that the hills were steep.

Sammi had her tonsils out. She'd had one bout of tonsillitis after
another. The doctor they went to at the Riverton Clinic was Ko-
rean. They had a little trouble understanding his accent. He told
them he didn't operate on tonsils unless a child had at least five or
six infections a year. Sammi had been through six so far this
winter. Tom told the doctor he could tell whenever she had one
because her breath just smelled terrible.

The surgery was scheduled at the county hospital in Plymouth
for a Friday afternoon. Sammi was excited. She was curious about
hospitals and surgery and she didn't mind being the center of
attention. The anesthetist who took her medical history the morning of the surgery was a sharp black man. She had to wait through
two previous patients before they wheeled her in. It wasn't so
much fun afterward, though. She threw up blood until two o'clock
Saturday morning. She didn't go to school until Tuesday. "She's
not talking much," Tom told Clarence. Both men remembered
having their tonsils out under local anesthesia, sitting up in a chair.
"I spit a lot of blood," Tom recalled, "but I didn't swallow any."
He didn't tell his little girl about his experience. He felt sorry for
her. He knew it hurt. But maybe she'd quit having all those sore
throats.

Rowland Howell set up a series of meetings around the county
during the winter to explain the new farm program. Tom and
Clarence went to the Plymouth meeting at the Lions Club hall on
the east side of town. The banks served supper—beans and ham in
broth, corn bread, coffee or tea—and they ate at long folding
church tables. The hall was about two-thirds full by supper time,
six thirty, well after dark on one of those long winter nights. It was
cold out, too. The coatrack over by the door filled up fast. There
was every color of seed cap stacked along the top. Most of the

attendees were men, but some brought their wives along. Not many women farmers in Crevecoeur County. You saw that more up in Iowa.

Rowland passed around a worksheet. "The handout has blanks on it," he announced from the speaker's table up in front. "We're going to go to school. I'm going to supply you with the numbers—my girls worked them out—so you'll see how the sign-up works.

"Let's take Sodbuster. A misconception of Sodbuster is, 'My God, I'll never be able to plow out sod again.' No. That's incorrect. We ask the public—and I represent the public—to help us out. The public's just saying that we want you to handle your land with good conservation practices.

"Let's go through what happens to you. You walk through the door of the ASCS office and you say, 'I want to sign up for the program.' We have to ask you some questions.

"One. 'Have you plowed out any ground that was planted to a conserving crop, grass or legume, in the years '81 to '85? Ground that you *have* plowed out or *will* plow out this spring?' That's a very fundamental rule to learn.

"Two. 'Are you going to convert any wetlands to the production of any agricultural commodity?' What's that mean? Say you've got a slough that you're going to convert to cropland. That falls under the Sodbuster program. I don't believe that applies to any farm in this county.

"The third question also deals with swampland.

"If you say no to all three questions, then we file the form and that's that. If you answer yes, then we have to pass you over to the SCS. Any land with a slope greater than three percent is almost certainly going to be considered highly erodible. Everything but bottomland and the tops of ridges.

"So. One. No plowed ground. That's okay. Two. Slough but not highly erodible. Okay. But, three, if plowed and highly erodible then SCS has to take over, to work out a conservation plan. What terraces and waterways and what crop practices. The law doesn't give you a choice. The law says you have to bring erosion under control to get *any* government programs. So my advice to you all is to get to the offices as soon as possible to get started."

Rowland was talking fast and hard. Tom had heard it before but it was new to Clarence and to most of the other farmers in the hall. Everyone was listening.

"Does this just apply to your farm?" Rowland went on. "No. It applies to your Social Security number. Every farm you have an interest in has to comply before *any* benefits can come to you. It's really an all-encompassing-type program, and I'm going to be brave enough to tell you that I'm in favor of it. I'm concerned with what kind of land we're going to have to farm fifty years from now.

"Where I see a collision coming—it's kind of like two bulls facing off and getting ready to collide. One is the Sodbuster program. The other is the feed grain program. I suggest you think meadow in the future as a rotation crop with corn and beans. Because corn and beans in rotation, even with terraces, isn't going to be enough to comply. So until those bulls collide I suggest you think meadow.

"Let me tell you, gang, it's time-consuming. It takes hours. We're going to have to put up cots and bring in sleeper vans the way it looks. And we're going to do it by computer this year.

"We estimate it's going to take eleven man-years to get all these conservation plans for the county together.

"Okay. I'm going to leave Sodbuster. Three years from now, all farms will be considered to be under the Sodbuster program, all land with slopes greater than three percent. We have four hundred five thousand acres in the county and more than three hundred thousand will fall under the program."

Sodbuster was the big new program, but Rowland had a list of smaller changes to go over. "Feed grain next," he told them. "The wheat program offers only one basic option and that's seventy-two point five percent. One of the fundamentals of the program is that you can't harvest grain in excess of seventy-two point five percent of your base if you want to participate in the program.

"But what's in it for you? Okay. How many of you think you'll see four-dollar wheat this year?" Someone snorted. No one held up a hand. "Three-dollar wheat?" No hands to that question either. "Right. Well, the government thinks two twenty-eight, and that's what you'll get if you sign up." The government price was still much better than market.

Rowland told them about set-asides, land set aside and not cropped for which they could earn compensation. "Set-aside comes to just about two hundred forty dollars per acre. How many think you can earn that for wheat? And your advance payment won't be reduced by Gramm-Rudman-Hollings.

"A couple of other areas in wheat I want to talk to you about. Wheat corn. Wheat beans. How many of you know what those are? They're corn and beans, right, allowed in *specific* fields normally part of your wheat base. I know of some farmers who sowed wheat in early January. I know why they did it: to get a deficiency payment. I've got a surprise for them. They ain't going to get it. The county committee established at the beginning of January that you reduce payment by one bushel for every day past November fifteen you planted. Wheat is unique. It doesn't exist unless it goes past June one. You got to let the wheat mature to grain. You got to combine it to get the payment. If you lose a crop you got to come to the office and we'll file a failed grain report. Then you get a deficiency payment. But those of you who planted wheat in January, don't tear out that crop until you check with us."

He told them about a sixty-five-percent corn option, a plan that encouraged them to plant only sixty-five percent of their corn base. "That's less corn if the market goes up, but a guaranteed deficiency payment regardless of what happens. I think this is going to be a very popular option. It has been so far, down at the office."

He described a special program designed to reduce their corn planting even further, 92/50. "If you take the sixty-five-percent corn option, then 92/50 only allows you to plant half of that. But if you cut down to only fifty percent of permitted acres then we'll pay you ninety-two percent of what we would have paid you under the sixty-five-percent plan. That's a little over six thousand dollars with only thirty-two and a half acres compared to seven thousand dollars for sixty-five acres. That other thirty-two and a half is idled land, what we call conserving-use acres. You can graze it and hay it without restriction, just so you don't plant it to a commodity. The 92/50 program is picking up popularity down at the office because we're reducing your risk and because you're going to pick up the difference on your wheat ground."

Rowland went on to take them through the worksheets, number

by number, working out the consequences of the various options the farm program offered. "We're going to enroll by computer this year," he reminded them again after half an hour of worksheet drill. "If you've made some decisions on options before you walk in the door it'll be very helpful. It'll save lots of time. And if you enroll and give us all the signatures and the paperwork, we'll get your advance payments out to you faster than any other ASCS office in the state. We think we've got the computer up and ready to go. The folder of forms for each of you is *that* thick. We're going to walk instead of run. But we're going to try to get you your checks and your payments within two weeks. I've just hired on some extra people to work on a night shift to get the payments out. Last year we had about ninety-seven percent of the ground that was eligible enrolled."

He shot them a last question. "Preventive planning: can you move your fields?"

Several farmers answered at once. "No!"

"Amen," Rowland ended his presentation.

Tom was impressed. He turned to Clarence. "You can tell that boy didn't ride into town on a load of cabbage."

Clarence was a rock-rib Republican, so he had his differences with the ASCS director, but he didn't see how he could disagree with that.

Sally got busy on taxes. She posted all their income and expenses for the year to new pages in the big ledger where she could accumulate the totals. They had income in the year just past from corn, wheat, soybeans, cattle, hogs, a little custom work, the PIK certificates and some interest. Gross income from hogs came to $50,527, from calves raised $14,825, from corn sold $23,402, from wheat sold $2,661, from soybeans sold $43,573, from custom work a little over $3,000. The PIK certificates had been worth nearly $11,000. Total gross income for the year with some depreciation figured in was $152,090.34.

That had to be set against expenses, though. Water for the year had cost them $587, farm electricity $1,274, home electricity $275. Their phone bill was $652. Insurance came to $1,014. Livestock feed cost $23,392, hired labor $1,309, machine labor $825.

They paid $17,329 in interest counting mortgage interest and $1,610 in taxes. The vet cost them $318. Seed was $3,134 but fertilizer and chemicals took $22,345, second only to livestock feed. Dues and subscriptions cost $100, fuel for farm use $7,396, truck expenses for four trucks $2,480, car expenses $217. They made donations of $908, paid doctors $2,761, paid $325 for tax preparation and $781 for storage and warehousing. Repairs— those combine pulleys and the big tractor—came to $10,514, supplies to about $4,500. Livestock cost $4,255. Depreciation on machinery came to $7,186 and Sally attached a long list of scrapped machinery and equipment. Total expenses for the year were $117,608, for a difference between income and expense of $34,482. They still had income and Social Security self-employment taxes. As it turned out, they cleared about $19,000 for the year. Farming was a good life, but it didn't make you rich.

TWO

"**I**f I had my choice," Tom told a friend once, "I'd raise just cattle. I like them. They're a lot cleaner than hogs. But hogs is where the money is." Tom had grossed nearly three and a half times as much from hogs last year as from cattle, and the net difference was even higher, but his formula for successful farming was diversity, and cattle were a necessary part of the mix.

In the middle of February, Tom decided it was time to sell some of his calves. These were mostly older animals that weighed about five hundred pounds apiece, calves he'd raised on shares with the Landers. He had fifty-four ready to sell. Whoever bought them would finish them to about a thousand pounds on corn in a feedlot. After finishing, they'd go to slaughter.

Tom liked the auction barn down in the stockyards in St. Joseph, Missouri, north of Kansas City two hours away by car. He'd done better by it in recent years than by auction barns closer to home. The day before the auction, he loaded his calves into a hired semitrailer and shipped them to St. Joe. For a fee, the yard there would hold them overnight and run them into the auction when it was their turn to be sold.

Tom and Sally got up early the next morning. Clarence was going along for the ride. They picked him up and took off for St. Joe. It'd been the home of the Pony Express once, a major jumping-off place to the West, and it was still a wild town. They had a six-foot ball of binder twine in the Pony Express Museum there that some farmer had spent a lifetime collecting and a reconstruction of the dental office of Walter Cronkite's father. Cronkite was a famous St. Joe native.

Tom had heard once about the escapades of one backwoods St. Joe family that still lived almost as much by hunting and fishing as it would have a hundred years ago. One of the boys in the family hadn't gotten his annual deer yet during deer season one year. This kid was supposedly driving down the highway one day when he saw a yearling buck caught up in a fence. The kid didn't have his rifle in his car. He was so desperate to get a deer that he swerved off the road, jumped out, extricated the animal from the fence and dragged it back to his car. He managed to get the trunk open without losing his hold and stuffed the deer in.

So here he came driving up to his mom and dad's place outside of town with this young buck making a tremendous racket rat-a-tat-tatting its hooves against the inside of the trunk lid. The kid ran into the house calling out, "Gimme a gun! Gimme a gun!" and not explaining anything. His dad handed him a rifle and some shells and he ran back out to his car. He must have figured he couldn't open the trunk or he'd risk the buck getting away, because he loaded the magazine on that rifle and proceeded to shoot the buck *right through the trunk lid*. The tattoo of hooves stopped abruptly and there the kid had his deer. That was St. Joe for you, not your uptown poker club kind of town but full of spirit.

When Tom climbed the wooden stairs to the open walkway above the outdoor holding pens at the sale barn that morning and looked down on his calves, he blew a gasket. The trucker had loaded a bunch of loose cattle in the upper deck of the semi and they'd relieved themselves all over Tom's calves down below. The animals looked like hell. Their hair was matted down. You'd think no one ever took care of them. "There's going to be words with that bastard," Tom swore angrily. "Them buyers don't want those shorthaired calves. They want the longhairs that show the breeding. These look bad. It's probably worth a couple of dollars a hundred. It just makes me sick." Clarence kept quiet. There wasn't much anybody could do at that late date. It was too cold to have the animals hosed off and they'd look worse if you did. The three of them followed the walkway around to the sale barn and went in, entering under the roof at the top of the stands.

The stands were wooden ledges like giant stair steps that curved around the full width of the hall. They were already filling up with farmers and commission men. They banked down steeply to the sale floor in front. The sale floor was oval, big enough to hold forty or fifty head of cattle at the same time, with a low barricade at one side like the barricade in a bullfight ring where the drovers could duck for safety if a sale animal got wild. The auctioneer's grandstand backed up to the wall opposite the stands. On each side of the grandstand there were doors cut into the back wall. Sale lots of animals would come in one door and go out the other. Fluorescent lights were suspended from the high ceiling on chains to light the sale floor. A warm gloom of dust and cigarette smoke hung over the stands. Over the grandstand, a big digital sign read out the number of head in the lot being auctioned and computed their average weight.

Selling had already started when Tom, Sally and Clarence came in. The assistant auctioneers were whooping and pointing from the sale floor, taking bids. They were selling open cows first, cows that weren't pregnant. Those went in lots and then they sold a few pound cows and a stray calf. The stray calf went for $105. Tom remembered the number since it measured more or less what a calf was worth by itself when you bought a cow with a calf at its side.

There wasn't a lot of shouting and waving. These old country boys played it closer to the vest than that. Someone would nod, someone would reset his cap or pull his ear, and the helpers would whoop and point and the auctioneer's chant would pick up a notch. He had his patter to keep them entertained while they bid. A new lot of cattle would come in, bursting through the left door, fanning out, spinning around to take up a defensive stance with rear ends together and heads facing out, the drovers breaking them up and moving them with their whips so that the bidders could see them on all sides and see them move, and the auctioneer would read off what they were and what condition they were in. When he got to pregnant cows, the lots were divided up into first, second and third trimesters—preg one, preg two and preg three. The question came up whether one herd of small heifers had been vaccinated for brucellosis and the auctioneer chanted, "Maybe, maybe not, only their hairdresser knows." Some wild young animals crowded in, kicking up their heels, and the auctioneer called, "Here's a green set of cattle, boys, I mean greener than a hoppin' gourd."

Clarence leaned over to pass along one of his jokes. "Say," he asked Tom and Sally, "you hear about the old farmer who had a bull that wouldn't breed? The vet gave him some special feed. Farmer fed it to the bull. Four days of that and it went out and banged six cows. Neighbor asked what was in the feed. 'I don't know,' the farmer told him, 'but it tasted like licorice.'" Sally rolled her eyes. Tom laughed, but Clarence just about convulsed. Nobody laughed as hard at his jokes as Clarence did himself.

The auctioneer turned to lots of cows and calves and came to a dispersion sale of Simmentals, a big breed of cattle from Switzerland that had become popular in the United States for crossbreeding with the traditional English breeds—Angus, Hereford and shorthorn. Tom didn't think much of the so-called exotics. He'd tried Simmentals and had major problems with calving. When the first lot of Simmental cows and calves trotted into the sale ring, the bidding immediately picked up. Tom gave Clarence a nudge. "Clem," he drawled, "they want them Simmentals, don't they? I believe I've had enough experience with them."

"I believe you have, Clem," Clarence agreed.

"It's what you take home that counts," the auctioneer encouraged. The barn was full now. The lot on the floor went out and a series of individual cows went by, all Simmental, all part of the same farmer's herd. The farmer took up an extra mike at the side of the sale ring and identified each cow and pointed out its breeding, any injuries, special points. All his cows had been bred by artificial insemination. He was obviously proud of them. Probably another older farmer with no children who wanted to carry on his life's work. "Now, boys," the auctioneer chanted, "take a look, getting to the heart of the watermelon here." Roan, chocolate or coffee in color the cows went by, big, long, most of them preg two or preg three, handsome.

Tom sat silent. He was worrying about his calves, but this Simmental business was too rich for his blood. Simmental cows were

going for seven hundred dollars or more when regular cows had
been selling before at a little over five hundred. Farmers got sucked
into fads just like everyone else and he figured exotics were pretty
much a fad. "A fella could spend a hundred thousand dollars here
today, easy," he complained to the smoky air. He lit a cigarette
and went off to look for his commission man. He wanted to talk
to him about the matted hair on his calves. He came back twenty
minutes later looking determined.

Bidding slowed down on the English-breed cows and calves.
That didn't mean they weren't a better deal. One lot of six cows
and six calves went for $530 per cow, which meant the cow cost
$425 if you counted the calf at the price the stray had sold for
earlier. It was a hell of a lot easier to make a profit on a $425 cow
that already had a calf at her side than a $700 preg three cow that
could lose the calf along the way, exotic or not.

Finally the feeder calves came along and Tom started paying
attention. "Here we are," the auctioneer announced when the first
lot ran in, "a set of cattle came off the grass, they're green as a
hound." A lot of twenty-one Angus steers caught Tom's attention.
They were comparable in age and finish to his. He leaned forward
to watch. They averaged 591 pounds each, the big digital sign
reported, total for the lot 12,410 pounds. The auctioneer took
them up, his helpers whooping and pointing. Farmers were moving
in and out of the aisles talking. The Anguses brought a good
$72.10 a hundredweight and Tom took note.

A bigger lot in, the biggest of the day, fifty-two head jammed
together into the sale ring, older animals too, average weight 723
pounds, total 37,600. "You talk about a smokin' good deal," the
auctioneer encouraged. This lot wasn't as popular. They went for
only $71 a hundredweight.

Then Tom and Sally's commission man came out from the holding area and they knew their calves were up next. The first nineteen
head ran out and swirled in the ring. "Here we are," the auctioneer
introduced them, "they're greener than a gourd. Got hair on them
a foot long, boys." So the commission man had talked to the
auctioneer about the hair problem. Tom thought they still looked
like hell. They weighed an average 566 pounds for a 10,760 total.
The bidding rolled right along. Tom's eyes were flicking left and

right as he looked to see who was bidding. Before you knew it they were sold, at $72.50.

"That's not bad," Sally said. "That wasn't as bad as I thought."

Six more of Tom's steers came in, 418 pounds each, 2,510 total. "That's the light end on the steers," Tom told Clarence. They brought a good price, $77.25.

Two heavier steers, 662 each, down to $70.75.

One bugeye at 410 sold for only $60 a hundredweight. They'd expected that.

"Here come the heifers," Tom announced. Nine at 486 pounds each. They sold at $68.25.

Another batch of twelve. "Here come the rest of them," Tom said. At 537 pounds each they brought $68.

When the next batch came in Tom nodded and smiled. "I forgot my little heifers," he said. The five averaged 327 pounds. The bidding didn't go as high as Tom hoped. "They're stealing them," he complained when the auctioneer began his final countdown. The little heifers went for $68.50. Tom looked glum.

After Tom and Sally's last lot was sold a new auctioneer took over with a delivery so fast he sounded like a machine gun. He auctioned off the cattle that had ridden above Tom's on the upper deck of the semi. They weren't much cleaner. "See how messed up they are?" Tom pointed.

Later, four heifers that averaged 378 pounds each went for $70. "They're just about identical to mine," Tom complained, "but they sold for that much more. That's the appearance." He wasn't going to be happy about the appearance. But it hadn't been a bad sale if you averaged all the animals together.

Clarence had another joke for Tom, to cheer him up. He told Tom and Sally while they were walking out after they'd collected their check. "There was two bulls that got together at the end of summer," Clarence began. "They asked each other how their summer'd been. One said he'd had a great summer. He'd been up in the mountains, the water was cool and they'd given him fourteen heifers to bang. 'Hell,' the other said, 'I had a terrible summer. I was down in Oklahoma, it was hot as hell, they gave me six old cows to service and some steer kept following me around complaining about his operation.'" That got a laugh.

Tom had been thinking lately about buying a bigger tractor. With a big four-wheel-drive job he could chisel and fertilize at the same time by hooking the implements up one behind another to the tractor. That would pack down the soil less and save labor and tractor fuel. Steiger made the best of the big four-wheel-drive articulated rigs. On an articulated rig, the body was hinged in the middle so that the front and the rear axles steered independently. A few years back, you could almost tell who was going to go bankrupt and lose his farm by who was buying new Steigers at ninety thousand each. Those guys were gone now and their Steigers were up for sale.

They still weren't all that cheap, though, and Tom didn't feel he could afford even a used one unless he could get it for under thirty thousand dollars. But another angle was a Ford FW60. It was just like a Steiger, 4WD, eight wheels, articulated, but it didn't have the same name value and usually sold for less. There was a Ford tractor dealer in St. Joe. Tom had called him and found out he had an FW60 on the lot. They detoured into St. Joe proper to look it over.

The FW60 was sitting off to one side. It looked as if it'd been outdoors awhile. Tom didn't make a fuss about it. He gave it a once-over quietly without climbing up to the cab to check the engine hours. Then the three of them hiked over to the showroom to talk to the dealer. It didn't look as if he was in a big rush. The FW60 was a consignment from a St. Louis outfit, he told them. It wasn't moving. He'd had it on the lot, in fact, for two years, and he wouldn't mind getting it off. But they wanted a lot of money for it and they didn't seem to care how long it took to sell.

Tom took down the name of the St. Louis outfit. He'd give them a call from home, he said, and see if they'd come down on their price. He thought the tractor could probably use some overhauling and the dealer admitted it probably could.

They talked away for a while and Tom finally asked the man how business was.

The dealer made a face. "I sold forty farm tractors last year," he said. "This year I sold two. I have trouble making a living on that."

They took their leave. Driving home, Tom speculated that the

man must have a pal in mind to buy the FW60 to be so discour-
aging of a possible customer. Let it sit on the lot until the seller
gave in on the price and then call up his pal. Tom decided he'd
wait and look farther for a big tractor. Maybe a better deal would
come along. Today they'd sold a bunch of calves. They'd made
some money instead of spending it. And before long they'd have
another frisky new crop.

THREE

Tom would have known spring was coming even if the calendar didn't say March. Before a storm brought driving cold rain now there'd be thunder rolling off in the distance and balmy air. There were dead skunks and possums again on the roads because the animals had started moving around again after holing up for the winter. Fred Siegelstecher had crews out planting hundreds of apple trees. The pastures were turning greener by the week and starting to fill up with calves.

Brett and Wayne were chiseling the fields whenever they could steal time from school. Tom could read the mildness of the passing winter in the gear ratio they had to use to pull the chisel plow. "The ground's chewy, rubbery," he told the members of the Elms Corporation at their formal annual meeting in the dining room of Donald Landers' house in Plymouth in mid-March. "My boys've had to drop a whole gear to chisel it. It didn't freeze and thaw enough this winter to heave itself loose." He'd have to chisel everything this spring to compensate for the lack of heaving. Normally, with some fields, you could go straight to disking and only chisel every other year. The big chisel plow, a Glencoe Soil Saver, had a row of twenty-two disks up front to break crust, then two gangs of chisels, six per gang, like thick, polished knife blades turned flat and bent into a curve, then a triple-set row of spring-loaded harrow spikes to tear up clods. Farmers didn't turn the soil over with old-fashioned plows anymore if they could avoid it. Minimum tillage saved soil moisture and left weed seeds near the surface where herbicides could reach them.

As long as they were chiseling, they went ahead and chiseled the garden. That was like using an elephant gun to kill a mouse, but it beat plowing out the garden by hand. The garden was Sally's department. She was especially proud of her asparagus. Nero Polotto had taught her how to grow asparagus. There was an old variety, Martha Washington, that grew wild along the fencerows in Crevecoeur County. Asparagus was a perennial. It took four years to establish itself to the point where you could harvest it. Nero had told Sally to dig up her plants from the fencerows. That way she'd have asparagus from the second year onward. He'd showed her how to plow a furrow for the row. He'd put chicken droppings in the bottom of the furrow. That was the kind of rich, acid fertilizer asparagus liked.

But his special secret had been salt. He'd said asparagus was a seaside plant in Italy. It loved salt. Keep it salted, he'd told Sally, and it would thrive. She salted the furrow when she planted and she side-dressed the asparagus bed with salt every year. The salt helped the asparagus and also kept down the weeds. People said Sally's asparagus was the best they'd ever tasted. It didn't taste bitter like store-bought asparagus from California. It tasted mellow and nutty.

Sally and Tom had battled with the power company over the asparagus bed a few years back. The power company needed to move the line that led to the house. They'd sent out a crew one day to set a new pole. Sally had looked out the window and found them setting the pole smack in the middle of her asparagus bed. She'd run out and asked them to move it and they'd told her it was too late. She'd called Tom on the two-way then. He'd come in from the field and argued with them. They hadn't listened to him any more than they'd listened to Sally. Tom was easy to get along with, but that kind of treatment made him mad. He'd decided that if they wanted to inconvenience him, he'd arrange to inconvenience them a little. So he planted a tree under the new power line.

Tom's duty with the Devon volunteer fire department generated another sign of spring, tornado drill. The Devon fire station was a prefab metal building put up new the previous summer. It didn't have a bathroom yet but all the materials were in, a stool and plastic pipe and partition boards. They had a Ford F-750 Big Job open-cab fire truck built in 1953 that they'd inherited from Grants when Grants got a new one. There were only a few thousand miles on the Ford and it was old-fashioned red. The big tornado siren was mounted on a telephone pole outside the station. When the central dispatcher in Grants called them on their home monitors, they'd meet at the fire station and run the truck out and hit the siren when the time mark came through on the radio. They practiced for fires, tornadoes and crashes of aircraft from the air base down the road that operated the missile field. Don't talk to the press, the Air Force officer had briefed them, don't try to put out the fire, just keep the crowds back and the jet fuel out of the creeks. Tom had a full fireman's outfit hanging in the mud room ready to jump into if he got a call.

At the Elms annual meeting, Donald Landers showed him the latest round in a battle the Landerses were having with a neighbor—a letter they'd had their attorney send. The neighbor's name was Higgins. He was a city man who'd moved to the country, years back. Tom liked to point that out because he didn't want to have to claim the bastard for a country boy. They'd caught Higgins red-handed trying to steal Landers land.

Even though everyone's property was deeded and platted and abstracted all the way back to the Indians, fences finally decided where one property line ended and another property line began. If two landowners stood facing each other square in the middle of a line of fence, each was responsible for all the fence to his right. If one man refused to maintain the fence, the other could back up three feet and build a fence all his own. Then the other man couldn't put cattle against it. If he wanted to run cattle he had to build his own fence on the property line. The three-foot space in between was called dead man's alley.

But once a fence was in place for ten years without being contested, it decided the property line. That was how someone could steal someone else's land. That was how Higgins had tried to steal Landers land. It was just pure luck he didn't get away with it.

Everyone knew the man was a thief. He wasn't much for fixing fence. When a fence washed out after a storm he'd call Tom and ask him to come help fix it. Tom would show up with a roll of fence wire and the necessary tools and Higgins wouldn't be there. That got old fast. Tom put up with Higgins' shenanigans twice in a row and then told Higgins to fix his own fence. Anyway, it looked as if Higgins let his fences fall down for a reason. A few years back, three of Tom's cows and calves had gone over to Higgins' land through a hole in a section of fence that Higgins was responsible for. They were animals Tom had just bought at auction on shares with Donald Landers' father, Eli, back when Eli was still living and running the farm. Tom hadn't marked the cows yet. They still had bright yellow auction-barn ear tags in their ears. Higgins claimed they were his. Tom went to see Eli Landers to decide what to do, but old Eli hadn't wanted any trouble. "God takes care of people like that," he'd told Tom. By the time Tom got back to Higgins' place, the cows had their tags removed and there wasn't anything he could prove. He lost the cows and calves and learned a lesson.

What Higgins did to steal land was to move fence. He'd moved fence on a kid to the east of his place when the kid was just starting out farming. Higgins had taken a line of fence that ran straight north and south along a body of timber and swung it out at an angle to enclose some of the kid's field. The kid hadn't known where the line was supposed to be so he wasn't any the wiser until it was too late. Higgins didn't even farm the land he stole. He just let it grow up into timber.

Tom had gotten wind of the claim jumping when a tree buyer had come by. The tree buyer had said he'd bought some trees from Higgins along Little Cebo Creek and wondered if Tom wanted to sell him some more from the Landers side of the fence. Tom had thought they might and had gone down to the woods to see. He'd found the fence moved three hundred feet onto what he was almost certain was Landers land. Higgins had painted little white numbers on the trees to be cut. There were nineteen trees that should have been Landers'. They weren't worth more than two or three hundred dollars.

Tom had called Donald. Donald hadn't wanted to accuse anyone until they were sure of their facts. He'd gotten out the survey map and he and Tom had walked off the distances and found the corner post. There wasn't any doubt then that the trees Higgins had sold were on Landers land and that he'd moved the fence to take them in. Donald was amazed. "I never walk down here, Tom," he'd said. "I haven't been in these woods since I was a boy."

"We was down here deer hunting," Tom had told him, "but I sure didn't look over this way. You don't expect your neighbor to be moving fence on you."

"If that tree buyer hadn't come by, Higgins would have gotten away with stealing the trees and the land both."

"He might have," Tom had agreed. "I don't know as I would have noticed it. I'd like to think I would have, but I don't know if I would."

Once they were sure where the fence line was supposed to be, Donald had studied up on the problem and consulted with the family attorney and had the man send Higgins the letter. "We threatened him just short of libel," Donald told Tom at the Elms annual meeting. "He called me a week later and apologized abjectly and profusely. He said he took down the fence to replace it."

"It wasn't his to replace," Tom said drily.

"You're damned right it wasn't," Donald agreed. The whole business warmed him considerably. "He said he thought the line was farther back. Said he remembered discussing it with my father."

"Maybe that was while he was stealing them cows and calves," Tom said.

"Oh, that's right," Donald said, his face getting redder. "I'd forgotten about that." He studied the attorney's letter, attached to a clipboard with a stack of other papers, then looked up at Tom again. "I told him I wanted him to meet me right on the property so we could straighten this business out. I'd like you there to back me up. Will you do that?"

"Sure," Tom said. He'd be glad to face the bastard down.

Tom went to the meeting with Higgins and came home with a story to tell. Sally couldn't wait to hear. "Higgins is about as big as I am," Tom told her. "Donald was scared of him. That's why he wanted me along. We met him down there by the creek. He's

real nice, you know. He's got that quiet, smooth voice that sounds
so reasonable. He's oily, though. Slick." Tom was good at imita-
tions, so good that even if you'd never met someone you knew
what he was like when Tom was done imitating him. He pursed
his lips and brushed his hand almost effeminately past his face.
" 'Oh yes, Mr. Landers,' " he imitated Higgins, pitching his voice
high, " 'how *are* you? Nice to *see* you, Tom.'

"Always smiling," Tom went on in his normal voice, "trying to
make it hard for you to get mad at him. How do you get mad at
someone who's smiling at you and agreeing with you all the time?
Donald was just telling him off, raking him up and down. I seen he
was getting mad, Donald was getting mad, he was shaking, and I
kind of took him aside and cooled him down.

"Higgins was just telling one lie after another. He showed us a
map and said it showed the corner as an elm tree. I said, 'That's
way back in 1927, and anyway, how come you put the corner
marker on a hackberry tree?'

"He said, 'Mr. Landers, I was just going to fix the fence,' and
Donald said, 'Then fix your own goddamned fence, this is our
fence to fix.'

"Donald just about couldn't talk by then, he was so mad, so I
took over. I said, 'Higgins, you're just completely out of line.
That's old stuff. That's the way they did things back at the turn of
the century. We don't work that way out here anymore. Anymore,
the name of the game is cooperation. If you weren't sure where the
fence line was, you should have gotten in touch with Mr. Landers
and we could have talked it over. What did you think you had to
gain? Everyone knows what you did to that boy to the east and
people are going to hear about this too. That's not the way we do
things out here anymore.' "

"That's plain old trashy," Sally agreed.

"I just stay away from guys like that," Tom said. "They're just
rotten. You just don't do a neighbor that way. And for what? A
little old piece of timber. Down on a creek where it floods all the
time. It ain't worth it. I noticed he took black paint and painted
out all them little white numbers he painted on the trees. Donald
got him, though. The fence at the edge of the timber, between
Higgins' land and Landers', was just nailed to the trees. It's been

there more than ten years. Higgins' property line actually comes out about six feet into Landers' pasture. Donald and them was going to let him put that fence back where it belonged. Now Donald told him just to leave the fence where it was. So he lost some land because of what he was trying to pull instead of gaining it."

Cleaning drain tiles was a chore that came up every spring. It had to be done, but no one much wanted to do it. Trees liked tile. Normally a tile ran full with water all year round, carrying off the underground flow, good water for tree roots. The drain tile that Tom and Wayne drove over to the Elms to fix on a cold, wet day in the middle of March stuck out the side of a steep bank of dirt at the edge of a field, a length of white plastic pipe about three feet long. It barely flowed a trickle of brownish water into the pool it made in the runoff channel below. Tree roots had clogged it. Up in the field there was a slough formed where the slope came down.

Tom had his Indian tricks for cleaning out drain tiles. He'd loaded Babe with a coil of flat steel tape fifty feet long and a length of heavy barbed wire. Standing in his rubber boots in the cold pool below the drainpipe, he bent the barbed wire into a loop and hooked it to one end of the steel tape. He handed the coil to Wayne, who backed down the channel uncoiling it as he went.

Tom fed the barbed-wire loop into the drainpipe. Wayne twisted the steel tape. The twist made the tape corkscrew and drove it up the drainpipe. After they'd fed in a few feet of tape they'd feel the barbed wire catch inside and the tape would get hard to turn. They'd wind it as tight as they could and then slowly draw it out. They did that nonstop for an hour. Each time, as they drew the tape out, they'd feel whatever it was hooked into give way and the barbed wire would emerge with a wad of wispy roots caught up on the end but no main plug. The water would still be trickling out instead of flowing full flow. The air was full of a cold mist blowing in from the north. They were standing in cold water, their faces dripping wet and their buckskin gloves soaked from handling the wet steel tape. That was the kind of work you did in the spring.

They came back from dinner with a plumber's snake. They wired the plumber's snake to the front section of the steel tape, along with the barbed wire, and started in again to work. It took another half an hour of twisting the tape and the snake up into the white pipe, getting a little farther up each time, pulling out wads of roots, and then Tom felt the wire bite into something big. They twisted it as tight as they could, hearing the snake taking up the twists inside the pipe, scraping and twanging, and then they started pulling the whole mess out. It gave a little at a time, like pulling something apart. That was the little roots tearing one by one to loosen the big wad.

When it finally tore loose, the surprise nearly knocked Wayne down. He staggered back, though, and kept his footing, taking the steel snake with him, and out slipped a black plug of wadded roots as big around as a man's hand and six feet long. It looked like nothing so much as the world's biggest blacksnake. Wayne let out a whoop.

But the water still wasn't flowing. They chewed around some more and after a while they decided there must be a second plug higher up. They worked another cold hour pushing and pulling, cranking the tape clockwise and then counterclockwise. Finally it caught. This time they pulled out a thicker but shorter plug. Behind it came a flood of dark brown water spilling out a good six feet into the runoff pool. That would clear the slough.

If the previous tenant had put a final hundred feet of unperforated tile under the edge of the field where the trees were, Tom told his son, then they wouldn't have had a drain problem. The tree roots couldn't have gotten in. When you can't use your brains, you have to use your back.

Tom kept watch for cows that were springing. A cow that was within a week of calving had a dropped bag and a soft, loose vulva. If the udder was dropped but the vulva was still tight and closed, the cow might be in trouble. Tom watched those cows in particular.

He had cows calving at home and cows calving at Landers'. He checked them two or three times a day. It was smart that he did. Late one morning, when it was raining hard, he'd driven to the Elms with Clarence to check a cow. He'd noticed the cow getting ready to calve in the pasture, down in the hollow below the barn, behind the feedlot where he'd confined the older calves earlier in the winter to wean them. He was driving the GMC. He stopped at the feedlot gate to lock in the four-wheel drive so he wouldn't get stuck in the mud. Inside the gate he shifted into 4WD and drove out into the greening spring pasture. It was spread with dark brown clumps of straw-matted manure in wide bands that ran back and forth from the feedlot. Scraping up cattle manure from the feedlot and spreading it on the pasture was another spring chore Tom had been performing. He had an old manure spreader he pulled behind one of his smaller tractors, an iron-wheeled wagon with an endless chain of scraper bars built along its bed that moved manure to the rear, where an arrangement of screws and paddles flung it out behind. Spreading manure was old-fashioned, but Tom couldn't see wasting a feedlot full of free fertilizer. Better to hook up the old turd hearse and spread it on the pasture.

Coming over the rise, Tom spotted the cow. It was down in the hollow a little into the brush, a few feet beyond the mowed edge of the pasture. It had just dropped its calf and was getting up. Tom looked for the calf and spotted it on the ground. It didn't seem to be moving and for a second he thought it might have been born dead. Then he saw it had a caul over its head. He slammed to a halt, threw the gearshift lever into park so fast that the truck rocked back and forth, jumped out without a word and ran down the hill in the rain to the calf. The cow backed off a little ways and then inched up to watch while Tom pulled the wet, bluish caul off the calf's head. The tough, sticky mass clung to his hands and he had to fling it away. As soon as his hands were free he grabbed the calf by its hind legs and swung it around in a circle, mucus flying from its nose and mouth. When he thought he'd cleared its passages he laid it down and stood back. The cow came up and licked it. She got to the afterbirth and started eating it. The calf was wheezing and sneezing but it was strong despite its ordeal. It was already trying to get up, propping one long spindly leg and then another.

"We just got here in time!" Tom called to Clarence. Clarence could tell he was excited. "Five more minutes and we'd of lost it!" Tom strode back up the slope to the truck and stooped to wipe his bloody hands on a clump of dead grass. "Nice big calf," he told Clarence. He heard it still wheezing. "Reckon I ought to pick it up some more?" he asked.

"Nah, it's okay," Clarence said. "Get it on its feet here, it'll be all right."

"Yeah," Tom agreed a little doubtfully. He didn't want to lose it after he'd just saved it. "You know, Clarence, we ain't had any of them breech births this year. Had all kinds last year."

"It was them bulls you used," Clarence said, watching the calf.

"Same bull," Tom corrected. "No, I think it was that ice last year. Cows would slip on the ice and wrench that calf around inside there. The mild weather this year is what did it."

The cows and calves were a Hereford-Angus cross, black-bodied with black-and-white faces. Tom and Sally liked to watch the calves run late in the afternoon when they'd nursed and were feeling their oats. Speeding, Tom called it, running around the big lot to the south of the house. The cows knew their calves first of all by their voices when they bleated, but they'd check them close up by sniffing them before they allowed them to nurse. Some calf was always trying to steal a meal. Tom had one all-black cow that was mean. She'd paw the ground whenever she saw him in the lot. He didn't mind. She was a good mother.

Tom fed the newborn calves a solution he made up to get them started growing. Cows produced colostrum the first few days before their milk came in. The calves needed it for the immunities it carried, but it wasn't very nourishing. He supplemented it with a bottle of starter made up of salt, baking soda, fruit pectin and consommé mixed with water. A calf had to learn to loop its long, narrow tongue around one of its mother's teats to nurse. If it didn't learn within twenty-four hours of birth it was in trouble. Tom would rope the cows if that happened and teach the calf to nurse, prying open its mouth, stripping milk from one of its momma's teats and squirting it in.

Before dinner one wet, balmy day, on a routine check of the Landers cows, Tom found a problem with a small Angus that he'd been expecting to calf. Her milk was down, dripping from her teats, and there was mucus hanging from her vulva, but she wasn't in labor. That could be serious. He herded the cow into a ten-by-twelve wooden holding pen and called Doc Mitchell at dinner-time from the house. They agreed to meet at the Elms after dinner to see if they needed to pull the calf.

It was breezy. The sky had opened to patches of blue with scudding puffs of white clouds. Doc drove up in his muddy pickup right after Tom. He took his lariat, climbed into the holding pen and roped the cow. As soon as the little Angus felt the rope around her neck she began shaking her head. Tom had the end of the lariat outside the pen. He and Doc started hauling on it. The cow braced herself with both forefeet, hauling back, but the two men won the tug of war. They cranked her over to the fence and tied her close.

Doc pulled on an arm-length blue poly glove, soaped it with Ivory Liquid, bunched his fingertips together and worked his arm up above the elbow into the cow's vagina. She squirmed but stood her ground. "Full dilation," Doc told Tom. "The calf's in position. The uterus isn't contracting."

"What is it?" Tom asked. He was standing behind Doc, out of the cow's line of sight.

"Uterine inertia. We'll have to pull it."

Now that they knew there was a calf on hand they were suddenly in a hurry. Doc had brought a calf puller. He strapped the harness onto the cow's hindquarters while Tom screwed together the brace and chain. The brace, like half an iron barrel hoop, fitted against the cow's rear. An iron pipe with a handle bolted onto the hoop. A light steel chain led from a crank back at the handle through the brace. Tom set the brace against the cow's hindquarters and Doc immediately began guiding the light chain inside. When he had it looped around the calf's front hooves he brought it back out the cow's vulva and anchored it to the brace.

His knees flexed, leaning back, Tom began turning the crank. Doc guided the calf. The cow felt the pull and arched its back and started bellowing. The two men and the cow strained together to birth the calf. When it came, it came all in a rush, slipping out long and thin and cylindrical like the plug of roots that had slipped from the tile pipe, partly covered with placenta shining purple-white.

As soon as the calf was out, the cow stopped bellowing. Tom hurried to dismantle the calf puller. Doc dropped down to work

over the calf. He cleaned it off, grabbed its hind legs, hauled it upside down into the air and began swinging it back and forth to clear its mouth and nose. Its hooves were bright yellow, coated with wax to protect the birth canal. Abruptly it began to blink and breathe, gasping at first, sneezing mucus from its black nostrils. Doc lowered it to the ground and got out of the way. Tom released the cow and she spun around to inspect her calf, sniffing it from one end to the other and poking at it with her nose. Satisfied, she began licking it. The afterbirth still hung from her vulva. She had an eye on the two men still in the pen with her. She started bellowing. The other cows in the lot trotted over.

"That's her danger call," Tom told the vet. "We ought to get out of here."

Doc nodded, still watching the calf. Tom climbed over the top of the pen and the vet followed. In between licks, the cow was butting the calf now to encourage it to stand. It tried once, all legs, got nearly up and then flopped over onto its side and stared. The cow went back to licking. After a while she butted the calf again. This time it got to its feet and stood, looked around, found what it was looking for and headed for her udder to nurse.

"I like spring and fall best," Tom told Doc out of the blue then, grinning, another calf saved. "You can see where you're going."

FOUR

Tom planted corn before soybeans because corn had the longer growing season. Corn germinated at fifty-two degrees, which translated to a soil temperature at a depth of three inches of fifty-five degrees. In central Missouri, the soil warmed up to that temperature by April 13 at the earliest, so April 13 was the earliest Tom could expect to plant. Before then he had more than enough to do to prepare the ground. Every field, regardless of what he'd plant in it, had to be chiseled, disked and fertilized. Wayne and Brett helped when they could. Brett even stayed home from school one day to get the bottomland field on the Dixon place chiseled before it rained. But most of the work was Tom's.

One sunny morning early in April he chiseled the bottomland field on the home farm. It was one field south of Camp Kooka-munga, across the fence from some set-aside land, the first field he'd reclaimed with tile when he and Sally had bought themselves a farm of their own. Level, with just enough slope for good runoff, it was a beauty. It sloped gently south toward Little Cebo Creek and the creek defined its southern end. The creek line was marked with sycamores, as running water always was in Missouri. Syc-amores grew taller than the other second-growth timber along the creek and their bark was mottled white, so they stood out from the background.

The soil in the upper half of the bottomland field was Marshall silt loam, the deep, wind-deposited loess off the old glaciers that thousands of years of prairie grasses had worked to fertility. The lower half of the field was Kennebec, another good silt loam deposited by flooding and also worked by grass. Kennebec was rich enough, and it broke up well under the chisel and the disk, but it dried out faster than Marshall. They were both close in color, a dark brown. Turning them with the chisel plow released their winy, complex smell. A man would almost be at a loss to describe it, but a good nose could pick out smells mixed together of caramel, potatoes, algae and pond water and very lightly of shrimp, all touched with something peppery. No surprise that the smell was so complicated. A lot of different things went into making soil.

Soil was first of all rock. Weathered rock particles made up the mineral part of soil. Sometimes the rock weathered in place and the soil it formed was like the underlying bedrock. Sometimes, as with Marshall silt loam and Kennebec, the soil blew in or flooded in from somewhere else and overlaid the bedrock. The three major mineral components of soil were sand, silt and clay, and their relative proportions were basic to determining the soil's qualities, especially its ability to hold water. Rock was important for its capacity to support plants and trees physically, to give them anchorage. But if anything was to grow in it, soil also had to contain water. Water adhered to the rock particles and was incorporated into other soil components. Too much water was as bad as too little. Plants couldn't live in saturated soil. There had to be space among soil particles for air as well. Plant roots took up oxygen from the air spaces in soil and exchanged carbon dioxide.

Sandy soils were the most porous, silt next, clay the most impervious. A gram of medium-sandy soil might contain no more than six thousand sand particles with a surface area of about 45 square centimeters. A gram of silt—rock particles fine enough to feel smooth, like powder, rather than abrasive, like sand—contained some six million rock particles with a total surface area for water retention of about 454 square centimeters. A gram of clay soil, by contrast, contained some ninety billion flat, crystal-like, microscopic clay particles with a total surface area of 8 million square centimeters. That much surface area would hold a lot of water. Clay was fine for ceramics. It wasn't much use for farming.

Soils evolved and had histories. The soils on Tom's farms and the soils on the orchards north of the federal highway were different because their histories were different. Soils like Tom's that formed under grass contained about twice as much organic matter as soils like the orchards' that formed under forests. The organic matter in such soils was typically as much as five hundred to two thousand years old. Grass roots died every year across that long space of time and decomposed to organic matter, but tree roots were long-lived. The total amount of organic matter in a forest and on a grassland was similar, but most of the organic matter in a forest was bound up in standing trees, while ninety percent of the organic matter on a prairie was in the soil. The pioneers who first encountered the great tall-grass prairies of the Middle West thought they were barren because they were treeless. "If it ain't fit for trees, it ain't fit for plowing" was a rule of thumb that Tom had heard people once used. Such people had learned farming on forestlands in England and Europe. When they finally essayed to plow up the prairie, they discovered that its soils were much more fertile than forest soils. Even today, after a hundred years of use, prairie soils yielded ten to twenty percent more corn on the average than forest soils.

An acre was an area of land a little more than 208 feet on a side, equal to about one and a half football fields squared off. A seven-inch-deep plowed layer of soil from that acre weighed roughly two million pounds. Of that two-million-pound furrow slice, about twenty thousand pounds would be organic matter. About sixty percent of the organic matter in soil was from plant residues, ten percent of it cellulose, fifty percent lignin. Lignin was the woody part of plants, inedible and slow to decay. Thirty-five percent of the remaining organic matter was protein from soil microorganisms.

The material that held most soils together was microbial gum, ropy or netlike molecules of complex sugars secreted by soil bacteria or decomposed from their cell walls. Organic matter usually darkened soils. In the Midwest, darker soils usually contained more organic matter than lighter soils, color to some extent measuring fertility.

Life below ground was as various and lively as life above. An acre furrow slice of soil contained about two thousand pounds of living bacteria, some billion bacteria per gram. It contained at least as many pounds of living fungi and almost as many pounds of actinomycetes, fungilike thread bacteria. Algae and protozoa were usually minor components. Disease organisms were minor but important. Tetanus lived in soil. The lockjaw its toxins caused was once a serious hazard of barefoot farming. A piece of cast-off wire or a dirty nail could kill.

Nematodes, microscopic worms that fed variously on decaying organic matter, earthworms, other nematodes, plant parasites, bacteria and plant roots, were the most abundant animals in soil. From the point of view of farming, they were more often parasites than partners. Farmers liked earthworms better. Two hundred to a thousand pounds of earthworms worked an average acre furrow slice, work that loosened the soil and improved its porosity. The commonest variety of earthworm, which was originally imported to the United States from Europe, dug shallow burrows and foraged on plant wastes at night. Other kinds of earthworms ate their way through the soil underground, breaking down organic matter, absorbing some and passing the rest through reworked as excrement. Charles Darwin studied earthworms and discovered that they deposited some ten to fifteen tons of excremental castings on an acre of ground every year, turning over an inch of soil every twelve years and slowly burying the old soil surface.

Arthropods, animals with external skeletons and jointed legs, lived everywhere in the soil. Springtails and mites, insects and their larvae, centipedes, millipedes, spiders, slugs, snails and wool lice fed on plants, organic matter and each other. White grubs ate plant roots, fed moles and emerged as May beetles and June bugs. Ants and termites competed with earthworms in the amount of soil they turned over and moved around.

Some larger animals inhabited the soil, including moles, mice, ground squirrels, gophers, marmots and prairie dogs. Other larger animals worked it, digging burrows and dens. The most active of those was man.

Plants took three basic nutrients from the soil that had to be replaced for continued production. They were the three nutrients

with which Tom was most concerned when he fertilized. One
hundred fifty bushels of corn, the yield of one good acre, 8,400
pounds, contained about 135 pounds of nitrogen, 23 pounds of
phosphorus and 33 pounds of potassium. Standard dry fertilizer
was usually a mixture of compounds of those three elements, their
proportions varying according to the characteristics and deficiencies of a particular soil. The same 150 bushels of corn also contained about 16 pounds of calcium, 20 pounds of magnesium, 14
pounds of sulfur, and trace amounts of boron, iron, manganese,
copper, zinc, molybdenum, cobalt and chlorine. The absence of
trace elements caused deficiencies in plants just as they did in
people.

Soil was a living body. Tom respected it as such.

Chiseling was hard work on the tractor. Turning over the dirt a
foot deep pulled rugged in second gear. As he always did when he
was running one of the tractors for an extended period of time,
Tom wore earplugs made of foam that wadded up like bread
dough and then expanded once they were in place to fill the ear
canal. Without the earplugs the engine would have been a steady
roar. Too many farmers over the years had lost their hearing
running noisy machinery. Tom was beginning to be concerned
about the tractor he was driving. It had hours on its diesel engine
that would amount to half a million miles if it were a car. It was
close to needing a major overhaul.

The dirt the chisels were turning was cold, about forty degrees
by Tom's reckoning, too cold for planting. Seed would lie there
and rot. He knew some old boys who were already planting, taking
a chance that the weather would keep warming and the seed would
hold out and give them an early start. Tom didn't see the sense in
gambling. If you gambled wrong you lost your seed and had to
plant all over again.

Over the winter, the corn stobble from last year's crop had
rotted. That was rot Tom wanted, to break down the stalks' fiber
and release their nutrients back into the soil. The disks on the
chisel chopped the rotten, softened stalks and turned them under.

Tom was chiseling the field from north to south and back again,
turning around in a tight circle at each end and following back the
edge of the dirt he'd worked on his last pass. Alternating back and

forth was the most efficient way to work the soil. It wasted the
least time and fuel. A steeper field, with terraces to control soil
erosion that had to be followed out, would take more time and
waste more time to work. That was why Tom liked the lay of this
particular land.

There was a big badger hole in the fencerow at the north end of
the field, a mound of loose dirt the badger had excavated and a
tunnel running in under the fence. The chisel turned over rabbit
nests, holes the rabbits dug in the open ground that they lined with
fur from their crops. They'd drop their litters into the nests, cover
the nests over and go off to forage, come back and nurse just by
lying over the hole. The baby rabbits could nurse that way, from
below, without being seen.

Killdeer skimmed the chiseled field under the blue sky for insects,
calling *Kill deer deer, kill deer deer.* A sulphur searched the clover
in the set-aside land next door, a butterfly version of the killdeer
skimming nearer the ground. In the timber along the creek there
were purple and white wildflowers blooming and a patchy ground
cover of pink-flowering weeds in the field itself. Tom was working
in an enclosed cab, but when he got down to relieve himself at the
side of the tractor he smelled wild garlic from the grass along the
timber. He noticed stumps among the trees pointed like pencils
that beavers had gnawed off.

He was going to plant this field to beans, rotated from last year's
corn. There wasn't much corn on the ground. He'd turned the
cows into the field over the winter and they'd cleaned it up, leaving
behind manure that helped fertilize it. He rotated his crops primarily to keep down disease. The boys who farmed the Missouri
River bottomlands didn't like to rotate. Beans were cheaper to put
in than corn and there was less risk if it flooded. But cheaper
wasn't always better. The beans got a nematode infestation that
built up when you didn't rotate. You'd see big patches along the
river where the nematode killed everything. It could take out a
whole field. If they'd rotated they wouldn't have had that trouble
so much.

The next morning, sunny again, forty-eight degrees going up to
sixty, Tom was out early. The fields of the Dixon farm had already

been chiseled and disked. Today he'd start knifing in anhydrous. Anhydrous ammonia was a gas, eighty-two percent nitrogen, the rest hydrogen, that was fixed from the air in reaction with steam and natural gas. Tom had bought his supply this year from MFA in Osage Station. MFA furnished the gas pressurized to a liquid in a white, capsule-shaped pressure tank twenty feet long. The co-op also loaned farmers the rig for knifing the fertilizer into the soil. Tom pulled the whole setup behind his big Oliver tractor. The rig had a gang of knives that cut into the soil about six inches deep. Hoses carried the anhydrous from the tank to the knives. When Tom opened the valves, the gas jetted from small holes near the tips of the knife blades. The gas combined with hydrogen in the soil water and stayed where Tom put it. Later on, after the corn was planted and growing, he could tell almost to the day when the corn roots reached the layer of nitrogen. Up to that point the young corn would have been medium green. As the growing roots took up the nitrogen, the whole field turned a green so dark it was almost black. Every farm kid at one time or another had dribbled granulated nitrogen fertilizer on a patch of grass to write his name. After a rain, the fertilized grass would turn dark green and stay that way most of the summer.

Anhydrous was another reason why tractors needed enclosed cabs. It was dangerous. It reacted with water, so it went for the eyes and if it got into them it burned them badly. Every anhydrous tank had a safety pod attached to one side with goggles and gloves and a water reservoir with a hose you could grab to flush your eyes if you got gassed. Tom knew a guy over in Franklin who was blind from anhydrous. Tom watched the wind when he was knifing in anhydrous and turned into the wind to avoid driving through a cloud of the stuff. It was a good deal, though. It was cheaper than dry fertilizer and something you could inject down at the plant-root level where it did the most good. It didn't need rain to activate it.

MFA delivered a second tank of anhydrous later that morning. Tom worked as fast as he could. He'd ordered his fertilizer first, way back in December, so he'd gotten first call on the knife rig, but there were lots of other farmers waiting in line.

The waterways were greening. So were the earliest trees. There was a smell of wild garlic in the air again and sometimes a whiff of ammonia from the anhydrous. Bees worked the wildflowers along the edges of the field. Molly, pregnant again, raced ahead of the tractor. She'd learned to stay well away from the anhydrous. Blaze had gotten a whiff that morning when Tom squirted the gas to test the valves and had run off sneezing to rub her eyes in the grass.

Midafternoon, Tom headed for the gate to trade tanks. He'd left a couple of strips of field along the waterway unfertilized so that he wouldn't have to deadhead. He'd knife the last strip with anhydrous on his last trip out. Molly stopped to sniff the remains of a rabbit in a terrace channel, fur and a little blood a hawk had left.

Tom donned safety goggles and heavy green rubber gloves to switch tanks. He shut off the gas at the knifing rig, bled the line, disconnected the hose and hooked it back onto its trailer. Then he drove the tractor around to the new tank and hooked it up. A hoot owl hooted from the timber. Twenty minutes after he started he was back at work. There was smoke in the air, someone to the north burning off a field. Down in the bottomland field, below the one he was fertilizing, he'd found broken pieces of crockery once among the arrowheads. He figured settlers had taken over an Indian campsite and built a log cabin.

A few days later, when Tom had finished knifing anhydrous on the Dixon place, he disked the bottomland field on the home farm that he'd chiseled before. The weather had turned cooler under a hazy sky. Disking went a lot faster than chiseling. The disks didn't turn the dirt as deep. Molly ran ahead. He disked the outside perimeter of the field first to make a turnaround lane, going clockwise following the fence and the edge of the creek timber. Flooding had washed a pile of cobs and stalks against the fence in the southwest corner of the field. He'd lit the pile the day he'd chiseled. It was still smoldering but it was mostly ash. He went over it with the disk a couple of times to turn it under.

Once he had a turnaround lane, Tom began disking straight north and south, the way he'd chiseled before. At the end of a pass he'd drop the tractor's high-low gear lever to low, hit the lever that raised the disk out of the dirt up onto its rubber tires, throttle back

the engine, hit the wheel brake in the direction of the turn to keep the turn tight, straighten out as he came around, throttle up, hit the hydraulic lever again to time the lag so that the disk dropped parallel with where it had come out before and advance the high-low to high. The high-low changed the gear ratio without Tom's having to push in the clutch and shift the regular gearbox. On a tractor, with all the drag of the implement it was usually hauling, pushing in the clutch usually stopped the machine dead in its tracks.

Yellow flowers had come into bloom on the waterways. The fields had started to look currycombed.

Two coyotes came out to watch the proceedings. Tom had seen the bitch before and suspected she had a litter somewhere in the neighborhood. Molly chased the coyotes into the timber. She was always chasing whatever turned up in a field when he was working, mice or rabbits or deer. He went on about his business.

On the next turnaround he saw the little black dog high-tailing out from the timber. It looked as if there was something wrong. When she got closer he saw that her neck was bloody. She went on running ahead of the tractor. After a while he started worrying about her. Her neck was swelling. It was pushing her head side-ways. Tom figured she must have gotten into a fight with the coyotes and they'd torn up her neck.

Then she was staggering. She acted as if she was in pain. He didn't believe in free rides and he'd never been sentimental about pets. She was the runt of the litter. She was pregnant again. They'd wormed her twice but she'd never grown up to her potential.

Molly fell down then and couldn't get up. Tom made a face. He'd have to put her out of her misery. He stopped the tractor. He left it roaring behind him and did that hard work and went back to disking.

While he was getting ready to plant, Tom was buying and selling. He and Donald Landers consulted nearly every day about wheat futures. They'd sold half their wheat on futures contracts already and were thinking about contracting more. Tom followed soybean futures at the same time. The market had been creeping up for two weeks. It got to $4.78 one day and he decided to sell some contracts. Sally was over to her brother's ceramic shop and he didn't check it with her. He figured she'd trust him on it. He contracted a thousand bushels each of his, Landers' and Ward's beans, about a quarter of the forty bushels per acre that was the worst he'd ever gotten in the way of yield.

"I don't feel as confident this year as I did with my Chernobyl beans," he told Clarence that afternoon in the workshop, cleaning a peck of dirt out of the tractor cab filter. "The weather pattern looks like it did in 1980 when we had that bad drought. It's warmer right now in Montana than it is in Miami. That may be what's spurring this market. But the Chinese done sold more corn to Japan than they can deliver. Argentina and Brazil got a dock strike that's holding back shipments. I think that's what's pushing the price up. I don't know. Maybe I'm being too conservative. I guess I can always sell some more later if it keeps on. Sally'll have a fit when she gets home. She'll say, 'You haven't even planted and you've already sold them.' "

In the middle of all the selling, Tom took delivery on the seed corn he'd ordered. He bought his seed corn from his brother Dale, and exactly on April 13, Monday morning, Dale arrived in his pickup with the camper shell full of fifty-pound bags. Tom had him back up to the door of the shed behind the workshop where he kept his seed. He'd already taken delivery on his soybean seed. He bought half his soybeans as certified seed every year and used his own seed beans, the ones he'd stored in the grain wagon at the Elms, for the other half. That way he was never more than one generation away from certified. Since he planted hybrid corn, though, and hybrids were sterile, he had to buy all new seed corn.

The two brothers looked over the soybean seed Tom had bought before they unloaded the corn. It was a Jacques variety. Dale was interested in seeing its quality. Tom opened one of the bags of soybean seed at the back of the shed and took out a handful. The beans were dyed purple to indicate they'd been treated for fungus. They were Missouri-grown beans, guaranteed eighty-eight-percent germination. Tom looked for a place to spread them out. Dale offered a buckskin glove. They searched the beans and found some that were shriveled. Dale raised an eyebrow, but he didn't say a word.

Tom dumped the soybeans back into their bag and then the two men began unloading the seed corn, Dale handing the bags off the pickup and Tom in the shed stacking. Tom had bought ten bags of Funk's 4500, fifteen bags of Funk's 4513 and twenty bags of Funk's 4560, three different varieties with three different maturing dates, to build in a safety factor. If drought came and one variety was burned out at tasseling time, another might be spared. The stack of bags made a solid pile about as big as a single bed. At the cost of $2,850 worth of seed, human labor, fertilizer, machinery wear and tear and diesel fuel but with free water and free solar energy, the bags of seed corn would multiply to fill grain bins the size of houses. Farming created capital. It didn't just transfer it from one pocket to another. Tom worked every day with his hands plunged deep into the real world. That was probably why not much ever got him down.

He'd bought a new planter. He'd been harassing the dealer up in Franklin about it for weeks. The man had it on his lot but hadn't finished a conversion yet that Tom had ordered on it. Every few days Tom would call. "Clyde," he'd say. "This is Tom Bauer. I figured you done forgot my phone number." Tom would recite his phone number just for the fun of it and then they'd talk about when the planter would be ready.

Finally the dealer got the conversion done and sent the planter out on a flatbed. It was a beauty, a Kinsey eight-row. "Last year everything was okay," a neighbor told Tom with a twinkle in his eye after he'd inspected the new machine. "This year you ain't anybody if you don't have a Kinsey eight-row planter." It was all hydraulic and electric, twice as wide as the old one Tom had been using and foldable. Its steel frame was made up of two L-shaped beams that came together to form a T hinged along the length of the long axis. The planting units attached along the cross-beams, which rode on rubber tires. The long beams hitched to the tractor. With the long beams hinged like wings, the two L's rotated up and down independently. Tom could plant along a terrace and one L would hinge up to cover the terrace slope while the other L ran level along the channel. He could plant right over the top of a terrace and the two L's would flap down to follow the slopes. The whole operation was twice as fast and that much more flexible. Enclosed wheels, mounted vertically up under the seed bins, picked up individual seeds in notches along their edges and carried them down to tubes that dropped them behind the small cultivators that opened up the seed channels. There were electric eyes in the tubes that counted the individual seeds as they dropped and sent a signal to a computerized display box that Tom had mounted on the hood of the tractor directly in front of the steering wheel. Every time a seed dropped past an electric eye, a display diode flashed. Tom could tell almost instantaneously whether the seed was dropping or when a seed tube was clogged and he got a digital readout on the rate. The seeds were fluorescent pink, treated with insecticide to protect them in storage from corn maggots.

With the soil ready and his planter finally at hand, late in April, Tom started planting. He finished the Landers fields in two days. The third day of planting, the twenty-fourth of April, he moved to the forty acres. He started early enough, pulling the planter folded up behind the tractor, to arrive by eight fifteen, but MFA hadn't shown up yet with the truckload of granulated fertilizer he'd ordered. He radioed Sally to call the co-op and get them into gear. They'd had truck problems, she reported, but the load was on its way. Tom waited. The morning was cool, the sky was clear and there was a breeze out of the north.

The truck arrived and began spreading fertilizer. Tom allowed it a good lead and started in himself. He was still new to operating the planter. The trickiest part was the end of the row. The planter had a small outrigger disk on each side, mounted on a long, hinged, hydraulically operated arm. It scratched a dark line of unplanted soil as the planter went along down a row so that the operator had a line to follow coming back up. Coming to the end of the row, Tom had to haul in the marker he'd been using, slow down, cut off the seed delivery, turn around an implement twice as wide as the one he was used to hauling without running into the fence, get everything going again and lined up and drop the other marker into place. The long marker arms looked like the arms of a praying mantis hinging up and down as he turned. "You got to have all your oars in the water when you're running this thing," Tom would say.

He used an open tractor to plant. He could see better that way. The day was warming up. Coming out on 24, he'd found the apple orchards in bloom north of the highway, white bloom against trees beginning to leaf out a darker green. The perfume blew across the highway mingled with diesel smoke from the tractor exhaust.

The wheat field directly to the west of the field he was planting was lush green. The wheat was about a foot high now.

The fertilizer truck finished. The driver honked and waved and went off. Tom was alone in the field, nothing but fields and empty road as far as the eye could see.

A coyote appeared on the terrace dead ahead. It stood and watched the advancing planter, then circled around to the next terrace west and paused to see if the machine would kick up any mice. Tom watched back, wondering when the coyote would catch his scent. When it did it turned and trotted on southwest to the corner of the field, looked back once more, jumped the fence and was gone.

You ate some dust planting with an open tractor, but Tom liked the exposure. There wasn't a better time of year than spring. A few rounds after the coyote, a Cooper's hawk came skimming low over the wheat field. Tom figured it was looking for baby rabbits. A Cooper's hawk would hover right over a tractor, waiting for you to scare up some game.

Tom doubted if anyone who wasn't born on a farm could understand how he felt about the land. "Why, hell," they'd say, "it's just a piece of dirt." It was more than that to him. He knew every piece of it and how it laid and its problems and all. But he couldn't explain it and he didn't see how anyone could understand it who hadn't lived it. Even Sally couldn't quite see it. "You know what you're going to do on that land," she'd tell him. "How can you be sure it'll come out the way you see it?" He just was. He was just plain old Tom. He didn't have no fancy words. He didn't have no fancy clothes. He just wanted to take care of his family and do his best. But he had the land he farmed in his head. That Dixon farm, he'd walked the whole thing, hunting. Hunting rabbits. He'd seen the things that need fixing, improving—erosion, drainage, problems.

You got so you knew every terrace, every row. A farmer didn't

have pretty hands. There wasn't no way he could keep his finger-
nails clean. But when he fixed something he could look back and
see where it was and the whole history of it and he knew he'd
made it work. That was a great satisfaction.

He remembered the seventies. He'd spent a lot of money in the
seventies. They'd never owed more than twenty-five thousand dollars at a time, but they'd borrowed again just as soon as they got
something paid back. A new tractor, the feeding floor, ten thousand dollars to fix up the house. Hogs had paid for a lot of it. They
were a stinky animal, not so pleasant to work with, but they'd sure
done well by him. He'd been in the black every year, but they'd
lost nearly half their net worth anyway. He blamed Reagan most
of all for that.

They'd bought a nice piece of land a while back on Highway 24
near Plymouth, a little piece of woods. He'd be forty-seven this
year. He'd figured they could move up there by the time he was
fifty or fifty-five. Sell the house and the outbuildings for sixty
thousand dollars or so and build a nice house. Rent the farm. He
could come out and cut weeds along the fencerows and help keep
things up. It didn't look as if they'd be able to do that now, the
way things were. He'd seen these farmers getting old. They slowed
down, let things slacken because they couldn't keep it all up anymore. He didn't want that to happen to him.

Maybe he'd stop by and see the retirement land next time he was
in the neighborhood. The old Santa Fe Trail ran right through it.
There was a marker about it out on the highway. The trail got used
so much in the old days it was worn down below ground level. A
man could stand in it and barely see over the top. He liked being
hooked up that way with the old pioneers.

He had an idea for the bottomland on the Dixon place. He used
to get standing water there when there was the least extra rain. He
wanted to put in more tile, really cover the field, and fix it so that
he could pump water back up into the tiles when there was
drought. He'd have an underground irrigation system then with no
evaporation and no runoff. He figured it would cost him about six
thousand dollars. It'd pay itself back. You'd always know you had
a crop unless it missed germination. So you could soak the fertilizer
to it and probably get two-hundred-bushel corn out of it.

Maybe he wouldn't get it done but maybe his son would. Farmers were just stewards. It wasn't their land. They owned it for a while, but it was for their children and grandchildren.

He had sows farrowing, the farrowing house filling up again with pigs. He'd found an 8.5-percent mortgage at the Federal Land Bank to replace the 12-percent he'd been carrying on the Dixon place. The other day he'd turned the cows and calves out into the new spring pasture. It was the first time the calves had ever been on grass. They'd shot out of the lot ahead of their mommas, kicking up their heels and flagging their tails. A little ways out they'd caught themselves, turned and raced back to their mommas to check in. Then off again speeding. The cows kicked up their heels, too, for the pleasure of the new grass.

Sally was home redoing Sammi's bedroom, putting up new wallpaper and re-covering the floor with reconditioned carpet she'd bought at a garage sale. Wayne was doing well in college. Brett was getting excited about his People to People trip come summer to New Zealand and Australia. That looked as if it was going to be a thousand dollars well spent. The new planter was a honey and planting was going fine. Tom had worried a lot more back in the early eighties than he did today. He could see a direction now. So here they went round again. Seedtime and harvest.

He was a happy man.

EPILOGUE

The next year, Tom decided to give up the Landers place. Clarence was going to semiretire. Besides his own place, he'd been working a farm north of 24 on shares for an outfit out of St. Louis, Carter's, that managed farms for banks. He recommended Tom to take his place. "After Clarence Galen was through with him," Sally told people, "this guy from Carter's thought Tom Bauer walked on water." The new farm laid a lot better than the Elms. The Landerses were sorry to see Tom go, but they'd kind of been expecting it.

Rain hadn't been a problem this last summer. The problem had been drought. Tom wasn't sure at first but that he'd lose his entire crop, but as the summer burned on and the whole country got to hurting, he'd been lucky. Rain had come just when the crops needed it to flower and make seed. "We're the Garden of Eden around here compared to them old boys back in Indiana and Illinois," Tom summed up. They didn't qualify for enough drought aid to make it worth the trouble to fill out the papers. Corn came in at around a hundred bushels to the acre, beans at about forty, but prices were up enough to make up the difference. At one point, beans were selling above nine dollars a bushel.

The hybrid wheat hadn't worked out. It didn't yield much better than certified seed despite its higher cost. The farmers who'd

329

bought it agreed they wouldn't plant it again without a demon-
stration.

Tom quit smoking. Once he'd lived through the nervous part
and got used to doing without, he felt a lot better. He chewed some
gum, but it wasn't hard to stay off cigarettes. He'd been ready to
quit. Sammi was proud of him. Sally cut down. That helped.

A tornado tore through the Dixon place one spring day. It took
the roof off the old barn, exploded the walls, carried the roof
down the hill and dropped it in the timber along the creek. Everyone was away from home at the time except Sammi. She went
down into the basement and hid out under the stairs. No one saw
it happen except their neighbor to the north. He saw the tornado
just lift the roof off the barn and spin it through the air down the
hill. The combine was stored in the barn. The tornado damaged
the body some, several thousand dollars' worth, but it didn't hurt
the works. It broke up the header, though. Tom bought a new one
that was smaller and fit his fields better. He would have bought a
used header, but nothing used was available and he got a good
deal. With the insurance money for the barn, he and Sally decided
to add a heated garage to the house. That let them park their car
and the GMC in the garage and freed up the workshop implement
shed for the trucks, which made room in turn for the combine to
be parked up at the Ward place. The garage was a beauty. It
doubled as a party space in the summer.

If his new header was smaller, the disk Tom bought was larger
than the one he'd had before. He found a used thirty-foot disk
with new replacement disks for just two thousand dollars and the
trade of his old disk. The replacement disks alone were worth
more than two thousand. The disk was a White and so big that
most farmers couldn't use it. Tom couldn't have used it if he'd kept
the Landers place, but the farms he worked now laid well enough
to take a disk with a thirty-foot spread. It would have cost him
twenty-four thousand dollars new.

Tom and Sally made their last combine payment. Sally kidded
Tom that he'd probably want to buy another combine now, but he
said he liked the one he had just fine. The new tax law set them up
to need some new depreciation, so he bought a new tractor, a
White 185 with front-wheel assist. Front-wheel assist was almost

as good as four-wheel drive. The White 185 was half again as big as his big Oliver. It had a computerized display that you could program to show a map of the field you were working and then would keep track of what you'd done and how much you had left to do. Tom could do that in his head. Mainly the new tractor was big enough to go over all the ground he had to work.

They'd adopted a couple of coyotes, a male and a female. Tom had dug out the pups the day they were born. You had to catch them when their eyes were still closed or they'd never tame. They kept them in a cardboard box in the kitchen for the first weeks and fed them out of a doll baby bottle. Now that they were grown, they lived around behind the new garage and played with the dogs. Blaze was gone, succumbed to old age. Tom and Sally had taken on a beagle and a new black Labrador pup. The coyotes treated the dogs about the way people treated dogs, as pets. Compared to the coyotes, the dogs were dumb. The coyotes were the size of miniature collies, fluffy, wiry and quick, with narrow muzzles and shrewd yellow eyes. They walked almost on their toes, sort of sideways, skittering around wary and alert. If Tom held a plate of food full reach above his head, out of sight, one of them would leap straight up eight feet into the air just to take a look. They had that kind of curiosity. Tom thought they were great. They weren't confined. They roamed off during the day and came back at night to their food bowls. He'd watch them playing out beyond the garden. What a life they had, free as the birds!

Sammi was a teenager now. She'd shot up a foot in the last year and gotten slimmer. She was almost as tall as her mother. She'd started on braces. She was trying to decide what she wanted to be. For a while she wanted to be a scientist. Then she wanted to be a lawyer. Sally said it was something new every day. Sammi's latest was that she wanted to go to Harvard. When the time came, she probably would. She was smart enough. Harvard could use a smart farm girl from Missouri.

Wayne had come up against a wall his last year in school. He'd gotten a job at a new factory in the town where he went to college and had tried to go to school and work the job at the same time. His diabetes had flared up. He'd realized then that he had to slow down to at least ordinary mortal status, so he was taking fewer

courses. He had his senior year yet to do and six hours beyond
that. Then he'd get his degree. He'd found a steady girlfriend. She
lived in Plymouth. She was still in high school. She doted on him.
He understood that he wasn't going to farm.

Brett had returned from New Zealand and Australia a lot more
grown up than when he'd left. He'd had a great senior year in high
school, playing football and dodging girls. He'd joined the Air
Force in March of his senior year with his induction scheduled for
the following December, just before Christmas. He wanted to be a
jet mechanic. *Top Gun,* the movie, had partly sold him on it. He
even looked a lot like Tom Cruise. He had an Air Force uncle's
career in mind as well.

Tom and his younger son had worked together all last summer.
Brett showed a lot more interest in farming than he ever had before
and took more responsibility. "A man's got to have pride if he's
going to do a good job," Tom said of his son. "Brett's got pride."
They had a great time together. "He plays with me like I'm a
younger brother," Tom told Sally. It must have reminded Tom of
when he'd been the youngest boy in the family, growing up.

Toward the end of the summer Brett even confided in his dad, "I
don't know, maybe after four years in the Air Force I'll be back
here farming." That was all Tom needed to hear. When the op-
portunity opened up in the fall to take on another farm, he did.
"I'm planning ahead," he told Sally. "Just in case the boys come
back. You can't just go out and rent a farm. This here Johnson
place needs lots of work. I'll put that work in and if the boys don't
come back I'll let it go." The farm was one of seven that belonged
to a ninety-three-year-old banker who still wrote his own checks.
He'd inherited the farms and they laid like a dream but he'd ne-
glected them shamefully. The main waterway through the farm
that Tom took on was actually grown up in timber twenty feet
high. The biggest field needed tiling to come even close to its
potential and there were lots of weeds—cocklebur, morning glory,
shattercane. Tom would have a hell of a job just getting rid of the
shattercane, which was a primitive sorghum, a grass like corn.
Since any herbicide that would kill it would also kill corn, it had
to be rooted out by hand. He managed to convince his new landlord to invest twenty-one thousand dollars over the next three

years in improvements. That was Tom's price for taking on the farm at all. He was up to 1,250 acres of land he was responsible for now. One man.

Three days before Brett was due to be inducted into the Air Force, just this last Christmas, he tripped on the edge of the new driveway and nearly broke his ankle. It was badly sprained. It swelled up instantly into an ugly knot. Brett was beside himself. He was afraid he'd have to delay his induction and miss all the schools he'd signed up for that started six months later, after basic training. He was determined he'd get his ankle back into shape no matter what. The emergency room doctor in Plymouth was an osteopath. He asked Brett why he was so determined to use his ankle again so soon. Brett told him his story and the osteopath said he'd played a basketball tournament five days after he'd had a bad ankle sprain just like Brett's. He told Brett how he'd done it.

So Brett came home and followed the osteopath's advice. The man had told him to chill his ankle four times a day for twenty-five minutes in a bucket of ice and then go outside and walk up and down on it. Brett did. It was so painful, Sally didn't see how he could stand it, but he didn't miss one treatment. In the meantime he was home for a week laid up and his girlfriend and everyone were doting on him. Sally called the Air Force recruiter. The man arranged a five-day delay, not enough to screw up Brett's schools, and came all the way out to the house from Plymouth to finish Brett's papers.

The ankle turned every shade of blue and purple, but by the end of the week Brett could more or less walk on it. He hobbled in to the air base to catch his flight to San Antonio. The Air Force doctors weren't going to let him go. He bulled his way through. He called Sally from San Antonio and told her, "I'm here, Mom, don't ask me how I did it but I did." The first doctor who'd seen him had told him his ankle was too bad to pass. But Brett noticed the doctor didn't write anything on his records. So he took his records to a second doctor, who did the same thing. The third time through, Brett found the head doctor. The head doctor examined the ankle and then looked Brett in the eye and asked him if he was determined to go through basic training regardless. Brett looked him right back and said absolutely he was. So the head doctor signed his papers and let him go. Luckily for him, he had three days of processing before basic training actually started. He'd been conditioning himself for the Air Force for nearly a year before he was inducted, lifting weights and running. His pulse was so low they were worried he had a heart problem until he told them about his conditioning program. A few weeks into basic, with the ankle still black and blue, he got called over to base headquarters. He'd been volunteered for the base tug-of-war team.

Brett still hadn't made up his mind one way or the other about farming. An Air Force career had its advantages. "I'll be retiring just about the same time you do, Dad," was the last thing he'd said to Tom on the subject. Tom encouraged him to sign up for the Air Force's college support program. If he wanted an Air Force career, it ought to be as an officer, and to be an officer you had to have a college degree. They didn't promote officers from the ranks anymore.

Tom had taken Brett's leaving pretty hard. When he found a pile of traps the boy had left out by the barn, he came in and sat down at the big kitchen table and cried. Sally rolled her eyes. "He didn't *die*, Tom," she told her husband, "he just joined the Air Force." The air base down the road that operated the Minuteman missile field was scheduled to become a major base for the new Stealth bomber. Brett hoped he'd be transferred back there eventually and get to be a mechanic on the Stealth.

With the boys gone and Sammi soon going into high school, Sally decided to give up working at her brother's ceramics shop and come home. Tom could use her help. She also saw he'd need the company.

The annual deer hunt went on. The year after the accident, when Tom called Cowboy to invite him up, Cowboy paused and put a twinkle in his voice and said mock-gravely, "Tom, I'd be glad to come deer hunting if nobody will shoot at me."

The biggest news of all was that Tom and Sally had decided to pull all but two of their farms out of government programs entirely. The conflict that Rowland Howell at the ASCS office had seen coming between grain bases and Sodbuster had arrived full bore. To participate in the government programs nearly every field on every farm had to be set up on a federal conservation plan. That

meant a rotation system that would take the erodible part of the
field out of row crops entirely for at least one year out of five and
put it into meadow, into clover, which thoroughly screwed up a
man's cash flow. You had to file paperwork on every field and
carve each field out into pieces according to their degree of erodibility. Either you rotated each piece separately or everything had
to be rotated according to the conservation plan. Tom knew one
farmer who'd spent a full week doing the paperwork for *one* field.
He didn't see the point. He hadn't gone into farming to become a
bureaucrat pushing paper. He and Sally pro'd and con'd it for
weeks. Grain prices were trending up. They first decided they
could pull out entirely. Then the drought got them worried and
they decided to go partway. They had to file conservation plans on
two farms they kept in, but they didn't have to bring them actually
into compliance for five years. For the price of doing the paperwork they left themselves room to wait and see.

So the days of PIKs and set-asides and deficiency payments and
crop loans were over on some of their land. They'd take their
chances on the open market and hope for the best. If they couldn't
make it as independent farmers they could always start a farm
management company. Crevecoeur County didn't have one of its
own. Tom could manage the farms and Sally could do the books.

But they didn't think it'd come to that. Not every farmer in
America was going bankrupt. Some of them were surviving and
even prospering. Tom and Sally Bauer stood well up on the list.

Kansas City, Missouri–Cambridge, Massachusetts
August 1986–January 1989